BUSINESS AS A LEARNING COMMUNITY

BUSINESS AS A LEARNING COMMUNITY

Ronnie Lessem

McGRAW-HILL BOOK COMPANY

London · New York · St Louis · San Francisco · Auckland · Bogotá · Caracas
Hamburg · Lisbon · Madrid · Mexico · Milan · Montreal · New Delhi · Panama
Paris · San Juan · São Paulo · Singapore · Sydney · Tokyo · Toronto

Published by
McGRAW-HILL Book Company Europe
Shoppenhangers Road, Maidenhead, Berkshire, SL6 2QL, England
Telephone 0628 23432
Fax 0628 770224

British Library Cataloguing in Publication Data
Lessem, Ronnie
  Business as a Learning Community:
  Applying Global Concepts to
  Organizational Learning
  I. Title
  658

ISBN 0-07-707787-3

Library of Congress Cataloging-in-Publication Data
Lessem, Ronnie.
  Business as a learning community / Ronnie Lessem.
    p. cm.
  Includes bibliographical references.
  ISBN 0-07-707787-3
  1. Organizational change. 2. Learning. 3. Employees—Training of.
  4. Continuing education. I. Title.
HD58.8.L468 1993
650′.071′5—dc20   92-44981
                                                                        CIP

1234 CUP 9543

Typeset by BookEns Limited, Baldock, Herts.
and printed and bound in Great Britain at the University Press, Cambridge.

Contents

To Reg Revans,

*originator of the
learning organization*

Acknowledgements

Practically, I am indebted to my collaborators on this book: Mary Coles, Project Manager in the Borough of Ealing Social Services Department; Conrad Fernandez, European Marketing Manager at Lecroy Electronics in Geneva; and Brian Johns, Actuary and Departmental Manager at Norwich Union.

Intellectually, I am indebted to Robert Reich and Shoshana Zuboff at Harvard; to Peter Senge at MIT; to Reg Revans in Britain; and to Elliot Jaques, who regularly commutes between Britain and the USA.

Emotionally, I am indebted to my MMBA students and colleagues at the Management Education Centre, and to my own family.

Preface

Theory in practice

In preparing this book I felt rather like the little child in Hans Christian Andersen's famous children's story, who declared that the emperor was wearing no clothes. Everywhere I turn, at least in the Anglo-Saxon world, I hear of people and organizations creating learning environments. I remember, for example, being enthralled at the first mention of the 'Rover Learning Business', in the early nineties. I have been similarly impressed, over many more years, by the great advances made by the Open University. Here, one might argue, is a learning organization, if ever there was one.

However, over the course of the nineties my initial euphoria has been tempered by realism. Whenever I am asked to provide an example of an authentic learning organization, that is, one which is wholly engaged in processes of individual and collective learning, I am lost for words. Such an entity just does not exist, notwithstanding the abundance of wishful thinking around us. Therefore, in the absence of a solid empirical base for that potentially all-important (though currently still embryonic) learning enterprise, I set out to do three things.

The emergent learning society

First, I wanted to establish the social and economic *context* in which business as a learning community may be set. In that respect I have drawn extensively on the work of Harvard's Professor of Government, Robert Reich, now Clinton's leading economic adviser, the leading American management thinker of our time. Reich distinguishes our emerging era of 'human capital' from past eras of enterprise and management. Whereas the former is knowledge centred, the latter were founded upon materially based resources.

The emergence of management thought and practice from its materially based resources – physical, economic and human – to its knowledge orientation is the subject of Chapter 2. Here I draw on the four elements of knowledge processing that Reich associates with the contemporary 'symbolic analyst'. These functions of experimentation, abstraction, systems thinking and collaboration replace those of marketing, financial, operations and human resource management. I also demonstrate the way in which Reich's four symbolic functions draw, respectively, on Anglo-Saxon, Gallic, Germanic and Latin approaches to business and management.

In Chapter 3 I demonstrate how, within our own consortium-based development programme at City University, we have reconceived business as a learning community. Drawing upon the dual heritage of that Elizabethan merchant adventurer Sir Thomas Gresham and his contemporary scientific thinker Francis Bacon, this book charts a new learning-based course for business.

Seminal concepts of learning

Such a course, having been contextually set, is conceptually pursued. What has struck me, above all, among would-be learning organizations around the world is that they lack any profound conceptual base. Whereas there are any number of worthwhile texts on management or marketing, on quality circles or on customer service, the literature on business as a learning community is still very sparse. Therefore I sought out those seminal management thinkers who have placed particular emphasis on a learning orientation. Moreover, I wanted to ground their work, to some extent at least, in live business practice.

Reg Revan's action learning

The obvious place for me to start, as someone resident in Britain, was with Reg Revans's *action learning*, described in Chapter 4. For me, Revans has been the greatest management thinker that the UK has produced. His idea that effective management, intelligent counselling and scientific achievement are a result of the same 'action learning' orientation reflects the pragmatic orientation of his fellow-citizens. Furthermore, his insistence that one cannot change a system in any significant way unless one also changes oneself serves to combine individual and organizational learning, albeit within a personalized context. Finally, Revans, devoted to linking scribe and artisan, thought and action, knowledge and experience, maintains that we learn much more from comrades in adversity than from teachers on high.

It seemed appropriate therefore to draw on the developmental activities of a social work department, in an inner-city area of London, for an action learning-based approach to organization development. For here the 'artisan' – the man and woman in the street – and the 'scribe' – the social worker – are inextricably intertwined. One such scribe, Mary Coles, has spent the last few years attempting to turn her own project team into a real learning enterprise, using an action learning approach.

Elliot Jaques's organizational stratification

Just as powerful a management thinker as Revans, but with a strongly rational as opposed to pragmatic outlook, is the Canadian Elliot Jaques. Whereas Revans focuses on managerial learning, Jaques is oriented towards *organizational stratification*. For Jaques, therefore, the path to organizational learning is laid by those capable of handling extended 'time spans of discretion'. Moreover, such a 'requisite' organization, described in Chapter 5, is one that can measure up to the cognitive capabilities and personal expectations of those in it.

Because such an orientation towards rationally based management comes more naturally to the French than to the British, I chose a high-tech company in Geneva as a focal point, although its headquarters are in America. In fact, by virtue of being in the instrumentation business, such an enterprise lent itself to learning-based treatment. Its marketing manager, Conrad Fernandez, had extensive experience in high-tech businesses, where managing complexity was of the essence. Innately interested in the dynamics of learning organizations, he had, since moving to Geneva, been focusing upon linking the action-centred Anglo-Saxon approach with the rationally based Gallic orientation.

Peter Senge's fifth discipline

While Revans and Jaques both have world reputations as management thinkers, the American Peter Senge is a rising star. In fact he is probably the best known of the management consultants currently concerned with the development of businesses as learning communities. Moreover, having spent many years with the Systems Dynamics group at MIT, Senge is very much a systems thinker. For him, a learning organization is inherently systemic (Senge's fifth discipline) in orientation, albeit that such an institution also requires personal mastery, mental modelling, team learning and shared vision if it is to realize its learning potential. These five disciplines are described in Chapter 6.

While action learning can be associated with free enterprise, and organizational stratification with 'requisite' organization, an interdependent learning system, for me, is closely associated with business 'union'. In fact, in nineteenth-century Britain the insurance industry was largely founded upon such mutual principles. One of these, the Norwich Union, forms the basis of our would-be learning system, and one of its actuarial managers, Brian Johns, has been particularly concerned with the revitalization of this mutual systemic view in the nineties. As we shall see, it is a long and arduous process to turn a bureaucratic organization into a learning system.

Shoshana Zuboff's 'informated' community

Like Peter Senge, Shoshana Zuboff, from the Harvard Business School, has devoted many years to uncovering the dynamics of businesses as learning communities, with a particular emphasis – in her case – on the role of information technology. For Zuboff, it is the 'informating' (as opposed to automating) function of IT which paves the way towards communally based learning. Such learning, for her, becomes the pivotal factor of production in the emerging technology-based enterprise. While, in Reich's terms, Revans focuses primarily on experimentation,

Jaques on abstraction and Senge on systems thinking, Zuboff is especially concerned with collaboration. Her approach is described in Chapter 7.

I had the good fortune in the sixties, without realizing it at the time, to apply much of Zuboff's thinking to our own family business in South Africa. In the course of installing a newly computerized system into our supermarket operation based in Johannesburg I attempted to build elements of a learning community into this multi-racial enterprise. Subsequently, and much more recently, I was engaged as a consultant, again in Southern Africa, to do something similar. In this case, although the company involved has been fictionalized in this book, we created a stage play of the emerging (and duly informated) learning community.

Business as a learning community

In the final section of the book I provide a series of creative and analytical tools for reconceiving a business as a learning community and for turning a learning-based idea into a reality. In Chapter 8 I reproduce the stage play that was used to create 'informated consciousness' in our so-called Clothes-Town in South Africa. In Chapter 9 I first illustrate the way in which we, at City University Business School's Management Education Centre, have worked analytically with individuals and organizations to foster individual and collective learning. Second, I have broadened the base of my analytical approach to incorporate action learning, organizational stratification systemic learning and an informated community. The exercises in this chapter should serve to enhance the reader's business as a learning community. In Chapter 10 I suggest the development of business as a worldwide learning community and highlight its particular implications for the Anglo-Saxon world.

We begin then, in Chapter 1, with an initial overview of the emergent learning society, drawing upon the work of Robert Reich, which is set to a large extent, in an American context.

Part 1

Part 1
THE EMERGENT LEARNING SOCIETY

1.
The next Anglo-American frontier

Introduction

As we began to write this book, in the spring of 1992, the world in general, and the Anglo-Saxon part of it in particular, were in a state of deep recession. A colleague of ours, Steve Gatley, Marketing Director of a young biotechnology company, based in France but operating throughout Europe, put matters very succinctly.

> In France the recession, as far as the general business community is concerned, is perceived to be the result of a freeze in government investment during the Gulf War. In Germany it's not so much seen to be a recession as a particular problem caused by the absorption of the former East German economy. In Italy there isn't really a recession as such. Family businesses appear to find ways of improvising, and of creating opportunities for themselves. As for Britain finally, well there the recession has really bitten into people's psyches.

As the politicians of different persuasions, in both Britain and America, launched their respective election manifestos, supporting or against tax cuts, government intervention in the economy, or the power of trade unions, all had an inordinately hollow ring to them. Both Conservative and Labour, Republican and Democrat came across as punchdrunk. As each desperately tried to deliver that final, telling blow, many of us had that uncanny feeling that it would never come. Could it be that the Anglo-Saxon world has entered the kind of structurally based recession that cannot be circumvented by any of the conventional wisdoms? It is our intention, in this book, to address this structural problem head-on, and thereby to help managers, organizations and economies, particularly in Britain and America, to evolve. Specifically, the direction of such a development, as we see it, is, first and individually, from entrepreneurially based self-help to managerially oriented self-development.

Second, and organizationally, the evolutionary thrust is from an economically based free enterprise to an information-centred learning organization; third, and societally, the line of development is from a financial orientation to one centred upon human capital. This development is focus, from financial to human capital, has been best charted by Robert Reich and his evolutionary perspective will form the substance of this first chapter.

3

In the chapters that follow, therefore, having set the scene for a learning society on a predominantly American stage, we shall subsequently outline the theory and practice of the learning organization in a more global setting. In so doing, while remaining most true to the Anglo-Saxon heritage out of which the learning organization has evolved, we shall turn towards more diverse contexts. More specifically, and drawing on Reich's own symbolic terminology (see page 20 below), we will move from characteristically Anglo-Saxon *experimentation* to typically Gallic *abstraction*, and from characteristically Germanic or Japanese *systems* thinking towards typically communal *collaboration*. We start, though, with Reich's socio-economic thesis, which has developed in America over the last decade.

The next American frontier

Three eras

In the early eighties, as the hitherto vibrant American economy began to falter markedly, Professor Reich introduced us to his initial approach to crossing the next American frontier. Reich's orientation, which applied more or less equally to the UK, involved the identification of three eras in the recent evolution of business enterprise, the first two of which he considered to be becoming obsolescent.

The eras in decline he described as, respectively, *entrepreneurial* and *managerial*, whereas the next frontier that American was beginning to cross he associated with *human capital*.

The first entrepreneurial era

In the eighteenth and nineteenth centuries the first American era, as had also been the case for Britain, was, for Reich, pre-eminently entrepreneurial. Watt and Stephenson on one side of the Atlantic and Edison and Rockefeller on the other became legends in their own lifetime. These were self-made men who thrived on free enterprise, inventors and entrepreneurs who made their own independent fortunes. Moreover, to this day, every time an Alan Sugar or a Steve Jobs creates a flourishing new business we Anglo-Saxons continue to celebrate the triumph of the individual. However, around the turn of the nineteenth century the entrepreneur's bell was already beginning to toll.

The entrepreneur no longer occupied centre stage in the economic state of the nation. It was the less glamorous but now more effective professional manager, according to Reich, to began to take pride of place. In effect, the organizational fluidity that had allowed entrepreneurs to summon quickly the nation's resources had become for Reich by the first decade of the new century a fundamental weakness. Once summoned, America's human and capital resources had no coherent structure into which to fit themselves. The nation's nascent private enterprises and government institutions were simply too decentralized, idiosyncratic and unreliable to handle a suddenly complex industrial society. According to Reich:

The tension between the advantages of a loose network of government, business and social organizations that let people and capital be easily 'unglued', and put more to productive uses, and the need for coherent and reliable institutions to stabilize the economic and social environment for high volume production formed the central dilemma of the first era.

The great increase in productivity of the late 1880s and 1890s in fact, had been due to an extraordinarily efficient mobilization of resources into high-volume production. Machinery incorporated new technology, there were disciplined workers from the farms and from overseas, and advances in communications enabled goods and materials to flow continuously through the manufacturing process and into distribution. But the process underlying the increase in mobilization could not sustain the dynamic they had set in motion. In sum, for Reich, the problems that stalled the next stage in industrialization stemmed from failures in organization. When America's new engine of production began to overrun its capacity to distribute, market and consume, business sought to remedy the problem through mergers and consolidations. But this reorganization did not suffice.

The second managerial era

At the turn of the century America was singularly well suited to the high-volume production of standard goods. Capital and labour, unlike in Britain and Europe, were uniquely mobile. The country was large. Its material resources were untapped and its energy resources were cheap and plentiful. Its potential market was almost beyond imagination. America's emphasis on personal determination and strength of character, Reich stresses was also consistent with the job of transforming invention into high-volume production:

> So the logic of routine, large scale manufacturing first shaped America's business environment and then permeated the larger social environment. And American society embraced and duplicated it because it was the engine of prosperity.

The managerial form of organization was the most efficient structure, Reich therefore maintains, for organizing the performance of an iterative set of simple, repetitive tasks. Managers concerned themselves exclusively with the efficient pursuit of productivity, as was expected, and they were rewarded for doing so.

The manager's professional code was built upon the ideal of efficiency, and the enterprises they worked in, along with the people they controlled, were cast as agents for achieving that ideal. Such a management science, incorporated into a canon of principles applied by professional managers, determined the shape of America's organizations for half a century. Scientific management, for Reich, rested upon three basic principles: *specialization of work* through the simplification of individual tasks; *predetermined rules* to coordinate the tasks; and *detailed monitoring* of performance. In the half century following the Second World War these principles were applied to almost every large enterprise in America.

Reich's management era, therefore, saw America's economy, much like Britain's, come to depend on the strength of large industrial enterprises producing long runs of standardized goods. Capital-intensive industries, like steel, automobiles, chemicals, textiles, rubber and electrical equipment, combined large-scale machine production with scientific management to achieve extraordinary efficiency. Specialized machines meshed with simplified jobs as the whole production process was guided, coordinated and monitored by professional managers and their professional staff. These remarkable efficiencies depended on huge investments in plant, equipment, and professional talent.

The third era of human capital

Managerial impasse
The management era, according to Reich, ended in 1970 for America. Its decline began, ironically, as many Europeans were coming to view the mastery of high-volume production as the 'American challenge' which either Europe had to emulate or to which it had to succumb. The proportion of US manufacturing capacity employed in production which had reached 86 per cent in 1965 fell to less than 70 per cent in 1982.

Yet large-scale manufacturing enterprises, such as Ford and General Motors, were finding it difficult to adapt to their 'leaner' and more flexible counterparts such as Honda and Toyota. While the latter focused on upgrading human capital, the former remained fixated upon financial matters.

Flexible system production
The unit costs of producing standardized products such as basic steel generally decline more with long production runs than with improvements in the production process. Manufacturers of these products therefore do well to emphasize large capacity, cheap labour and cheap raw materials rather than flexible systems. However, to the extent that a financial orientation is replaced by a developmental one, these industries become gateways through which new products and processes emerge.

It is far easier to move into flexible system production, Reich maintains, by upgrading manufacturing skills and knowhow and by elaborating existing networks of suppliers, distributors and customers. This can be contrasted with leaping into a totally unchartered sea of products and processes unrelated to a past industrial base. Rather than abandoning older industries, companies and countries should seek to restructure them towards higher value added and technologically more sophisticated businesses, Reich argues, such as speciality chemicals, synthetic fibres and precision-engineered automobiles and components. In this new era of human capital, which Reich believes all industrialized nations are now entering, high-volume standardized production will therefore be replaced by flexible system production, in which integrated teams of workers identify and solve problems. This new organization of work needs to be more collaborative, participatory and egalitarian than its scientific predecessor, for the simple reason that initiative, discretion and responsibility must be more widely exercised within it. Since its success, moreover, depends upon quickly identifying and responding to opportunities in its rapidly changing environment, the flexible enterprise cannot afford rigidly hierarchical chains of authority.

In the final analysis, then, while for Reich all industrialized nations have been entering an era of human capital – as opposed to entrepreneurship or management – the Anglo-Saxons are in an especially ambivalent position. On the one hand, they are lagging behind the Japanese and the industrialized Italians, in particular, in flexible production systems. On the other, their individualistic perspective favours the conversion of standardized production into individualized service. To the extent that the evolutionary journey from standardized product to individualized service has not been undertaken so there will have been a failure to adapt, culturally and hence economically, to the new era. The decline of Britain's Labour Party is one symptom of this cause.

Ironically, the key to such economic, technological and commercial adaptation is held by the group rather than by the individual, in the social rather than in the personal. These group norms are subject to broader societal norms and values, duly reflected in cultural mythology. Reich therefore, in his second major work in the mid-eighties, turned to America's prevailing cultural and economic parables, with a view to renewing them. While Reich regarded them as typically American we see them as intrinsically Anglo-Saxon, although there are some variations on the themes of the myths. What, then, of Reich's 'tales of a new America'?

Tales of a new America

The four parables

Origins and renewal
Cultural parables, for Reich, come in a multitude of forms. In modern America, the vehicles of public myth include the biographies of famous citizens, popular fiction and music, movies, feature stories on the evening news and gossip. They may also take more explicitly hortatory forms in judicial opinions, political speeches and sermons. In whatever form they are transmitted, they shape our collective judgements. What gives them force is their capacity to make up, and give coherence to, common experience. Even when a culture's parables lose their vitality – their compelling connection with the broader reality in which they find themselves – they may continue to inform and enchant.

Cultural myths are no more 'truth' than an architect's sketch is a building. Their function is to explain events and guide decisions. Thus, Reich argues, while it is pointless to challenge myths as unrealistic, it is entirely valid to say that a culture's mythology serves it well only to the extent that it retains its connection to the reality the culture faces. '*Myths must evolve as the context evolves. Stories that stay rigid as realities change become ever less useful cultural tools.*' The problem, according to Reich, comes when a changing environment outpaces the political culture. When people become so enchanted with our fables that they fence them off from the pressures for adaptation the stories may begin to mock reality rather than illuminate it. Instead of cultural tools for coming to terms with challenges people face, these fables become means of forestalling them. Conversely, a living political mythology, while retaining its roots in the same core themes, is constantly incorporating new stories that manifest basic values and beliefs in new and more fruitful ways.

This is what the major political parties, on both sides of the Atlantic, patently fail to do. Let us now, with Reich, uncover each of the parables in their original form.

The mob at the gates
The first mythical story is about tyranny and barabarism that lurk 'out there'. It depicts America – or Britain, for that matter – as a small island of freedom and democracy in a perilous sea. The parable gives voice to a corresponding fear. America must beware, lest the forces of darkness overwhelm it. Its liberties are fragile. Its openness renders it vulnerable to exploitation or infection from abroad. Hence, as Reich sees it, America's endless efforts to isolate itself from the rest of the world – or Britain's effort to isolate itself from the European Community – and to convey its lessons with missionary zeal. The American amalgam of fear and aggressiveness towards 'them out there' appears in countless fantasies of space explorers who triumph over alien creatures.

The triumphant individual
This is the story, for Reich, of the owner of a small business who works hard, takes risks and eventually earns wealth, fame and honour. It is the parable of the self-made man who bucks the odds, spurns the naysayers and shows what can be done with enough drive and guts. The theme recurs in the tale of Abe Lincoln, log splitter from Illinois who goes to the White House; in the hundred or so novellas of Horatio Alger, whose heroes all rise promptly and predictably from rags to riches. It appears in the American morality tales of the underdog who eventually makes it, and, as we shall see in Chapter 4, forms the stuff of Samuel Smiles's 'self-help' philosophy in Britain. Think of Rocky or Iacocca, Branson or Harvey Jones. Regardless of the precise form, the moral is the same – with enough gumption, anyone can make it on their own in the Anglo-Saxon world.

The benevolent community
The parable of the benevolent community alludes to the nature and extent of Americans' obligations to each other. Like the other myths, this one has altered

over time. During wars and depressions, in a typically Anglo-Saxon context, the theme has been social solidarity, mutual sacrifice and joint progress. In more recent years, for Reich, it has been a tale of America's charity and compassion towards the poor, and of their dependency and the stubborn persistence of poverty: 'Yet as the stories we tell about obligation and benevolence have shifted, the instruments of benevolence – the programs we enact and fund – have come to have less to do with aid to the poor and more to do with redistribution among the relatively comfortable majority of Americans.' Most of the social programmes, then, are based on the idea of insurance – tax-favoured pensions, tax-free health insurance and even financial help with tort suits. The system of social benevolence, then, is tilted less towards bringing those born into poverty out of it and more towards sheltering the rest of America from insecurity, and from the malevolence of others.

The rot at the top
The fourth of Reich's parables is about the malevolence of the powerful elites, be they wealthy aristocrats, rapacious business leaders or imperious government officials. There are no workers against capitalists at the heart of the American story. It is rather a tale of corruption, decadence and irresponsibility among the powerful. This morality tale has repeatedly provoked innovation and reform. For example, America responded to the increasing concentration of private economic power by introducing antitrust laws. The moral for Reich is clear. Power corrupts; privilege perverts. This morality tale, admittedly, is more distinctly American (and Australian) than British or Canadian.

The conventional wisdom – 'us' and 'them'

Conservatism
All the four lessons convey much the same moral. America, and for our purposes Britain, is, according to Reich, in danger of losing its way. Americans consider it necessary to impose discipline and responsibility on 'them' (malign outsider, free-riding worker, welfare cheat, bureaucrat and politician) in order that the nation may fulfil its grand destiny. According to Reich:

> The parable presents an intricate blend of dissenting Protestant theology and social Darwinism. The overwhelming lesson is clear. Its power lies in its simplicity, and in its evocation of unarticulated fears and hopes.

This may be why the Tories retained power in Britain in the 1992 election. Their message was simple. The maligned outsider was the Labour Party, in conjunction with the Inland Revenue!

Liberalism
Reich's prevailing liberal story draws upon the same morality tales as does conservatism but interprets them in the radically different terms of altruism and conciliation. First, the mob at the gates must be treated with understanding and

tolerance. Poorer nations deserve America's aid. Second, individuals rarely triumph when they cannot get work. Economic policy should ensure full employment so that every citizen can find a market for his or her labour. Third, the nation as benevolent community should contribute more to common purposes. Finally, it is scheming economic elites who create the rot at the top. They must be constrained by a strong and compassionate government empowered by and dedicated to the common people. This is the position, more or less, that Britain's Labour Party adopts. So much, then, for the old parables. How can they best be renewed to bring them into line with contemporary circumstances, in Britain and America, and in the world at large?

The emergent wisdom – we win or lose together

Beyond the mob – Born-again cooperation

To a greater extent and for subtler reasons than either modern conservatism or modern liberalism appreciate, life on this planet, Reich argues, has become less a set of contests in which one party can be victorious and more an intricate game which we win or we lose together. Britain's economy is independent of but also interdependent with that of Germany. From such interdependence the two-party first-past-the-post system precludes us, despite the fact that the world has moved on!

America or Britain or a Tory Party, then, cannot withdraw in fear and distaste from the mob at the gates. Its interests are too intimately bound up with theirs. Nor can the Anglo-Saxon world, or the Japanese for that matter, boldly assert its will. Either's control over the rest of the world, according to Reich, is too contingent and tenuous: 'Rather, we must seek our possibilities for mutual gain. The world has evolved beyond the point at which either assertion or isolation is a tenable option.'

By 1986, by way of example, almost every American industry, with a history of bitter conflict with Japan, was seemingly showing signs of 'born-again cooperation'. Similarly, Anglo-Japanese cooperation had gained apace. Therefore Reich argues, for example, trade names were becoming irrelevant for distinguishing Japanese from American products. General Motors was buying diesel engines from Isuzu, Ford was buying key parts from Mazda and Kodak's copiers were being made by Canon. As an overall pattern, though, Americans took charge of the two ends of the production process, the major research innovations and the final assembly and sales, while the Japanese concentrated on the complex production in between. This division of cultural labour has emerged out of the individual ingenuity in America and group effectiveness in Japan.

Beyond the triumphant individual – collective entrepreneurism

The Horatio Alger cosmology presented America, as Samuel Smiles's 'self-help' might have done in Britain, with a noble ideal, a society in which imagination and effort summoned their individual reward. The key virtue was self-reliance. The goal was to be one's own boss. Such a myth, of the triumphant individual, may have been appropriate, Reich maintains, to a simpler and more insular economy. But within a complex economic system, with so many potential bottlenecks and critical levers, so many transactions to be coordinated among so many people, opportunistic individualism more often than not short-circuits progress rather than advances it. Each party is led to limit his or her own responsibility and commitment, and to take refuge in explicit contracts, rules and other guarantees. Thus the current version of the myth of the triumphant individual may have outlasted its time.

Managers have sought stability by resorting to intricate, economically sterile legal and financial schemes that loads risk onto employees, suppliers or investors. Investors, meanwhile, have rewarded managers who cut short-run labour costs. Workers have absconded with valuable training and experience. The frequent result has been gridlock. The resulting loss is largely invisible, Reich claims, because we cannot see the potential in an economy that remains unfulfilled.

What is required, in effect, is mutual investment for long-term gain, through what Reich terms 'collective entrepreneurship'. While owners continuously invest in workers by giving them training and experience in new technologies, workers invest in one another by sharing ideas and insights. Suppliers of materials and parts invest by committing to produce specialized components. Creditors supply capital without requiring a rigid projection of how the funds will be used. What distinguishes these investments from the standard form is that they rest primarily on trust. Each party trusts that its contributions will eventually be reciprocated. In this case of collective entrepreneurism, for Reich, all those associated with the firm become partners in its future. Each member of the enterprise participates in its evolution. Business becomes part of a benevolent community.

Beyond the benevolent community – towards mutual gain
Compassion and generosity, according to Reich, are still sentiments that America can endorse and act upon when it is a matter of charity concerts, cake sales and other such voluntary activities. But when it comes to government welfare programmes the consensus has dissolved. It is widely accepted that welfare does not work, but there is no alternative vision of public action that might. The benevolent community is bereft of any guiding philosophy for demarcating public and private responsibilities. As private individuals, Americans understand their obligations towards the poor; as citizens they are frequently baffled, disappointed and suspicious.

A society premised solely upon the principle of selfish interest, for Reich then, even of the enlightened variety, cannot summon the shared responsibility upon which any scheme of social insurance or social investment can depend. But it is equally true that a society premised upon altruism and compassion toward others cannot sustain those noble sentiments when the going gets tough. The former arrangement asks too little of its citizens; the latter too much. A truly benevolent community must both inculcate mutual responsibility and simultaneously celebrate the resulting mutual gain. To be motivated, in the final analysis, to contribute rather than to exploit, people need more than good health and education. They must feel that they are members of a society that respects them, and whose respect is worth retaining. For this to occur both business and government have their part to play.

Beyond the rot at the top – reconnecting business and government

For Reich, the liberal version of the 'rot at the top' typically concerns itself with the business exploitation of the wider community; the conservatives are similarly alarmed by the meddling of government. The common error of both variants, for Reich, is the rigid delineation of 'us' and 'them'. The conservative morality tales speak of 'their' strength and deviousness; the liberal morality of 'our' weakness and need. Neither feature stories of mutually rewarding encounters, or common efforts to overcome perils. It is here, in the premise of generally opposed interests, that the prevailing myths seemingly serve worst as guides to reality. For the *reality involves an overlap of interests*, in common cause that transcends each side of the public–private divide. For example, according to Reich:

> The key to Japan's successful industrial policy has lain not in any elaborate plans emanating from MITI, but in an industrial structure that has been designed and redesigned for the express purpose of pushing Japanese industry (and Japanese workers) into *ever more complex and efficient production*, thereby extending their experience and extending outward the frontier of their production capacities as quickly as possible. Their rules of the game – taxes, public procurement, the organization of banks and labour – are tilted in favour of the rapid accumulation of new knowledge and skills.

The current version of rot at the top, then, and the sharp division between business and government, undercuts any rational assignment of their responsibilities. Business has no clear mandate for the development and deployment of workers; government alone lacks the competence to take on the task. It is this conundrum that led Reich, five years after writing his tales of a new America, to publish his treatise on 'the work of nations', taking up perhaps from where Adam Smith left off. Reich also leads us, at this point, right into the learning society, via the 'work' (if not directly the 'wealth') of nations.

The work of nations

Citizens' skills as primary assets

For Reich then, as he sees things in the 1990s,

there will be no national products or technologies, no national corporations, no national industries. All that will remain rooted within national borders are the people who comprise the nation. Each nation's primary assets will be its citizens' skills and insights.

As borders become ever more meaningless in economic terms those citizens best positioned to thrive in the world market are tempted to slip the bonds of national allegiance, and by so doing disengage themselves from their less-favoured fellow-citizens. The future American standard of living, therefore, like that of any other nation's citizens, depends upon the country's capacity to moderate its overall consumption (both public and private) while simultaneously making investments in its unique resources – people and infrastructure – and thereby attracting global investors to do the same.

The real economic challenge facing America in the years ahead, according to Reich, is to increase the potential value of what its citizens can add to the global economy by enhancing their skills and capacities (human capital) and by linking those to the world market. The standard of living of all citizens is coming to depend less on the success of a nation's core corporations and industries, or even on something called the 'national economy', than it is on the worldwide demand for people's skills and insights. At the same time, economic success lies in adding such value to enterprise webs.

The high-value web of enterprise

The new barrier to entry, for Reich, is not volume or price; it is skill in finding the right fit between particular technologies and particular markets. In the high-value enterprise, profits derive not from scale and volume but from continuous discovery of new linkages between solutions and needs. Thus the key assets of what Reich terms 'high-value enterprise' are not tangible objects but the skills involved in linking solutions to particular needs, and the reputations that come from having done so successfully in the past. Power is diffused, depending not on formal authority or rank but on the capacity to add value to enterprise webs. Points at the periphery where a few threads once intersected evolve into new webs. Such webs centre on groups of people who create the most value and attract the most talented followers.

These new organizational webs of high-value enterprise, Reich claims, which are replacing the old core pyramids of high-volume enterprise, are reaching across the world. Thus there is coming to be no such organization as an 'American' (or British or French or Japanese or German) corporation, nor any finished good called an 'American' product. In such global webs products are international composites. What is traded between nations is less often finished products than specialized problem solving (research, product design, fabrication), problem identifying (marketing, advertising, customer consulting) and brokerage (financing, searching, contracting) services, as well as routine components and services, all combined to create value. Such value, in effect, arises out of learning.

Because Reich's high-value enterprise is based on skills and insights, the highest returns and the greatest leverage belong to skilled people within the web (including the licensees, partners or subcontractors) rather than to shareholders or executives occupying formal positions of authority. No longer should other countries, Reich argues, be seen to be taking over America's assets. Instead, they should more accurately be perceived as helping the country to become more productive and its people to increase their personal worth.

Increasing personal worth

The transformation of work

As corporations of all nations are transformed into global webs, the important questions – from the standpoint of national wealth – is not which nation's citizens own what but *which citizens learn what to do what*. As such, Reich maintains, they are capable of adding more value to the world economy and *therefore increasing their own potential worth*. Today no more than 3 per cent of the price of a semiconductor chip goes to the owners of the raw material and energy, 5 per cent to those who own the equipment and facilities and 6 per cent to labour. More than 85 per cent, according to Reich, is for specialized design and engineering services and for patents and copyrights on past discoveries made in the course of providing such services. Unlike machinery that gradually wears out, raw materials that become depleted, patents and copyrights that grow obsolete and trademarks that lose their ability to comfort, the skills and insights that come from discovering new linkages between technologies and needs increase with practice. By 1990 routine production work comprised about one quarter of the jobs performed by Americans, and the number was declining. Service industries accounted for about 30 per cent. Symbolic-analytical services formed the third category. These services do not enter world commerce as standardized objects but as symbols, data, words and visuals.

The sinking ship of routine producers

The ship containing routine producers, for Reich, is sinking rapidly. Twelve thousand people are added to the world's population every hour, most of whom eventually will work happily for a small fraction of the wages of routine producers in America. For example by 1990, American Airlines were employing over 1000 data processers in Barbados and the Dominican Republic to enter names and flight numbers from used airline tickets.

Also vanishing are lower- and middle-level management jobs involving routine production. Between 1981 and 1986 more than 780 000 foremen, supervisors and section chiefs and section chiefs lost their jobs. As America's core pyramids were transformed into global webs, many middle-level routine producers were as obsolete as routine workers on the line.

The gradual demise of 'in-person service'

The second of the three ships, carrying what Reich terms 'in-person servers', is sinking as well, but somewhat more slowly and unevenly. The fiercest competition comes from labour-saving machinery, such as automated tellers, robotized vending machines and self-service petrol pumps.

The rise of the symbolic analyst

Unlike the ships of routine producers and in-person servers, however, the vessel containing what Reich calls 'symbolic analysts' is rising. Worldwide demand for their insights is growing as the ease and speed of communicating with them steadily increases. The formal education of an incipient symbolic analyst, moreover, entails refining Reich's four basic skills: abstraction, systems thinking, experimentation and collaboration. For Reich:

> The fortunate student gains from formal education the techniques and habits of abstraction, system thinking, experimentation and collaboration – all of which are prerequisites for a lifetime of creative problem solving, identifying and brokering. From then on, learning comes from doing. The struggle over complex problems yields new insights and approaches relevant to even more complex problems, and so on, as learning builds on itself. Abstraction becomes more sophisticated; system thinking expands and deepens; the repertoire of experimental techniques widens; collaborative skills improve.

The rise of the symbolic analyst

The habits and methods of *experimentation*, first are critical for Reich in the new economy, where technologies, tastes and markets are in constant flux. So the cinematographer tries out a new technique for shooting scenes; the design engineer tries out a new material for fabricating engine parts. Such experimentally based 'action learning' will be the focus of Chapter 4, and is pre-eminently Anglo-Saxon. Second, Reich's capacity for *abstraction*, for discovering patterns and meanings – pre-eminent in the Gallic world – is the essence of symbolic analaysis, in which reality must be simplified so that it can be understood and manipulated in new ways. The symbolic analyst therefore wields equations, formulae, analogies, models, contrasts, categories and metaphors in order to create possibilities for reinterpreting and then rearranging the chaos of data swirling around us. How to learn to cope with complexity, at a 'requisite' managerial and organization level, will form the substance of Chapter 6.

Third, *systems thinking* for Reich, strongly engrained in the Germanic culture, carries abstraction a step further. To discover new opportunities one must be capable of seeing the whole, and of understanding the processes by which parts of reality are linked together. In the real world, issues rarely emerge predefined and neatly separable. The symbolic analyst must constantly try to discern larger causes, consequences, relationships. Such a systemic approach is represented in Peter Senge's so-called 'fifth discipline', described in Chapter 8. Finally, there is Reich's communal capacity to *collaborate*. Symbolic analysts typically work in teams, spend much of their time communicating concepts and then seek a consensus to go forward with the plan. In the best classrooms, students learn to articulate, clarify and then restate for one another how they identify and find answers. They also learn to work together.

In Chapter 10 we shall review such a collaborative approach, in learning-based terms, drawing particularly on the work of Harvard's Shoshana Zuboff. Her learning community, in fact, is not unlike Reich's 'symbolic-analytical zone'. In his new economy replete with unidentified problems, unknown solutions and untried means of putting them together, mastery of old domains of knowledge is not nearly enough to guarantee a good income. Nor, importantly, is it even necessary. Symbolic analysts often can draw upon established bodies of knowledge with the touch of a computer key. Facts, codes, formulae and rules are easily accessible. What is much more valuable is the capacity to use knowledge effectively and creatively. Such knowledge is most prolifically generated in (and disseminated from) what Reich terms 'symbolic-analytical zones'.

Symbolic-analytical zones

Los Angeles in music and film; Boston and San Francisco in science and engineering; New York and London in world finance; Paris and Milan in fashion – such symbolic-analytical zones cannot easily be duplicated elsewhere. While specific inventions and insights emanating from them cross the world in seconds, the cumulative, shared learning on which such ideas are based is far less portable. Each of these zones, Reich maintains, represents a complex of institutions and skills which has evolved over time. They serve as design centres, development laboratories and strategic brokerage hubs for worldwide operations. The plans, designs, images, formulae and strategies that spring from them enter global webs. There they are added to the high-value concepts issuing from other symbolic-analytical zones and to high-volume objects fabricated and assembled around the world. The symbolic-analytical zone, for Reich, functions as a large, informal organization all of its own, where members' skills are combined in certain ways for particular projects and subsequently recombined in different ways for others. Information travels quickly within this fluid organization. In this highly efficient but informal system, talents and abilities shift to wherever they can add the most value.

Conclusion

In conclusion, and for Reich, we are now presented with a rare historical moment. Although localized conflicts are sadly proliferating, the threat of world-wide conflict seems remote. Moreover, the transformations of economy and technology are blurring the lines between the industrialized nations. For Reich:

> The modern nation state, some 200 years old, is no longer what it was. Vanishing is a nationalism founded upon the practical necessities of economic independence within borders, and security against foreigners outside. There is thus an opportunity for us, as for every society, to redefine who we are, why we have joined together, and what we owe each other, and the other inhabitants of the world. The choice is ours to make. We are no more slaves to present trends than to vestiges of the past. We can, if we choose, assert that our mutual obligations as citizens extend beyond our economic usefulness to each other.

Reich sees 'positive economic nationalism' as an orientation whereby each nation's citizens take primary responsibility for enhancing the capacities of their fellow-citizens for full and productive lives. At the same time, they work with other nations to ensure that these empowerments do not come at the expense of others. This form of nationalism seeks to encourage new learning within the society, to smooth the transition of the labour force from older industries, to educate and train the nation's workers. It seeks to improve the nation's infrastructure and to create international rules of fair play for accomplishing all these things. Such a learning society – within which individual, organizational and systemic learning would prevail – sets the scene for our next chapter. Within it, we shall outline the major concepts of institutional learning, set within the context of the evolving business enterprise.

REFERENCES

Reich, R., *The Next American Frontier*, Penguin (1984).
Reich, R., *Tales of a New America*, Times Books (1987).
Reich, R., *The Work of Nations*, Simon and Schuster (1991).

2

The next business frontier

Learn:

> To gain knowledge by study or experience; to develop an ability by practice or training; to modify existing knowledge, skills and habits; to become practised in a specific field; to become aware.
>
> *Webster's New International Dictionary*

Introduction

Anglo-Saxon myopia

Economic myopia

While there has been substantive rethinking among farsighted management academics, in the Anglo-Saxon world, the prevailing economic and business views have hardly changed at all. British Chancellors of the Exchequer and American Secretaries of State for Commerce continue to focus on financial – as opposed to human – capital, alongside tax and interest rates. Similarly, their business leaders concentrate on the financial bottom line rather than upon the human factor.

Furthermore, in the world at large, the triumph of capitalism, and supposedly of the market economy, has resurrected our collective faith in the powers of free enterprise. Alongside such enterprise, in our newly invigorated and classically based economies, stand the traditional, physically based factors of production. *Land* is represented in contractually based property rights; *labour* is embodied in a freely marketable 'workforce'; and *capital* is transacted in the world's financial markets. Our overall economic, commercial and industrial perspective, at least in the Anglo-Saxon world, has not changed in any significant way for over two hundred years.

Business myopia

Within businesses, and business schools, the foundations have remained equally unmoved, at least over the course of the last century. It was in the early 1900s that Henri Fayol, the French engineer and industrialist, wrote his seminal work *Industrial and General Administration*. In this he divided the business functions between *technical* activities, including production; *commercial* activities, including buying, selling and exchange; *financial and accounting* activities, including the procurement, allocation and divestment of monies; and so-called *security* activities, including the protection of property and persons. Finally, Fayol incorporated *managerial* activities as the integrating function, including planning and organizing, command, coordination and control.

Apart from the transformation of the ill-fitting 'security' function into today's human resource management, the basic activities of business have not been substantively reviewed for a hundred years. The era of human capital may be upon us, together with its constituent knowledge workers, but our underlying business and economic perspective has remained remarkably unchanged. It is our intention here to make due amends, with Reich paving the way, rather than laying the actual foundations for our business and economic renewal.

From mass to information

Knowledge work and the information economy
'The era of human capital', as we saw in the previous chapter, represents the next American frontier, surpassing the hitherto-dominant epoch of enterprise and management. Moreover, Reich's is not a voice heard in the American wilderness. For no less an authority than Peter Drucker, 'Knowledge now has become the real capital of a developed economy'.

While knowledge, then, is seen by both Drucker and Reich to be the real human capital of a developed economy, information has recently been viewed, by Californian economist Paul Hawken, as the critical factor of production:

> The mass economy is being replaced by an economy based on the changing ratio between mass and information contained within goods and services. While the former was characterized by economies of scale, by many goods being produced and consumed by many people, the latter is represented by people producing and consuming smaller numbers of goods that contain more information embodied in design, utility, craft, durability and knowledge added to mass.

How, then, is this brought about?

The symbolic analyst in the work of nations
For Robert Reich, within the context of the information economy, the key player is neither manager nor entrepreneur, but a symbolic analyst, who engages in four key tasks (Figure 2.1). These tasks have emerged for Reich as if out of the American blue. Conversely, in Europe, as we shall soon show, they directly relate to the major knowledge domains, or philosophical systems, that have emerged over the past few hundred years. What, then, is the Western connection?

From enterprise to learning
The emergence of the information economy, the knowledge worker and the

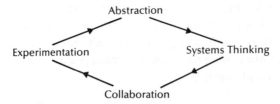

Figure 2.1 The functions of the symbolic analyst

symbolic analyst are symptoms of a larger cause, that is, the emergence of 'intellectual' – as opposed to material or financial – capital as the primary source of comparative economic advantage. In the process, the knowledge-based learning enterprise gains evolutionary precedence over the commercially or industrially based business enterprise.

As knowledge replaces land, labour and capital as the pre-eminent factor of production so the continuing renewal of our knowledge base – with a view to its commercialization – becomes a prime function of the learning enterprise. Such a knowledge base rests upon both the sciences and the humanities. Whereas the former, embodied in modernity, are converted into physical and social technologies, the latter, reflected in tradition, are transformed into management style and corporate culture. The Japanese, for example, have created learning enterprises which have recombined Western technologies, such as microelectronics and statistically based quality controls, with Eastern philosophies – Confucianism, Taoism, Shintoism and Buddhism. The most productive learning enterprises – as has been the case for the large manufacturing establishments in Japan – manage to fuse together, and indeed continually re-synthesize, modern technology and traditional culture. For we Americans and Europeans, on the other hand, our philosophical traditions and modern technologies have become increasingly disconnected, one from the other. Therein lie the origins of our structurally based economic recession. The time is therefore ripe for renewal, in the form of a collective learning enterprise.

Business and economic renewal

Economic renewal

Retracing knowledgeable steps

Therefore in order to convert the materially based factors of production into informational or knowledge-based ones, it is necessary for us to go back to the grassroots of knowledge. In so doing we shall find that Adam Smith's classical economics – from which came our definitions of land, labour, capital and enterprise – derived from a so-called 'empirical' tradition. Such empiricism, utilitarianism or pragmatism is only one of several knowledge bases that have prevailed in Europe since the Renaissance.

The four most pervasive sources of knowledge, or historically based European philosophies, as we see it, are *pragmatism, rationalism, wholism* and *humanism*. Those generic philosophies, in their turn, have created diverse economic concepts and applications that precondition business activity. Whereas English empiricism underlies the market economy and French rationalism underpins hierarchical bureaucracy, Germanic idealism underlies its integrated economic system and Italian humanism its family-based socio-economic network. As business and economy evolve, therefore, from a material to an information base, so a series of transformations take place:

- A market-based enterprise, marked by a horizontal exchange of goods and services, is transformed into a *learning company*, dominated by a negotiated exchange of knowledge.
- A bureaucratic hierarchy, marked by a vertically stratified organization of people, is transformed into a *learning organization*, characterized by a cumulative ordering of knowledge.
- An industrial system, with interdependent business functions and economic enterprises, is transformed into a *learning system*, characterized by combined knowledge disciplines.
- A family business network, with reciprocal personal and commercial relationships, is transformed into a *learning community*, characterized by the sharing of social, technical and economic knowledge.

During the course of this chapter we shall be introducing each of these in turn, and throughout the book we will elaborate upon both their conceptual foundations and their practical implications. We start with the conceptual foundations of the commercial enterprise, set within the pragmatically based market economy.

;matism – free market

> Relating to, or concerned with the practice or practical side of anything; the function of thought as a guide to action; one skilled in affairs of business; application of ideas or the practical bearings of conceptions or beliefs; truth is pre-eminently to be tested by the practical consequences of belief.
>
> (*Webster's New International Dictionary*)

'Pragmatism', the doctrine that all knowledge is acquired through experience, is firmly embedded in the philosophical soil of Britain, most particularly within England. The seminal philosophers Thomas Hobbes and John Locke, as well as the classical economists Adam Smith and Jeremy Bentham, were all of an empirical bent. Common law based on precedent, behavioural psychology based on directly observable phenomena and classical science based on visible blocks of matter, all stem from this Anglo-Saxon 'feet-on-the-ground' approach.

Classical economics, then, as preached by Adam Smith, and as practised by the empirically oriented Anglo-Saxons, converted the British experience – or rather what the British hoped would eventually emerge from the trend which they detected in their own story – into something very like the Platonic idea of capitalism. A picture emerged of a perfect market, unimpeded by the influence of any public authority, with a vast multiplicity of buyers and sellers, none of them strong enough to impose a desired direction on events. The marketplace, the small independent trader and the non-interventionist public authority were, and still are, indissolubly associated with political freedom. Not so in 'dirigiste' France!

Rationalism – 'Dirigisme'

The notion that reason is in itself a source of knowledge superior to and independent of sense perceptions, as contrasted against sensationalism or empiricism; knowledge can thereby be deduced from a priori concepts; such rationality is opposed to emotion or intuition.

(Webster's New International Dictionary)

Where pragmatism is inductive, rationalism is deductive. The seventeenth-century French philosopher, René Descartes, was as seminal an influence on the latter as Francis Bacon was on the former. Beginning in philosophy with clearly perceived institutions which he regarded as comparable to the axioms of geometry, Descartes, a mathematician of the first rank, constructed by deductive reasoning his complete cosmic theory. Analytical method, cognitive psychology and constitutional law all come naturally, therefore, to the rationalist.

In the economic arena the physiocrats, immediate predecessors of Adam Smith, were rationalists who set out to find self-evident truths in the light of reason rather than with the help of experience. However, the direct counterparts to the British classical economists were the French socialists. The best known of these is the nineteenth-century pamphleteer Henri Saint-Simon, who considered the forces of the market as conducive to anarchy rather than as instruments of discipline. Saint-Simon saw all producers, employees and employers as a very large class of 'industrialists'.

For the rationalists, then, whether in Paris or Stockholm, 'dirigiste'-style planning replaces free market economics, constitutional law transcends common law, cognitive psychology replaces the experientially based variety. Wholism, on the other hand, is oriented towards an idealistic, systematic approach.

Wholism – social market

Constituting an undivided unit; comprising the total sum or undiminished entirety; a coherent system of or organization of parts fitting or working together as one;

constituting a person in his full nature, development or relations; involving body, mind and emotions; comprising moral, social and economic activities.

(*Webster's New International Dictionary*)

Bacon in England, Descartes in France, Hegel in Germany – there lies a formidable European trinity. For Friedrich Hegel, the idealist, every condition of thought or of thing, every idea and every situation in the world leads irresistibly to its opposite, and then unites with it to form a higher or more complex whole.

The factors of production – in the German romantic tradition – are not land, labour and capital but *nature*, *man* and *the past*. The last includes all capital, both physical and spiritual, which has been built up in the course of time and is now available to help man in production. Economists, Adam Müller wrote in the nineteenth century, have tended to ignore spiritual capital. The fund of experience which past exertion has made available is put in motion by language, speech and writing; and it is the duty of scholarship to preserve and increase it. All these elements collaborate in production.

As a result, industrial collaboration in pursuit of long-range objectives is fostered by powerful trade associations in certain industries, in Germany as is the case in Japan. Moreover, these advocates of the collective view have a direct *entrée* to the government machine. German *Verbande* (trade associations) have traditionally seen themselves as guardians of the interests of the nation's industries. Italy has communal similarities.

Humanism – socio-economic network

Pertaining to the social life or collective relations of mankind; devoted to realizing the fullness of human being; a philosophy that asserts the essential dignity and worth of man, relating to the arts and humanities, to the 'good' things of life.

(*Webster's New International Dictionary*)

Renaissance humanism was, first and foremost, a revolt against the other-worldliness of medieval Christianity, a turning away from preoccupation with personal immortality to making the best of life in this world. For the Renaissance the ideal human being was no longer the ascetic monk but a new type – the universal man, the many-sided personality, delighting in every kind of earthly achievement. One such man, Ferdinando Galiani, an eighteenth-century Italian abbot in diplomatic employment in Paris, condemned the dogmatic rationalism of the French physiocrats, and he called for flexible policies in line with historical and geographical conditions rather than for adherence to immutable principles of allegedly universal applicability.

Galiani's historical sense made him see value not as an inherent quality of goods but as one that will vary with our changing appreciation of them. He recognized the effect of social forces and stressed the role of fashion as a determinant of human desires and thus value, as is eminently the case today in the Italian textile industry. Employment today in Prato's textiles, based in central Italy, has remained steady while the industry has declined in other developed countries. Prato's success is due to two factors: a long-term shift from standardized to fashionable products, and a corresponding reorganization of production. This involved a move from large integrated mills to technologically sophisticated shops, specializing in various phases of production.

The story of Prato textiles can be retold, in Italy, for many industries: the mini steel mill of Brescia; the ceramic building materials industry of Sassuolo; the high-fashion silk industry of Como; the farm machine industry of Reggio Emilia; and the specialized machinery and motorcycle industry of Bologna. The humanistic Italian model, in effect, provides an example of an economic system whose strength derives, to a large extent, not from its differentiation but from its integration with the social structure.

Each member of our philosophically based quartet, then, has a distinct part to play, if they are to make good music together. The question is, how does such a process of integration come about? How does business renew itself in this wholly learning-based light?

Business renewal

Renewing the factors of production

Commercially based free enterprise, as we have seen, is a composite of those economically based factors of production – land, labour, capital and enterprise. In a rough sense these are reflected in the major functions of business. The technical function represents an upgrading of land into technology; the personnel function reflects a conversion of labour into human resources; the finance function upgrades capital transactions into management control; and the commercial function represents the conversion of enterprise into procurement and marketing.

At this point, however, we remain imprisoned within the materially based business and economy, as opposed to raising ourselves towards the 'informative' one. As we move out of the material world into the 'informed' one then, for Reich, physically based enterprise might be replaced by 'informatively' based experimentation. Second – in prospect if not in actuality – as the gold standard is replaced, according to financial analyst Adrian Hamilton, by an information standard, so finance becomes ever more of an abstraction. Third, as linear mass production is transformed into circular and so-called 'lean' manufacturing according to Womack et al., so technology lends itself ever more to systems thinking. Finally, as the physical image of a 'labour force' is transformed into Shoshana Zuboff's 'informated' image of a learning community, so individually oriented personnel management is turned into communally based collaboration. As indicated in Figure 2.2, and in the final analysis, the four knowledge domains – pragmatism, rationalism, wholism and humanism – respectively underpin our renewed factors of production.

Reconceptualizing business

As business academics, we have a continual responsibility for abstracting or reconceptualizing business, albeit with a view to active experimentation in collaboration with others, and in the context of the wider cultural and economic environment. Hitherto, the material grounds for conceptualization were contained within the traditional business functions – of marketing, operations, financial and human resource management – with an overlay of organizational behaviour and corporate strategy. At the same time, the Anglo-Saxon world has predominated in codifying business and management, with the functionally based MBA as its most pervasive influence. In reconceptualizing business for the information age we shall be developing Reich's basic framework in the light of our newly discovered knowledge domains, thereby proposing that it be:

- Individually grounded in the Anglo-Saxon world of pragmatically based *experimentation*, the concept of *action learning* replacing marketing management, and oriented towards the learning company.
- Institutionally grounded in the Gallic world of rationally based *abstraction*, the concept of *organizational stratification* replacing management control, and oriented towards the learning organization.
- Wholly grounded in the Germanic world of wholistically based *systems thinking*, the concept of *general systems* replacing operations management, and oriented towards a learning system.
- Societally grounded in the Romance world of humanistically based *collaboration*, the concept of *informated work* replacing human resource management and geared towards a learning community.

Capital – **Finance**
ABSTRACTION
Rationalism

Enterprise – **Markets**
EXPERIMENTATION
Pragmatism

Land – **Technology**
SYSTEMS THINKING
Wholism

Labour – **Human Resources**
COLLABORATION
Humanism

Figure 2.2 Business renewal

The learning company – exchanging knowledge

The philosophy of action learning

> Reg Revans, the originator of *action learning*, has followed in the empirical and experiential footsteps of Francis Bacon and Adam Smith. For Revans, self and system, manager and organization are irrevocably intertwined. In quoting from St James's Epistle in the Old Testament, he urges us 'to be doers of the word, and not hearers only, thereby deceiving ourselves'. Revans's commitment to self-in-action, through ongoing experimentation, assumes almost religious proportions.

The context of action learning

> Action learning, in effect, arises out of an exchange between fellow-learners, individually engaged in projects but regularly trading information, advice and ideas in so-called 'learning sets'. Such action learning groups form a 'level playing field', whereby the free trade of goods and services among free enterprises is supplanted by the free exchange of knowledge among free spirits!

> For Revans, then, within the learning set, it is not a matter of 'the blind leading the blind' but rather a case of individuals learning more from their 'comrades in adversity' – each pursuing their commercially and psychologically risk-laden projects – than from teachers on high! In other words, managers, in the spirit of free inquiry, exercise their 'questioning insight' among one another rather than looking to experts for their 'programmed knowledge' from the educational establishment.

> So much for the marketplace for learning, as it were. What about the concept of action learning, that is, the personal analogy to the impersonal market mechanism?

The concept of action learning

> For Revans, as for Francis Bacon before him, the process of learning involves, at the outset, a two-way flow between *action* and *reflection*. The actor changes the system; the reflector changes the self. Neither can operate effectively in isolation from the other. You can only learn from experience if you reflect on it. Unless you have experience, you have no foundation on which to base your learning.

> The model of the learning process that Revans puts forward is a particular application of general scientific method. It encompasses a survey (reflective observation), an hypothesis (abstract conceptualization), a test (active experimentation) and an audit (concrete experience).

> • *Survey* activity involves observing, collecting data, investigating, fact finding, becoming aware.

- *Hypothesis* making involves speculating, conjecturing, theorizing, design, invention, pattern formation.
- *Testing* involves trial and experimentation.
- *Audit* involves inquiry, inspection, scrutiny, verification.
- Finally, there is an integrating *control* phase where an attempt is made to improve general methods following the particular experiment.

Revans's approach to learning focuses on the managerial personality. Conversely, that of Elliot Jaques is oriented towards the impersonal organization.

The learning organization – ordering knowledge

The philosophy of organizational stratification

The functioning of social institutions depends, for Elliot Jaques, on more than having the right individuals; it depends, to begin with, on having the 'requisite' *organizational stratification*. As far as leadership is concerned, moreover, it is impossible to describe or define what is meant by the right personal competencies until the nature of the task has been defined and the organization designed and constructed to enable the work to be done. Finally, it is through work at a matched level of individual and organizational cognition, Jaques argues, that a person maintains a primary sense of reality.

The stratified work context

Stratified work bureaucracies are, by definition, hierarchical. They contain a range of different levels, reflected in different strata of work. This work, moreover, mediates between an individual's internal mental processes and the external organization's requisite functioning. For Jaques therefore, the hierarchal levels of control are preconditioned, in such a 'requisite' case, by strata of information-processing capacity.

Jaques maintains, as a result, that there is a universally distributed depth structure of levels of bureaucratic organization, whereby natural lines of stratification exists at 3–month, 12–month, 2–year, 5–year, 10–year and even higher levels. The existence of the stratified depth-structure of bureaucratic hierarchies is the reflection, in social organization, of the existence of discontinuity and stratification in the nature of human capacity. The capacity is referred to as work-capacity, which is further analysed in terms of both a person's and an organization's level of abstraction, or ability to cope with complexity.

Stratified 'orders of complexity'

Orders of information complexity are the increasingly complex groups of data which an organization must take in, and subsequently use, to inform its cognitive

processing and thereby to solve its problems. The learning organization, therefore, is able to accommodate progressively more complex information, ranging
from the specifically concrete to the universally abstract. There are, according to
Jaques, four orders of complexity:

- First order *concrete* things, that is, specific things that can be pointed to. The
variables are clear and unambiguous – 'use this tool'; 'employ him, not her' –
they are not tangled together and are relatively unchanging.
- Second order *verbal* abstraction, through which managers are able to run
factories, design new products, discuss orders with customers, produce financial accounts, maintain information systems and generally carry out the
activities necessary to run a business unit.
- Third order *conceptual* abstractions involve, for example, balance sheet values
that bring together a wide range of accounting categories, which can in turn be
translated into specific and concrete assets and liabilities. the abstracted values
are characteristically very ambiguous, continually changing and inextricably
entangled together.
- Fourth order *universal* abstractions contain concepts that are grouped together
into the universal ideas that are required for handling the problems of whole
societies.

For Jaques, then, depersonalized structures and functions eclipse Revans's
personalized attitudes and behaviours. Peter Senge, as we shall see, combines
mental modelling with systemic thinking.

The learning system – combining knowledge disciplines

The philosophy of systems thinking

Peter Senge, drawing upon the spirit of wholism that has predominated within a
Germanic as well as oriental world view, has developed an approach to learning
that befits large-scale systems. The *general systems* approach brings together disciplines for seeing wholes. When an idea moves from an invention to an innovation,
Senge claims, diverse 'component technologies' come together. Emerging from
isolated developments in separate fields of research, these components gradually
form an ensemble of technologies that are critical to each other's success.

Five new disciplines are converging, Senge claims, to create learning systems. A
discipline, for Senge in this context, is a developmental path for acquiring certain
skills or competencies, based on a body of theory that must be
mastered. Such a 'discipline' involves a strengthening or even perfecting of mental
faculties and moral character.

The context of general systems

The general systems approach, in its turn, is the antidote to the sense of helplessness that many feel as we enter the age of interdependence. It is a discipline for seeing the structures that underlie complex situations, and for discerning high from low points of leverage. It is a framework for seeing interrelationships rather than things, for seeing patterns of change rather than static 'snapshots', for viewing causality in multidimensional and circular terms, rather than in unidimensional, linear ones.

The five disciplines conceptualized

A discipline involves a system of rules which Senge has developed to cover five related disciplines. These embrace so-called 'personal mastery', the development of 'mental models', the evolving of 'shared values', and the exercise of 'team learning', in conjunction with 'systems thinking' in itself.

- *Personal mastery* is the discipline of continually clarifying and deepening vision, of focusing energies, of developing patience, and of seeing reality objectively. As such, it is the learning system's spiritual foundation.
- *Mental modelling* is the discipline of working with mental models – of people and institutions – starting with 'turning the mirror inwards', that is, learning to unearth mental pictures of the world to bring them to the surface and hold them to rigorous scrutiny. It also includes the ability to carry on 'learning-based' conversations that balance inquiry and advocacy.
- *Shared vision* involves the skill of unearthing shared 'pictures of the future' that foster genuine commitment and enrolment rather than compliance. In mastering this discipline, leaders in certain organizations and in whole societies learn the counterproductiveness of trying to dictate a vision.
- *Team learning*, as a discipline, starts with 'dialogue', whereby members of a team, within and across organizations, suspend assumptions and enter into a genuine 'thinking together'. To the ancient Greeks, *dia-logos* meant a free flowing of meaning through a group, allowing the group to discover insights not attainable individually.
- *Systems thinking* is the fifth discipline. It is the discipline that integrates the four others, fusing them into a coherent body of theory and practice. For example, a visionary leader without systems thinking ends up painting lovely pictures of the future with no deep understanding of the forces that must be mastered to move from here to there. Systems thinking also needs the disciplines of building shared vision, mental models, team learning and personal mastery to realize its potential.

While Peter Senge places considerable emphasis upon individuals, if not also organizations, 'thinking together' in systemic terms, Shoshana Zuboff is somewhat more concerned with the way people 'feel together', in communal terms.

The learning community – sentient knowledge

The philosophy of community

> In his intricate study of communal activity the English political economist Ralph Glasser portrayed, in the seventies, life in a typical village – San Giorgio – in southern Italy:

>> San Giorgio insists that we see man in society in organic terms always, and that we demand to know, before anything else, what kind of emotional and spiritual life must underpin his workaday existence. It indicates compellingly that a certain type and size of small, self generating township – or growth unit – is the right social model to strive for, one that can be fully known to itself and therefore helps the individual to maintain the reciprocal relationships of obligation and response required to support the community's emotional network.

> In fact, according to Harvard's economic historian, J. L. Badaracco, business until the Industrial Revolution was enmeshed in relationships with families, because households were basic economic units. 'The core of a firm' was then and still is – he says, as an Italian-American – 'a dense web of longstanding relationships'.

The context of 'sentient' knowledge

> Shoshana Zuboff, also based at the Harvard Business School, describes how such longstanding relationships, for the traditionally based craft workers, underpinned their involvement with things, as well as with people. Such 'sentient' knowledge, she maintains, was filled with intimate detail of material and ambiance – for example, the colour and consistency of metal as it was thrust into the blazing fire, and the smooth finish of clay as it gave up its moisture.

> By redefining the grounds of knowledge from which competent behaviour is derived, new information technology, for Zuboff, lifts skill from its historical dependence upon a labouring sentient body. While it is true that computer-based automation continues to displace the human body and its knowhow (a process that has come to be known as deskilling), the 'informating power' of the technology simultaneously creates pressure for a profound reskilling of work. Zuboff quotes a paper mill engineer:

>> You have to be able to imagine things that you have never seen, to visualize them. For example, when you see a dash on the screen you need to be able to relate that to a 35 foot square by 25 foot high room full of pulp. I think it has a lot to do with creativity and the freedom to fantasize.

The concept of 'informated' work

> Zuboff's learning community of colleagues and co-workers, as opposed to the military terminology of line and staff, superior and subordinate, must engage in four key functions:

- *Informating strategy*
  For an organization or society to pursue an informating strategy it must maximize its own ability to learn. In the process it needs to explore the implications of that learning for its long-range plans with respect to markets, product development and new sources of comparative advantage. Some members will need to guide and coordinate learning efforts in order to lead an assessment of strategic alternatives, and to focus organizational intelligence in areas of strategic value.

- *Technology development*
  A new division of learning, for Zuboff, depends on the continuing progress of 'informating' applications. These include maintaining the reliability of the core electronic database while improving its breadth and quality, developing approaches to system design that support an informating strategy and scanning for technical innovations that can lead to new informating opportunities. This kind of technological development can only occur in the closest possible alignment with organizational efforts to promote learning and social integration.

- *Intellective skill development*
  The skills that are acquired at the data interface, nearest to the core of daily operating responsibilities, provide a coherent basis for the kind of continual learning that would prepare people for increasing responsibilities. The relative homogeneity of the total organizational skill base suggests a vision of organizational membership that resembles the trajectory of a professional career, rather than the 'two-class system'. The interpenetration between rings provides a key source of organizational integration.

- *Social system development*
  The abstract precincts of 'informated' work heighten the need for communication. New sources of personal influence are associated with the ability to learn and to engender learning in others, in contrast to an earlier emphasis upon contractual relationships or the authority derived from function and position. The demands of managing intricate relationships reintroduce the importance of the sentient body. The body now functions as the scene of human feeling rather than as the source of physical energy.

Conclusion

In conclusion, we have four world views. Each is comprehensive in its own right but respectively biased towards individual, organization, system and community.

The concepts of *action learning, organizational stratification, general systems* and *informated community* replace the commercial, financial, technical and personnel ones to which Fayol originally alluded, and which are illustrated in Figure 2.3. The knowledge domains of pragmatism (experiments), rationalism (abstraction), wholism (systems) and humanism (collaboration) serve to transcend the more

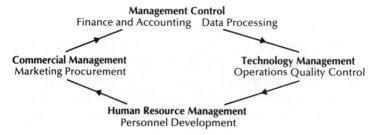

Figure 2.3 The functionally based organization

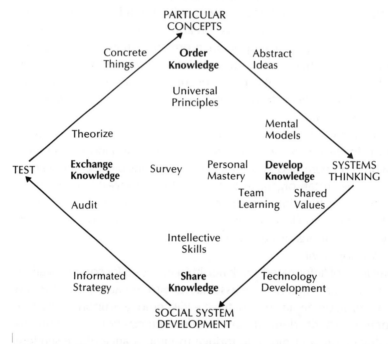

Figure 2.4 The knowledge based organization

narrowly, and materially based factors of production, that is, enterprise, capital, land and labour (Figure 2.4).

Pragmatism, experimentation and the horizontal exchange of knowledge through the learning company replace sales-oriented commercial management. Rationalism, abstraction and the vertical ordering of knowledge through the learning organization replace finance-based management control. Wholism, systems thinking and the circular combining of disciplines through the learning system replace technology-based operations management. Finally, humanism, collaboration and the networked sharing of knowledge through the learning community replace personnel-oriented human resource management.

We shall soon examine each of these learning orientations in turn, first in theory and then in practice. Before doing so, however, we need to establish the learning context in which both concepts and applications have been set.

REFERENCES

Badaracco, J. L., *The Knowledge Link*, Harvard Business School (1991).
Drucker, P., *The New Realities*, Harper and Row (1989).
Fayol, H., *Industrial and General Administration*, in Pugh, D., (ed.), *Writers on Organizations*, Penguin (1971).
Glasser, R., *The Net and the Quest*, Temple Smith, (1977).
Hamilton, A., *The Financial Revolution*, Heinemann (1987).
Hawken, P., *The Next Economy*, Ballantine Books (1983).
Jaques, E., *Executive Leadership*, Blackwell (1991).
Lessem, R. and Neubauer, F., *The European Quartet*, Unpublished Manuscript, IMD (1992).
Revans, R., *The ABC of Action Learning*, Chartwell Brett (1982).
Senge, P., *The Fifth Discipline*, Random Century (1991).
Womack, J., Jones, D. and Roos, T., *The Machine that Changed the World*, Macmillan (1990).
Zuboff, S., *In the Age of the Smart Machine*, Heinemann (1988).

Introduction

Gresham's call

Before investigating in much greater depth the four generic concepts of the learning organization that emerge from Reich's experimentation, abstraction, systems thinking and collaboration, we need to establish the overall learning context within which we have placed them. Late in the eighties, something began to stir within the City University Business School. Conscious of their school's local and world significance in London's financial centre, a 'pragmatic' Professor of Export Marketing, soon joined by a 'wholistic' Reader in International Management, set out on a long journey together. Whereas the former was something of an English merchant adventurer, the latter – of both African and Germanic stock – saw himself as a conceptual activist.

The Business School, originally established in the City's Gresham Street, traces its origins back to Sir Thomas Gresham. In Elizabethan times this formidable Englishman had expelled the Lombards from their dominant position in the 'Square Mile' and reinstated his country's influence. While in his lifetime he created the Royal Exchange, forerunner of today's International Stock Exchange, upon his death he bequeathed his fortune to the advancement of learning. Since then, Gresham Fellows have devoted themselves to the sciences, though not to business. Gresham, in fact, albeit unconsciously, had stumbled upon a connection between business and learning, almost as if the one was the other's 'alter ego'. For 300 years his vision of business as a learning community lay dormant, until the entrepreneurial professor saw the light.

The future of his country lay in the education of its managers, and the professor tried to enlist the support of the Gresham Trust to further his purpose. In the true spirit of Bacon and Revans, action was not to be divorced from learning.

Time for a rethink

To quote Murray, it was time for a rethink about the role of business schools in general and the MBA in particular. For the marketing professor the inductive and empirical English tradition lent itself much more readily to project-based education than to a classroom-oriented teaching. Moreover, the exercise of practical skills in the business field could not be separated from the acquisition of knowledge. In this respect the traditional case study was, at best, a half-way house on the road to Xanadu.

The vision, however, was not yet fully formed. Gresham made some signs of acknowledgement, in his grave, but he was not sufficiently moved. So attention was transferred to the participating companies themselves, forming a shadow board of prospective clients. In the interim the professor managed to win over the University's senate after a prolonged exercise in internal marketing.

Freeing enterprise

The fact that the professor of export marketing was very much an entrepreneur in his own right was somewhat unusual for an academic, though less so in a 'nation of shopkeepers' than in other parts of the world. During the course of his own life he had continually juxtaposed business and management, management and education. Enterprise was his lifeblood. He was a true descendant of Adam Smith and Samuel Smiles.

By 1988 the Management MBA (MMBA) was under way, the first step in a process established to develop business as a learning community. The International Stock Exchange, American Express and the food retailer Sainsbury's had become the founder-members of the original consortium. Interestingly enough, the nation of shopkeepers, straddling the two sides of the Atlantic, was well represented. At the first induction programme, beautifully located at Sainsbury's management training centre, the selected participants – together with their in-company coaches and academically based educators – came together to dream up their prospective projects. These three practically based projects, in fact, were to become the fulcrum of the programme. At that point there was no curriculum, other than a requirement that each manager complete 20 days of courses any-where, at any time. Finally, there were to be no formal examinations. Successful completion of the course, from both a practical and a theoretical perspective, depended upon the delivery of satisfactory projects.

At this initial point the educational programme truly embodied those principles that Adam Smith had enshrined into his 'wealth of nations'. As we shall see in Chapter 4, human conduct, for Smith, was naturally activated by six motives; self-love, sympathy, the desire to be free, a sense of propriety, a habit of labour, and the propensity to exchange one thing for another. Given these springs of conduct, each man was naturally the best judge of his own interest and should therefore be left to pursue his task in his own way. The MMBA participants, then, were motivated to get on with their projects by self-interest, in their own way and at their own time, as long as they worked hard at it and exchanged information and ideas with their educators and coaches.

Promoting self-help

If left to themselves, Smith argued – as did our professor – people would not only attain their own best advantage but would also further the common good. The result would be achieved because providence had made society into a system in which natural order prevailed. Each individual was led by an invisible hand to promote the interest of society or, in the MMBA case, the interest of the sponsoring company.

The spirit of self-help then, as shown in the energetic action of individuals, has always been a marked feature of the Anglo-Saxon character. Schools, academies and colleges, for Smiles, give but the merest beginnings of a culture. Far more influential is the life education daily given in people's homes, in the streets, behind counters, in workshops, at the loom and the plough, in counting houses and factories, and in the busy haunts of men. For Smiles, man perfects himself by work more than by reading. It is life rather than literature, action rather than study and character rather than biography which tends perpetually to renovate the human race.

Within the MMBA specifically, as for organizational learning generally, it is the workplace rather than the classroom which formed the base for learning, and the work-based project more than course-based reading. The initial curriculum, therefore, was located not in a marketing text but in the marketplace; not in an 'interpersonal skills' course but in real-life interactions. Through their projects, managers would be called upon, via educator and coach, to reflect upon their everyday actions and so conceptualize and internalize them.

The advancement of learning

Whereas our Professor of Export Marketing is an extrovert our Reader in Cross-Cultural Management is an introvert. While Adam Smith and Samuel Smiles focused on the extroverted processes of business enterprise and individual self-help, Francis Bacon was oriented towards the introverted processes of individual, institutional and societal learning. In his so-called 'device' of 1592, Bacon analysed the problem which confronted his age. The learning of the day bore little relation to the productive processes of industry. That proclamation has a familiar ring to it some four hundred years later!

The story of Francis Bacon, in effect, is that of a life devoted to one great idea. The idea gripped him as a boy, grew with the varied experience of his life and occupied him on his deathbed. It was simply that knowledge should bear fruit in works, that science should be applicable to industry, that people should organize themselves, as a sacred duty, to improve and transform the conditions of life. Up to this point, both Professor and Reader were at one with Bacon, their illustrious English predecessor.

The reader from the African south had linked up with the professor from the European north six months after the programme had got off the ground. He liked the smell of it! He was in love with education, and business, for him, was merely a means to an end, that is, the pursuit of individual freedom. Having been born in Zimbabwe, as a member of a ruling white minority that had oppressed the black majority, freedom was dear to the reader's heart. Having emigrated to Britain in the early seventies, he had become progressively more dismayed by the contradiction between England's bottom-up individual predilections and its top-down educational institutions. Immediately, he recognized the potential of the professor's project-based, and duly individualized, approach.

He had, before now, been particularly struck by Francis Bacon's exhortation: 'May God the Creator, Preserver and Restorer of the universe, protect and guide this work both in its ascent to his glory and in its descent to the service of man.' The ascent to glory is the inductive process leading to the highest axioms; the descent to the service of man is the deductive process by which science is applied to works. The reader could now see that project-based learning was inductive, from which could be deduced the highest managerial axioms, and project management was subsequently deductive.

Fortunately also, over the course of the previous decade, our reader had been involved with a colleague, and psychologist. Kevin Kingsland had developed a 'spectral' approach that served to calibrate Bacon's ascending (inductively based learning) and descending (deductively based innovation) processes. This became our own integrated approach to individual and organizational learning, setting the stage for the more clearly differentiated approaches to follow (Chapters 4, 6, 8 and 10).

Managerial learning and innovation

Managerial learning

The inward journey
Operating initially within a predominantly Anglo-Saxon environment, our development programme was originally oriented towards individually based managerial learning. As is indicated in 'Total Quality Learning', learning and innovation – in a managerial context – constitute, respectively, an inwardly reflective and an outwardly active journey for either the individual manager or for the managed organization.

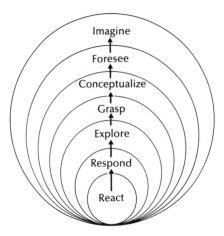

Figure 3.1 Learning and development

Both journeys encompass the full range of the individual and the organizational personality, learning being introverted and innovation extroverted in nature.

The inward journey – learning and development – begins with our five senses and culminates in our creative imagination. Along the way, as we build up our developmental repertoire, we react physically, respond socially, explore mentally, grasp intentionally, conceptualize analytically, foresee insightfully and then finally imagine creatively (Figure 3.1). We, begin, then, by physically reacting.

Physically react
Individual learning, that is, when we are literally starting from scratch, begins with an inward, and sensual *reaction*, that sets our adrenaline flowing. For example, we start out on our financially oriented business journey by being so weighted by numbers (the effect literally pains us) that we have a physical urge to do something about it, for fear of being left behind our much more numerate colleagues. Our professor first set out, in the mid-eighties, on his adventure in learning, catching a boat that had seemingly gone astray; at least in management education and organization development, since the days of Samuel Smiles.

Socially respond
Once, as a manager, we are physically underway, but unaware which way to turn, we become dependent on others, *respond*ing enthusiastically to their every instruction. For example, in the sales context, we put out 'help me' signals to every salesperson around until we find one or more who will take us protectively under their wing. We become an enthusiastic apprentice, on the lookout for practical, specific instructions, not for 'heady' techniques.

In that context our professor used the shadow board that he had formed in 1986 as a prospective client group to whom he warmly responded. Prior to that he had apprenticed himself to a number of formidable salespersons/entrepreneurs. Moreover, his administrative assistant at the time provided the social glue that held his diverse activities and people together. This communal quality would subsequently stand the Management MBA in good stead, when professor and reader were to be joined by our animator. She was to become the heart of our learning community.

Mentally explore

It is only after we have acquired some concrete feel for the area of knowledge, self or skill that we are inductively ready to move on. As a would-be accountant we will have painstakingly learnt to do basic bookkeeping before wanting to intellectually *explore* the financial subject matter in greater technical detail. It is at this point that intellectual curiosity can and should get the better of us, as we begin to explore abstract financial techniques. We now seek out alternative books and courses and avoid instruction by rote. Our professor, as a marketing academic, has been an inveterate explorer of management education; our reader was an obsessive investigator of the learning organization. In fact the two of them were joined, at a later stage, not only by our animator but also by an IT-based project manager and agent of change.

Grasp wilfully

Once we have acquired the basic knowhow – whether related to finance or marketing, to the assimilation of knowledge or the acquisition of skill – we are ready to put it more purposefully to use. At this intermediate stage of managerial learning we begin *wil*fully to turn our feelings and actions to solving our own managerially based problems. Management now becomes a tool to be grasped to suit our own individual purposes. Any courses we attend or articles we read have to be customized to suit our own managerial predicaments. In our professor's case, over the years he had grasped the importance of internal as well as external marketing.

Conceptualize analytically

Once we have played with particular routines and acquired a firm grasp of their specific and alternative applications, we are ready to appreciate the overall *concept*s of, say, management accounting of influencing skill, or of entrepreneurial management – whatever the case may be. In our reader's case, he had dedicated his adult life to conceptualizing organization and management across cultures.

In fact, if we are exposed to concepts before we have acquired a personally and situationally specific set of circumstances in which to apply them, they will be rendered inductively sterile. A course on accounts will be of limited learning value if, on the one hand, we have no business to account for, and, on the other, we are unfamiliar with basic bookkeeping.

Insightfully foresee

Concepts can only be fully understood in context. It requires a particular brand of insight to appreciate the significance of, for example, the management of change in Japan versus in America. It takes *foresight*, born of a combination of intelligence in depth and experience in breadth, to manage in cross-cultural settings. Our professor foresaw that the standardized MBA was soon to peak in product lifecycle terms. At the same time, our reader foresaw that managerial learning – as a more evolved form of self-help – would ultimately be inhibited, particularly in the Anglo-Saxon world, in the absence of organizational learning. Such insight, moreover, does not arrive suddenly. It emerges after one has physically reacted, socially responded, mentally explored, wilfully grasped and thoughtfully analysed different cultures over an extended period of time.

Creatively imagine

The ultimate point in managerial learning – whether as an entrepreneur or animator, change agent or enabler, strategic planner or as a skilled motivator – is to be able to *imagine* oneself, as in the form of a motion picture, assimilating the knowledge or acquiring the skill. Such a capacity to imagine, to the full, represents the culmination of a process of learning, starting with our five senses and ultimately incorporating body, heart and mind. The image of the consortium-based programme, with managerial and organizational learning as its nucleus and knowledge-, skill- and personality-based competencies on the periphery, emerged ever more strongly over the years.

It is well known that champion skiers and great musicians can practise their art in their mind's eye. However, this only becomes possible once they have opened themselves cognitively, affectively and behaviourally to their particular pursuit.

Managerial innovation

The outward journey

Up to this point all the emphasis has been on the inward journey of learning, that is, the cumulative development of individual and organizational competence. It has involved the thoughtful assimilation of management knowledge and professionally based knowhow; the active acquisition of managerial skill and organizational capacity; and the felt realization of oneself as an evolved manager and our organization as an evolved institution. We now turn to the outward journey, that is, to cumulative innovation, through the transformation of competence (Figure 3.2).

Creatively envision

Whereas creative (or inventive) managers imagine the internal effect of their accumulated learning, they *envision* the external impact of their innovations. Their focus is extroverted and outwardly directed rather than introverted and inwardly directed. For example, they picture the marketplace being transformed by their innovative technology or creative approach to consumer retailing. While our professor envisaged a duly individualized management education that led to flexible organizational response, our reader envisaged a duly self-actualized man-

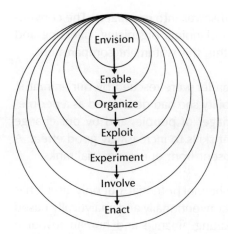

Figure 3.2 Innovation and transformation

ager, contained within a learning organization. Both visions encompassed individual freedom and both involved transformation. Neither were able to realize their own vision without the receptive influence of others. The vision subsequently projected encapsulates the thoughts, feelings and actions of their transformed customers. Such a vision transports others, in inspirational colours and tones, towards a new and promised land.

Insightfully enable

No matter how brilliant the individual manager's vision, it will fail to inspire others if it is not potentially accessible to them. Our entrepreneurial professor's vision of workplaced-based practically oriented management education served to inspire corporate sponsors and the in-company coaches. Our reader's vision of the self-actualizing manager served to inspire the participating students. Similarly, our animator's vision of a social community bonded together staff and students alike, while our change agent's vision of a networked community induced a gleam in many an IT manager's eye.

It is the function of an *enabling* technology, of an enabling organization or of enabling finance to provide the context in which the gap between vision and potential can be recognized and also bridged. Similarly, it is the developmentally oriented manager – deploying listening, facilitating, team building and joint venturing skills – who has a particular part to play in this enabling process. In transforming oneself from being a visionary into playing the role of an enabler one is moving against the innovating grain. As we move from a predominantly active to a primarily receptive outlook on innovation we let go of envisaged action and adopt, instead, enabling insight.

Methodically organize

Visionaries and enablers are rare managerial breeds, at least in Europe and America.

Both find great difficulty in transforming themselves into *organizer*s. The conventionally based principles of management – planning, organizing, directing and control – are all methodically contained within this watertight compartment.

In this methodical respect, professor and reader were rescued by our animator, who began to translate the organizational ability she had developed as a people-oriented administrator into those of a manager of people, and by our change agent, who applied her project management skills to increasingly good effect. A 'true-blue' organizer, however, remained absent from our managerial ranks.

Such organized management is required to channel potential, but only after it has been created, recognized and tapped. The conventionally and analytically based business functions – operations and marketing, finance and human resource management – serve that methodical end, as do the skills of organizing and directing and the analytical manager, from an individual, albeit impersonal, perspective.

Wilfully exploit

The entrepreneur wilfully, and often ruthlessly, *exploit*s products and markets, if not also people, in pursuing competitive managerial and strategic ends. Such entrepreneurs or intrapreneurs are the champions, the 'winners', the games people or the raw 'jungle fighters' who bring in the resources in cash or in kind. Creative scientists often rely on such enterprising managers to champion their products in the same way as analytically based executives often depend on an entrepreneurially inclined sales force to 'make a killing' in the marketplace. Moving from analytical into enterprise management, once again, involves going against the innovative grain. The traditional tension between operations and sales, and between finance and marketing, arises out of these contradictory styles of management. Skill in influencing people now predominates over organizing, or even creative skills. Our professor was innately skilled in that influential respect, and he left his team members to get on with the developmental and organizational activities.

Experiment continually

It is Reg Revens, as we shall see in Chapter 4, who claimed that learning must be greater than the rate of change if the individual manager is to survive in today's business world. In fact 'the management of change' is probably the buzzword of our day in British management circles if not worldwide.

Revans, like David Kolb, his colleague at the MIT, has taken the scientific method and applied it to the process of management. For Kolb, managers' learning styles are determined by their relative preference for one of the four components of scientific method – active experimentation (test), concrete experience (audit), reflective observation (survey) and conceptualization (hypothesis). For Kolb, as for Revans, the management of change and the capacity and inclination to adapt are related to the managers' ability to continually move around the above-mentioned cycle.

Movement within the cycle is the prerogative of the manager–learners on our development programme, facilitated by their academically based educator, their in-company coach and their learning set of 'comrades in adversity'. At the same time, and in order to ensure that our office learnt at a rate that was faster than the changed demanded by the learning community, the programme attracted two administrators – one a teacher and the other a psychology graduate – who were avid learners in their own right.

Involve people
The people manager is that socially skilled genuine people-person within the human resource management fold. Such an individual, or such a social part of our managerial being, is the one best able to carry other people along the outward and innovative journey. Our animator radiates this warmth, and those who joined us soon became equally radiant.

It requires a softness of approach, and a degree of comfort with the world of feelings, that is characteristically lacking among organizers and entrepreneurs, visionaries and change agent alike. The pain involved for such managers in moving against the innovating grain, from the worlds of thought and action to a world of pure feeling, is too great for them to bear.

Enact things
At the end of the managerial day, any process of technological innovation or organizational transformation requires a physical and tangible outcome. Action managers make it their business to make things happen. In fact, genuine visionaries have a strong streak of action within them whereby they have a relentless desire to turn vision into action. In their differently influential, developmental, flexible and practical ways, our entrepreneur, enabler, animator and change agent exemplified this action orientation. This action bias was reinforced in the early days of the programme by one of them subsequently leaving her administrative post to spend the next few years sailing, in a small yacht, around the world.

At such a time as our team would be able to take real account of Smith and Smiles, Bacon and Revans, we would inevitably transform management education. In the process, individuals would cross paths and organizational learning.

Organizational learning and innovation

Conceptualizing management and organization

The 'free-form' approach to their management education, in the early days, inevitably caused anxiety among the first MMBA participants. Interestingly enough, the most vociferous complaints came from a student and company director, whose business was based in France. It was indeed the French as we shall see in Chapter 6, through Henri Fayol, who first conceptualized business and management. Fayol, in the twenties, was followed by the Austro-American Peter Drucker, in the fifties, who made the next major impact on business and management theory.

In the same way as the British have, at least during the twentieth century, been more interested in commerce than in manufacturing, so the continental Europeans have made more inroads into shaping the form, as opposed to the substance, of business. Our reader, whose cultural heritage was primarily central European, was inclined towards substance. While, therefore, the business school began to make available to students intensive two- and three-day modules in the conventional areas of management knowledge and skill, both he and our professor began to explore ways and means of linking individual and organizational learning.

As will be indicated in Chapter 6, Elliot Jaques suggests that there is a universally distributed depth structure of levels of bureaucratic organization, of natural lines of stratification. The existence of the stratified depth-structure of bureaucratic hierarchies, he argues, is the reflection in social organization of the existence of discontinuity and stratification in the nature of human capacity. The capacity is referred to as work capacity, which is further analysed in terms of a person's level of abstraction.

For our purposes, being less exclusively cognitively oriented than Jaques, we were more inclined to draw on cognitive, affective and behavioural elements. In effect, the spectrum of personality identified above was such, and can be organizationally recapitulated.

Organizational learning

The inward journey
Organizational learning and development is individual learning writ large. In the summer of 1991 we launched a programme on 'Building a Learning Organization', out of which, ultimately, emerged much of the material for this book. Learning is a bottom-up process, ascending from reactivity to creativity. In Figure 3.3 the colours we associate with each level were developed for ease of recognition.

Physically react
Organizational learning begins when, threatened with extinction, the whole organism reacts instinctively, pulling out all the stops, drawing on its fighting spirit. This physical reaction may be called upon when survival is threatened at birth, as was the case for us, or at a point of imminent takeover. The more finely honed and sharply focused the senses of the corporate body at this time of

RED	Reactor	How does your unit keep itself collectively alert?

ORANGE	Responder	How do you attract to you communities that will enhance your organisational learning?

YELLOW	Experimentor	How does your organisation maintain your exploratory stance and institutional experimentation?

GREEN	Energizer	How does your organisation continually expose itself to commercially, technologically and culturally or socially risk-laden situations?

BLUE	Deliberator	How do you continually conceptualise your unit's activities, both in part, and as a whole?

INDIGO	Intuitor	How do you develop your powers of insight?

VIOLET	Inspirer	How do you draw out your people's and your organisation's origins, and consequent originality?

Figure 3.3

reactive learning – by touch, taste, smell, sight and sound – the better. This instant reactivity is contained within an environment in which people 'work hard/play hard'.

Socially respond

As the organization learns so it develops a feel for its people and product, both inside and outside, by dint of willing exposure. Physical reactions, to the extent that it learns against the grain, are accompanied by social responses; instead of being lean and mean it becomes warm and welcoming, of both people and things. The hard and aggressive qualities, acquired in the active struggle for survival, are counterbalanced by soft and receptive qualities, obtained in the process of bonding together, as a community of people and as a 'craft' guild. Such is the quality of an organization that warms to its staff, to its suppliers and to its clients.

Mentally experiment

Armed with direct experience of its community within and its industry without, the organization is ready to move on. To the extent that is willing to learn – against the grain – so the craft-based community will need to develop into a technology-based institution. Our own organization is tentatively reaching out towards the electronic village, with the first of our learning sets having recently become networked electronically.

This step from a people-centred to a knowledge-centred organization is a traumatic one to take. Parochial values have to be cast aside and universal ones put in their place. Yet, to the extent that the organization wants to retain 'that family feeling', the two modes of learning and development will need to co-exist. Having lost its old way, as a social community valuing people and things, it will have to find its new way, as a learning community of interacting 'human and machine intelligences'.

Wilfully energize

An organization, at this point, has acquired the instinctive aggressiveness, the communal responsiveness and the technology-based knowhow to take on allcomers. However, it has not yet acquired the corporate will to win, the emotionally laden desire to exploit situations to its own advantage and the kind of corporate power and influence that will beat off all the competition. The learning orientation required is acquisitive and intentional, physical and emotional, a combination of raw aggression and focused intent. To develop an organization in that wilful learning light a culture and reward system needs to be established through which individual and corporate egos are aligned. This is difficult to achieve within a conventional educational environment.

Deliberately conceptualize

The overtly competitive organization, accommodating expressively competitive individuals, will get so far and no further. For at a certain point the desire to learn is counteracted, rather than reinforced, by the will to win. Self-centred intrapreneurs begin to cancel out one another's efforts. Learning is inhibited by an unwillingness to share information for fear of one individual or group being overtaken by the other.

A quantum leap in outlook is required if this confrontational and highly personalized learning mode is to be outgrown and replaced by a more cohesive and relatively depersonalized one. Such a leap would represent a move against the organizational grain, from person-centred enterprise to organization-centred management. Slowly and unsurely, under the influence of our animator's personable administrative skills as well as our change agent's project management orientation, and faced with the organizational demands of its individual and corporate clients, our programme has moved onwards and upwards, in a reasonably methodical direction.

Insightfully intuit

Bureaucracies are notorious for insulating themselves from their all-too-often changing environments. Concepts of management or of organization, of centralization or of decentralization are conventionally static and narrowly prescribed, rather than dynamic and evolutionary in nature. In fact, general concepts tend to be ill suited to changing contexts.

The consortium is notably a partnership between academia, commerce and industry. Moreover, it is reaching out towards other lands – Europe and Africa, the Middle East and Australasia – with a view to drawing upon such diverse cultures. Organizations which consciously evolve, continually renewing themselves as their internal and external environments change, have the foresight to anticipate the future. Through continually interacting with the worlds around them they progressively extend their boundaries of operation, through merger rather than takeover, through interfusion rather than expropriation. The organization thereby assumes a form which is molecular rather than hierarchical, organic rather than mechanistic. In fact, significant organizational learning is required – against the grain – if the institution is to overcome the restrictions of rigidly defined time and space.

Creatively imagine

The manager's imagination, individually centred, can be likened to the corporate image, organizationally centred. Once the institution has neared the end of its inward journey it will have accumulated the necessary thoughts, feelings and behaviours which – when combined creatively – project its self-image. In other words, that image should project the full extent of what the institution knows, is, and does. Yet it is inevitably contained within the advancement of learning.

The creative leap of learning from an evolutionary awareness to full-scale image projection demands a marrying of thought and feeling with action. Image conveys not only the organization's inner being, or aspect, but also its outer doing, or impact. Image integrates past, present and future – inspirationally – invoking positive thought, feeling and action in relevant others. Such a potent image we have yet to project.

So much for the inward journey, through which learning and development has taken place inside the individual and the organization, but is yet to make its desired impact – in terms of profit or market share, social service or community development.

Organizational innovation

The outward journey

Organizational innovation, as was the case for individual creativity, is individual innovation writ large (Figure 3.4). Innovation, as we have now seen, is conceptually a top-down process, from vision to action. We now turn from organizational learning and innovation to a more wide-ranging systemic process.

Envisioning transformation

An organization infused with vision is collectively inspired. People's individual purposes are aligned with those of the organization, and vice versa. The business's purpose, moreover, is aligned with that of society at large – technologically and ecologically, economically and culturally. The solution of the world's problems (for example relating to global warming or to the progressive increase of urban slums) are high on the visionary's strategic agenda, albeit in a commercial context. Our consortium's business purpose, with its learning orientation, is closely aligned to the implicit (though not necessarily explicit) purpose of European civilization. In its practical orientation, however, it addresses an overt need, for the enhancement of business performance, of human capital, and of the learning community.

At this point the spirit of the organization and its environment rather than 'men, money, materials and machines' is envisaged as its most potent resource. It is the ongoing transformation of that spirit into new matter, and of that matter back into new spirit, which is therefore senior management's reason for being. Whereas the journey from matter to spirit represents learning or development, the journey from spirit to matter – turning dreams into reality – represents innovation or trans-formation.

Enabling development

The enabling organization has the task of establishing a commercial and social context through which the potential created by the vision can be actualized. Both internal and external environments need to be rendered receptive to the innovative thrust of a new technology or method of social organization. New linkages have to be established once the old ones have broken down in the face

VIOLET	Create Vision	What is the far-reaching mission of your part of the organisation (your unit)?

INDIGO	Enable Development	What market or organisational potential is your unit realising?

BLUE	Structure Methodically	What definable core function is your unit carrying out?

GREEN	Compete Aggressively	What special effort and reward is particularly associated with your unit?

YELLOW	Continually Experiment	How is your unit continually learning and growing?

ORANGE	Establish Shared Values	How does your unit effect shared values, whereby people co-operate with each other?

RED	Ongoing Implementation	How are people's energy levels kept from waning?

Figure 3.4

of the disruptively innovative force. Through the enabling organization people and products, businesses and markets are developed to fulfil their potential. People, products and roles evolve rather than become mobilized, immobilized or demoblized. Physical or human energy is recognized and harnessed rather than created, channelled or destroyed. Product families replace product lines; integrated systems displace separated products and services.

Enabling the development of individual managers comes naturally to those who step easily into facilitators' shoes, whether as educators or coaches. The enabler's primary task is to provide the environment in which such developmental activity is encouraged. Enabling the development of whole organizations and societies, although an aspiration, is some way from realization.

Methodically organize

A wealth of human, product or market potential can easily be squandered if it is not ordered, organizationally and strategically. Rules and procedures, policies and programmes, management by objectives and specialization by function all have their proper place in the natural order of things. Structures and procedures play the same stabilizing part in the human organization as does the skeletal system in the human being.

In the early days, our programme and process suffered greatly from lack of structure, or 'requisite organization', as Jaques would say, to accommodate the complexity of individual freedom. Gradually, however, a profusion of systems and procedures were developed and subsequently implemented.

An analytical approach to strategy and to structure thus creates method out of madness – bearing in mind that madness needs to precede method in the natural order of innovative things – before another kind of madness bursts onto the managerial scene.

Commercially exploit

In urging us to go 'back to basics', Tom Peters has invited us to transform bureaucratic organizations into enterprising ones. This is indeed a necessary part of the innovative whole, but only a part. In fact, on the outward journey from vision to action, enterprise comes half-way through, and only after the creative, enabling and bureaucratic phases along the organizational way.

'Enterprise culture', vividly depicted in wheeler-dealing, and characteristically measured in profitable sales, is the order of our Anglo-American business day. It comes naturally to the sales force and to new business ventures. It represents capitalism at both its rawest and at its truest. Without the competitive spirit, the urge to conquer commercially, where would free enterprise be?! Without our entrepreneurial professor's 'never say die' approach to salesmanship, where would the learning consortium be?!

Interactively experiment

The learning organization is able to adapt its systems and its methods at the drop of a hat. In Edward de Bono's terms it has built-in mechanisms for thinking laterally, and in Tom Peter's terms, it is full of 'ad hocery', favouring experimentation over deliberation. Such interactive processes are enhanced by information technologies.

It is important to note, however, that this generative capacity, important as it may be, is positioned towards the end of the outward journey. The capacity to envision, the enabling function, the conventional oranizational order and the enterprise culture, all precede situational flexibility along the road to innovation. In other words, thought, devoid of feeling or action, has its organizational place but it is a limited place in the transformational hierarchy.

Involve community

No enduring organizational transformation can take place without an organization providing the social glue that can bind a new community together, once it has been re-created out of the old. Moreover, without a display of genuine caring for those people who have been lost along the way, the depressed spirit of those remaining will drag down the organization. For spirit, like energy, cannot be created or destroyed. It can only be transformed from one state to another.

With the renewed interest of the management establishment in 'corporate culture', the role of animator has come back into the limelight. For, as the American culture gurus – Deal and Kennedy – have told us, a healthily growing organization needs not only its heroes but also its priests and its storytellers, its gossips and its whisperers, each playing their well-orchestrated part in the people-managed whole. A uniquely communal environment, then, has been created within our programme, with warmth and caring flowing over at the edges.

Bias for action

In converting a farsighted vision into everyday action an organization, engaged in continuing learning and transformation, will be actualizing itself completely. In so doing it will be employing a full set of knowledge-, skill- and character-based competencies. The urge to actualize, at this culminating end of things, will be stimulated by a sense of absolute urgency, a bias for continuous action and a spirit of physically based adventure.

Conclusion

Learning at heart

> In conclusion, our development programme has evolved out of managerial, towards organizational learning, but has not yet purposefully addressed societal learning, in Robert Reich's sense. In the chapters that follow we shall present the four major concepts of individual and institutional learning upon which this text is based. In so doing we shall consider Reg Revens's 'action learning', Elliot Jaques's 'requisite organization', Peter Senge's 'fifth dimension' and Shoshana Zuboff's 'informated community', in turn.
>
> In the practical chapters that follow each of the above four learning concepts, first, Mary Coles, a project leader in the social work department of a London-based local authority, will deal with managerial learning, drawing upon both spectral theory and action learning. Second, Conrad Fernandez, a marketing manager in a Geneva-based subsidiary of an international American instrumentation company, will deal with organizational learning, applying concepts of requisite organization. Third, Brian Johns, a manager of an actuarial department at Norwich Union in the UK, will be applying Senge's systemic worldview to his organization. Finally, Ronnie Lessem will apply Zuboff's ideas of a learning community to the computer division of a South African clothing retailer. Finally, in a concluding chapter, the implications for business as a learning community will be reconsidered.

REFERENCES

de Bono, E., *Mechanics of Mind*, Penguin (1971).
Deal, T. and A. Kennedy, *Corporate Cultures*, Penguin (1982).
Kolb, D., *Experiential Psychology*, Prentice-Hall (1984).
Lessem, R., *Intrapreneurship*, Wildwood House (1987).
Lessem, R., *Developmental Management*, Blackwell (1990).
Lessem, R., *Total Quality Learning*, Blackwell (1991).
Murray, H., *Time for a Rethink*, Internal publication.
Peters, T. and R. Waterman, *In Search of Excellence*, Harper & Row (1982).

Part 2
SEMINAL LEARNING CONCEPTS

4

Action learning –
individual learning and managerial development

A 'would-be' enabling organization

During the nineties the public sector in Britain, particularly in the National Health Service and local government, has been undergoing a transformation. Spurred on by the Conservative government's attempts to bring market forces to bear upon public services, old-style bureaucracies have been turned inside out, ostensibly into 'enabling organizations'.

Within such 'enabling' enterprises the emphasis has been shifted away from the lifetime employment of internal resources to a system of contracting-out services to private and voluntary organizations on an ever-increasing scale. In basic terms, there has been much in the way of marketing and little in the way of enabling. An enabling organization is one in which the potential of people and enterprises, of products and markets, is considerably enhanced. In that sense it is closely connected with a learning organization, in which the development of individuals and groups, of interpersonal and inter-organizational relationships, holds pride of place. Sadly, such a developmental nettle has not been grasped by many local authorities. As a result, the government's vision of an enabling organization, duly distorted by its market-based philosophy, has prevailed.

Reviewing social work

There have, however, been exceptions to this general rule. For example, in the London Borough of Ealing a project manager in a social work department, Mary Coles, has spent several years building up a learning community within her own team, making extensive use of Revans's concept of action learning. In fact, Mary has modified Revans's approach, including a nurturing element alongside the scientific one, thereby purposefully bringing the world of feeling into play to co-exist with thinking and doing. More recently, moreover, Mary has begun to transform the appraisal system in her department into a vehicle for conscious learning. In that context, performance appraisal becomes a part of a greater whole, that is, an integrated learning process.

In fact, Mary Coles has not been working in isolation. Brenda Malahleka, a colleague of hers in social services, has been developing quality circles to enhance the development of her staff and the functioning of her department. These circles of learning and development, management and organization, extend from the Borough into the surrounding community. The particular approach Brenda has used is drawn from her own African experience of 'the collective self'.

In the final analysis, though, the work that Brenda and Mary have been doing in social services is swamped by the overriding forces of traditional bureaucracy, on the one hand, and of the marketplace, on the other. In that context individually oriented action learning, as we shall see during the course of this book, needs to be supplemented with organizationally, systemically and communally based approaches. We shall start, however, with the action learning approach.

Introduction

The roots of action learning

The first of our four approaches to the learning organization is that developed in the sixties and seventies by Cambridge physicist and management philosopher, Reg Revans. Revans's approach is deeply rooted in English and scientific soil, that is, within empirical and pragmatic traditions. As such, it is strongly focused upon 'action' as an individual managerial activity and upon 'learning' as a social and organizational process. Not surprisingly, therefore, Mary Coles perceived that action learning would have a vital role to play in the development of an 'enabling organization' within the Borough of Ealing's Social Services.

Revans, moreover, has stood on the shoulders of three great British predecessors – Francis Bacon in the seventeenth, Adam Smith in the eighteenth and Samuel Smiles in the nineteenth centuries. Whereas Bacon spearheaded the advancement of learning from England, and Smith the wealth of nations from Scotland, Smiles was the chronicler of Victorian self-help. All three, together with Revans, were empirically oriented.

The idea of empiricism

'Empiricism', the doctrine that all knowledge is acquired through experience, is firmly embedded in the philosophical soil of Britain, particularly within England. To some extent, the Dutch and the Scandinavians within Europe, and to a greater extent, the North Americans and Australasians outside, share this action-centred, experientially oriented, philosophical outlook. In fact, embodied in private enterprise, in the free market and in capitalism, this economic orientation has dominated the world, at least prior to the emergence of the Japanese with their variation on the theme of free, individual enterprise.

Moreover, common law based on precedent behavioural psychology based on directly observable phenomena and classical science based on visible blocks of matter, all stem from this Anglo-Saxon 'feet on the ground' approach. The initiator of it all, following in Aristotleian vein, was Francis Bacon, the Lord Chancellor of England, in Elizabethan times.

Francis Bacon – The Advancement of Learning

Discovering the experimental method

The seminal influence on empiricism or pragmatism, from a managerial perspective, has been, surprisingly enough, Francis Bacon in the early part of the seventeenth century. His work on the inductively based *Advancement of Learning* did for the scientific revolution what Adam Smith's treatise on *The Wealth of Nations* did for the industrial one. Man, Bacon insisted, must ascertain the facts about the universe; he must maintain the great continuity and transmission of learning through universities dedicated not to the dry husks of ancient learning alone but to research upon the natural world of the present.

Mary Coles's management development

> Soon after I enrolled on the Management MBA I realized that my research requirements would be set not by the academics on high but by the emergent needs of the people around me. In that context, the university in which the programme was based, in association with the Borough of Ealing, was more in the way of an enabling organization than an educational institution.

Truth, to the medieval schoolmen, rested upon the belief that reality lay in the world of ideas largely independent of our sense perceptions. Whereas Elizabethan craftsmen or seafarers sometimes made discoveries, Bacon said, the experiments of those calloused hands were often scorned by 'medievally minded' gentleman. Francis Bacon, presented quite another 'engine', as he termed it, for the attainment of truth. In essence, his argument was as follows. *We must refrain from deducing general principles for which we have no real evidence in nature.* Instead, we must dismiss much of what we think we know and begin anew patiently to collect facts from nature, never straying far from reality until it is possible through close observation to deduce more general laws. This is Bacon's famous inductive method.

Project-based learning

> My first project arose out of my own need to make more sense of what I was doing, and my clients' needs to benefit more from the service we were offering. I realized that I needed to be more adept at putting my background and experience as a woman, as a mother, as a professional, and as a self-starter, to bear upon my work. What came out of the combination of action and introspection that followed was a

concept of 'action learning' that I dreamt up. Subsequently I discovered that I was not the first person to come up with the term!

The unlearned man, therefore, according to Bacon, does not know what it is to descend into himself, or call himself into account, whereas the learned man fares otherwise, forever interweaving thought and action. Though he sought to combine the discoveries of the practical craftsman with the insights of the philosopher, Bacon saw clearly that the development of the experimental method itself, the means by which 'all things else might be discovered', was of more importance than any single invention.

Building from the bottom up

So Bacon eliminated reliance upon the rare elusive genius as a safe road into the future, for, he maintained, it involved too much risk and chance to rely upon such men alone. One must, instead, place one's hope for Utopia in the education of 'plain Tom Jones and Dick Thickhead'. Bacon had an enormous trust in the capacities of the human mind, though he was at the same time well aware of its distortions. This English Lord Chancellor was more than willing, therefore, to build from common clay.

Built out of common clay

> I came from a family of thirteen children. Cheaper by the dozen the saying goes. We brought each other up, becoming parents and children at one and the same time. When I raised my own family, though we had fewer children, the same pattern of mutual support prevailed. In fact we took on boarders from all over the world to extend the family, as well as the household budget. So I started my social work training late in life, as a mature student, consciously building on the experience of life – both my own and others' – that I had built up along the way.

Francis Bacon, moreover, regarded learning as composed of two parts. First, it entailed the gathering together of existing knowledge, to be organized and disseminated through books and other forms of communication. Second, it involved the discovery of new knowledge through experience, indeed through experiment. Such experimentation involved turning everyday experience, and observation, into scientifically based insights.

Revans, three and a half centuries later, has transformed Bacon's discovery of experimental method in science into his own discovery of 'action learning' in management. Moreover, Bacon's distinction between existing and new knowledge has been turned, as we shall see, into Revans's differentation between programmed knowledge and questioning insight. However, Bacon was not Revans's only source of inspiration. The 'naturalist' school to which both belonged also included the noted political economist, Adam Smith.

Competition promotes liberty

The naturalist school of philosophy, originating with the ancient Greeks, came to full flower in the latter part of the seventeenth century. In essence, it relied on what is natural as against what is contrived. For Smith, only complete competition was consistent with natural liberty. Through such free competition everybody obtained the full rewards of their efforts, while also adding their full contribution to the common good.

Human conduct then, according to Adam Smith, was naturally activated by such a desire to be free, by a sense of propriety, by a habit of labour and by a propensity to truck, barter and exchange. Given these springs of conduct, each man was naturally the best judge of his own interest and should therefore be left to pursue his task in his own way. If left to himself he would not only attain his own best advantage, he would also further the common good. Each individual was led by an invisible hand to promote the interest of society. What Smith proposed, therefore, was a system of natural liberty, or *'laissez faire'*, as the best means of bringing about the wealth of nations.

Self-made man

> My father was a self-made man. With no formal education of his own he pulled himself up by his own bootstraps, and made a good enough living to support as large a family as ours. In many ways I have inherited his inclination to be a self-starter, albeit in the context of social work rather than business. It is this kind of outlook that I bring to my project team, with regard to not only our team performance but also our individual and group learning.

Revans likewise, as we shall see, advocated that individuals should pursue their own learning but alongside so-called 'comrades in adversity'. Such a learning 'set' would duly exchange information, advice and ideas, thereby engendering a social process of learning.

Promoting mutual exchange

Revans, in this respect, was linking the advancement of learning with processes of social, if not economic, exchange. Why then, according to Smith, was such social or economic exchange necessary?

In almost every other race of animals, Smith maintained, when it is grown up to maturity it is entirely independent, and in its natural state has occasion for the assistance of no other living creature. But man has constant occasion for the help of his fellow creatures. Among men, Smith maintains, the most dissimilar geniuses are of use to each other, being brought, by virtue of exchange, into a common stock. Every man thus lives by exchanging, or becomes in some measure a merchant, and the society itself grows into a commercial society. What Revans has done, therefore, is to shift his micro orientation from economic to social exchange, and his macro orientation from a commercial towards a learning society. In that context he is mirroring Robert Reich's shift in emphasis from financial to human capital. Between Smith and Revans, historically and conceptually, is Samuel Smiles.

Samuel Smiles – promoting self-help

Help from within

Samuel Smiles's *Self-Help* was published in 1859, the same year as Darwin's *Origin of Species* and Mill's *Essay on Liberty*. Smiles built the book on a series of talks he had given to young artisans who had formed, in the north of England, an evening school for mutual improvement. Cults of self-help and self-improvement were becoming widespread, representing the value of achievement over that of birth. There were in 1860 over 200 000 members of Mechanics' Institutes, combined with mutual improvement societies, lyceums and libraries, and adult education took place at most of them. In addition, there were three million members of friendly and provident societies.

Self-improvement

> I come from a whole tradition of self-improvement, what with my father as a self-made man and myself as an adult learner. There is something ingrained within us, an in-born desire to help ourselves, and in my case to help others help themselves along the way. In fact local government within this country was started by social entrepreneurs in the nineteenth century. People like Ebenezer Howard, with his Garden City movement, were very influential in the part of the world where I come from.

Smiles lauded individualism, unlike his Scottish predecessor, Adam Smith, not solely as a means to worldly gain but as the path to independence and to self-fulfilment. In that sense he constructed a bridge between commercial and personal growth.

For Samuel Smiles, in fact, the spirit of self-help is the root of all genuine growth in the individual. Exhibited in the lives of many, therefore, it constitutes for him the true source of national vigour and strength. Help from without is inevitably en-feebling in its effect but help from within invariably invigorates. National progress – for Smiles then as for Reich now – is the sum of individual industry, energy and uprightness. It follows that the highest patriotism and philanthropy consist not so much in altering laws and modifying institutions as in helping and stimulating people to elevate and improve themselves. It may be of comparatively little consequence how a man is governed from without, while everything depends, for Smiles, on how he governs himself from within. The solid foundations of liberty must rest upon individual character.

The school of labour

Schools, academies and colleges give but the merest beginnings of a culture. Far more influential is the life education daily given in people's homes, in the streets, behind counters, in workshops, at the loom and the plough, in counting houses and factories, and in the busy haunts of men. A man perfects himself by work more than by reading. It is life rather than literature, action rather than study, and character rather than biography, which tends perpetually to renovate mankind. For Smiles, then, it is in the school of labour that the best practical wisdom is taught.

School of labour

> I would reckon that it is 'the school of labour' rather than, say, the Labour Party, which has informed my character development during my life at work. In fact it was Ebenezer Howard who said: 'The true remedy for capitalist oppression where it exists, is not the strike of no work, but the strike of *true work*, and against this last blow the oppressor has no weapon. If labour leaders spent half the energy in co-operative organization that they now waste in cooperative disorganization, the end of our present unjust system would be at hand.'

Great men of science, literature and art, Smiles said, have belonged to no exclusive class or rank in life. They have come alike from colleges, workshops and farm-houses. Some of God's greatest apostles have come from the 'ranks'. Difficulties undergone evoke powers of labour and endurance, stimulating personal faculties which might otherwise have lain dormant. For example, Shakespeare's father was a butcher and glazier, and Shakespeare himself is supposed to have been a woolcomber in early life. He was certainly also an actor, and in the course of his life played many parts, gathering his wonderful store of knowledge from wide experience and observation.

Among the great names of the Industrial Revolution – symbolic analysts in Reich's terms – are those of Thomas Newcomen, James Watt and George Stephenson; the first a blacksmith, the second a maker of mathematical instruments and the third an engine-fireman. For Reich, with the benefit of twentieth-century hindsight, such innovators would have engaged in some degree of abstraction from their everyday reality, some kind of systems thinking in relating technology to society, and due collaboration with their fellow-craftsmen. Above all, though, they will have been engaged in experimentation.

The best of every man's education, for Smiles then, is that which man gives to himself. The education received at school or college is but a beginning. That which is put into men by others is always far less theirs than that which they acquire through their own diligent and persevering effort. Knowledge conquered by labour becomes a possession. A greater vividness and permanency of impression is secured; and facts thus acquired become registered in the mind in a way that mere imparted knowledge can never effect. The solution of one problem helps the mastery of another; and thus knowledge is carried into faculty.

Knowledge as faculty

> My social work training, initially, and my management education, subsequently, has taught me one and the same thing, that – as Samuel Smiles said many moons ago – the solution of one problem helps the mastery of another. In this way knowledge applied converts into ability. This process is as applicable to the development of interpersonal skills, in working with the public, as it is to the cultivation of financial skills, in working with managers.

Help from without

Finally, however, although much may be accomplished by means of individual industry and energy, Smiles emphasizes – as Revans does even more – that the help which we derive from others is of very great importance. From infancy to old age, Smiles argued, all are more or less indebted to others for nurture and culture, and the best and strongest are usually found readiest to acknowledge such help. One needs to be sustained not only by oneself but also by contact with one's colleagues in the business of life. For Smiles no individual in the universe stands alone; one is a component part of a system of mutual dependencies. To respect oneself, to develop oneself – this is one's true duty in life. And as one respects oneself, one is equally bound to respect others, which leads us on to Revans.

Do unto others . . .

> My project team hardly recognize me any more. They reckon that my whole attitude to management has changed dramatically over the past year. I used to be so involved with the professional work I was doing that I would virtually ignore the professional workers. Now, they say, I have developed a much greater awareness of my responsibility, as a manager, to carry other people with me, not only in the performance of the task but also in the development of ourselves as a group of 'action learners'.

Action learning

The vision: 'doers of the word'

> But be ye doers of the word and not hearers only, deceiving your own selves. For if any be a hearer of the word, and not a doer, he is like unto a man beholding his natural face in a glass. For he beholdeth himself, and goeth his way, and straightway forgetteth what manner of man he was.
>
> (*The General Epistle of James*, 1, 22–4)

Revans seems to have an almost religious *commitment to action*, as opposed to book learning. He argues that education has a role in helping the manager to build bridges between his subjective self and the world out there. For Revans:

> Human experience remains only partially accessible to external observation. Deep within the manager is the darkness of his subjective world. Education should play a part in helping the manager explore that darkness so that he may find his way through the solitudes of conscious experience.

Revans has, no doubt, spent many years exploring his own inner world. However, without the other, the self is incomplete. Revans alludes to learning situations in which there are neither Chiefs nor Indians. In this context, individuals, in seeking to enrich and enlarge their own subjective self, help, reciprocally, to enrich and enlarge the subjective selves of others.

Spiritual barter

> It is interesting to observe the changes I have gone through these past three years, since I consciously embarked on a programme of management development. Firstly, I have become much more purposefully introspective. I am much more aware of myself as a person and as a manager. I am also operating on an entirely different plane now from the one I inhabited three years ago. Before I would tackle day-to-day problems with little awareness of their broader implications on myself, on my workmates, and on the community as a whole. Now I feel I am operating on a different wavelength. I am engaging in people's work and lives at a much more intimate and profound level than I was doing before. Work has become a challenge to myself, via other people's selves, rather than a contest between my ego and my fellow professionals'.

Revans even refers to a process of 'spiritual barter', whereby our latent capacity for warm and genuine exchanges manifests itself. He alludes constantly, moreover, to comrades in adversity learning from and through each others' moving experiences. Revans's mission may well be reflected in the following quote from Toynbee's *A Study of History*:

> Real progress is found to consist in a process defined as 'etherealisation', an overcoming of material obstacles which releases the energies of society to make responses to challenges which henceforth are internal rather than external, spiritual rather than material.

This vision of Revans has evolved through a lifetime of action learning, undoubtedly shaped by his experiences as athlete, scientist, manager and coalface worker. He has devoted some fifty years to developing his ideas and testing them in companies, the hospital service, in government and education. Perhaps, more than anything, he has fought to close the gap, particularly in Britain, between the 'artisan' and the 'scribe'.

Context: linking artisan and scribe

Revans states in his book, *Action Learning*, that:

> It is a virtue of *action learning* that, like truth itself, it is a seamless garment. With its help, all parties alike, 'Scribe' and 'Artisan'; Manager and Workman, should tackle

their common foe – the External Problem. Their own opinions of each other – personal and interested, strained by the antipathies of unforgettable tradition, teased and exacerbated by every civilising process of the education establishment, reinforced by every decision of our Industrial Tribunals, may be pretty intransigent; advance will not be easy.

Linking thought and action

At a societal level, as we have seen, action learning attacks the root of our nation's problems. In his *The Rise and Fall of the British Manager*, Alistair Mant puts the matter succinctly. In fact he views Britain as being 'schizoid'. He describes a schizoid person or nation as one whose parts remain split, feeding off and sustaining each other. They are essentially unintegrated, incapable of resolution into a whole, fearing a fantasy of destruction. Such a nation, is, literally, without integrity.

Mant argues that the obvious split in Britain is that between owners and workers. Revans treats the whole question of integrity in both personal and social terms. Action learning is a means to link thought and action within the person and scribe and artisan within the nation. Mant describes this social process with vivid effect:

> People in clerkish roles do not have an experience of, and cannot therefore properly comprehend, the three-dimensional world of bulk, lumpiness, weight and unpredictability which lies outside their immediate preview. If there were two ingredients I most wanted to inject into clerkish veins, they would be inspiration and panic.

Inspiration and panic

> I am invariably struck by the inward looking nature of much of the bureaucratic activity that goes on within the corridors of power. For field workers like ourselves the world is filled with inspiration and panic, perspiration and manic. Our work is so full of unpredictability and change that unless we are continually learning, and developing, our stock of knowledge and our portfolio of skills becomes remarkably obsolete.

Learning > rate of change

Revans substitutes inspiration and panic with an ability to learn that exceeds the rate of change. He maintains that anyone who can't keep up with what is new will lose control of their surroundings. Someone capable of taking innovation in their stride will profit by being about to turn it to advantage. Therefore, according to Botkin *et al.*, in today's climate the advantage must lie with anyone able to learn.

When he was working with the National Coal Board in the fifties Revans saw how management–worker relations impaired the nation's economic performance. He recognized that the potential of management science was being virtually untapped. Initially, in the hospital service, where tensions between nurses and doctors and medical and administrative staff were rife, Revans used social science and statistical methods in order to research and act on the problems. As a result of this, in the sixties, Belgian industry seized upon Revans's 'product'. Belgian managers, in admitting the inadequacies of their country's own resources combined with its landlocked position, realized that the only way they could keep up was to learn faster than their wealthier European counterparts. How might this, in Revans's terms, come to be?

The concept: programmed knowledge and questioning insight

Management

According to Boddy:

> Professor Revans distinguishes between two kinds of learning, 'P' and 'Q' . 'P' refers to the acquisition of existing, programmed knowledge, while 'Q' refers to the acquisition of the ability to ask fresh questions. Both types of learning are necessary for Managers. They need to keep up to date with technical work, and also to develop the skill to cope with the ambiguities and uncertainties of innovation and policy making.

The action learning concept, from what we have seen so far, is a much richer one than is conventionally realized. The wider social significance of the approach is often missed because most of its advocates are either too practically or technique oriented. Moreover, because of the human relations bias of many of its interpreters, the 'management science' aspect is frequently diluted, and sometimes ignored altogether. Finally, Revans has drawn significantly from Francis Bacon. And interestingly enough Revans calculated six essentials of managerial concern: the *nature of values*; the nature of *information*; the logic of *systems*; the theory of *decision*; the extention of *uncertainty*; as well as adaptation and *learning*. What bearing, then, does Revans's analytical approach have upon a manager's work? How does it compare with the more conventionally based general management activities of planning, organizing, directing and controlling?

System Alpha

Revans represents the three principal influences on management as systems based on the use of information. 'We call them System Alpha – The Use of Information for designing objectives; System Beta – The Use of Information for achieving these objectives; and System Gamma – The Use of Information for adapting to experience and change'. System Alpha is probably the best known of all Revans's concepts. To be flexible, Revans argues, a course of action demands first that the manager *values* what he anticipates will be the outcome of the action; second, that he be aware of the *external difficulties* he will need to surmount in order to achieve this outcome: third, that he can find *internal resources* enough to deal with these difficulties at a cost consonant with the value of the outcome. Revans raises these questions on the manager's behalf, pertaining to his System Alpha, related to designing objectives:

- By what values am I guided?
- What is blocking their fulfilment?
- What can I do against the blockage?

or

- By what set of values am I guided?
- What is the chance to fulfil them?
- What can I do to seize the chance?

System Alpha

> Since deciding to embark on a career in social work, I have been strongly influenced by the ideal of social work, that is, my desire to be of service to those in need. The reality is, and as I discovered over the years, there is much more need than there is available provision. This leads many a social worker to burn out, through alienation or sheer desperation. Having been through a similar process myself I eventually came to realize that I had to go about more purposefully fulfilling my own needs before I could truly serve the needs of others. So, over the course of the past few years, I have become what some of my colleagues would describe as more self-centred. I would argue that I have been steering a more selective course towards self realization, and in the process hopefully furthering the self-fulfilment of others with whom I am closely connected. In that respect I have seized the developmental chance that my recent course of management development has offered.

Management objectives, therefore, should be designed to reflect pervading values, to take into account external difficulties, and to utilize internal resources.

System Beta

System Beta is concerned with achieving objectives. At its simplest, it involves five stages:

1. A *survey* during which an event is observed.

2. A *hypothesis* – through which a relation is perceived.

3. An *action* – in which a trial is made.

4. An *audit* – through which the results are analysed.

5. *Control* – whereby the whole process is assimilated.

System Gamma

Finally, System Gamma, which deals with aspects of individual learning, brings together the person and the situation. The manager, who is a quite unique being, confronts a problem in the field and absorbs the facts in a particular way. In effect, they are then processed by the manager's 'predisposing mental set'. His or her decision and learning are both conditioned by a perception of values, the external problem and the internal resources.

Revans claims that in management you need to design objectives, work towards their achievement and learn in the process. The media through which you work consist of values, information, systems, decisions, probability and learning processes. The relationship between the manager and the problem, mediated by the 'predisposing mental set', is of key importance. So, equally, is the organization's commitment.

The commitment: know, care, do

For Revans, action learning must be able:

> To enable every enterprise to make better use of its existing resources, by trying to engender within it a social process of learning calculated to help it identify its internal strengths and weaknesses, to understand better its inertias and dynamics, and in other ways to make more effective use of its stored experience.

Project-based commitment

Action learning, as we have now seen, is a vehicle for management development and a route to organizational learning. One cannot proceed without the other. It is critical, therefore, that the organization as a whole should subscribe to the learning objectives.

If a problem is seen as requiring a project report, this in no way interferes with the day-to-day operations of the company. However, according to Powell, if the organization is going to examine procedures, operations and methods, and subsequently, at the behest of the action learner, change them, there is a substantial threat of disruption to present operations. These must be anticipated and negotiated. Organizational commitment to learning must be developed. In any dealings between educator and institutional client, Revans has itemized fourteen matters for consideration:

1. The choice of problems around which to form projects.

2. The role and responsibility of clients.

3. The qualities and selection of action learning participants.

4. The monitoring of projects.

5. The development of set (small-group) advisors.

6. The representation of the firm in any consortium of learning organizations.

7. The role of training staffs.

8. The induction of fellows into their projects.

9. The continued academic support for participants.

10. The continued role of line management in projects.

11. The supply of appropriate technical knowledge.

12. The extension of one project into another.

13. Issues of cost and benefit.

14. The concept of the whole organization as a learning system.

Commitment to organizational learning

> Our local authority falls far short of an overall commitment to organizational, as well as to individual learning. That having been said, I know of no other organization in this country which had made that kind of learning-based commitment. On the one hand, then, I have been very contented with the projects I have undertaken, both from my own point of view and from the organization's. I have also been fortunate in the academic and line management support that I have received. On the other hand, the borough is far from seeing the whole organization as a learning system. That is one of the reasons I set my own project team on such a deliberately learning-based course, so as hopefully to trigger off our whole system towards its supposed transformation into an enabling organization.

A participant in the GEC Action Learning Programme, one of the most extensive such programmes run in Britain in the seventies, highlighted three considerations as being critical for both participating organization and manager. For Casey and Pearce:

> Participants should be given projects that are *major business problems*. Simple problems, involving tedious clerical work will not train future senior managers. They must also be *important problems* for the client, so that they are determined to get them fixed. Learners should be told that there will be *new jobs* at the end of the programme, and these should be arranged as soon as possible.

An action learning consortium
While action learning has made great inroads among management in Belgium, its influence in Britain has been sporadic, albeit widespread. The responsibility for spreading word and action has been largely that of individual management trainers and consultants, polytechnics and a few companies. The trouble is, according to Morris, people want something tangible that they can relate to, rather than a supposed cure-all which will develop the organization as a whole. As Casey shows, the sponsors of an Action Learning Programme Consortium, a group of companies in the Midlands in the seventies, tried to overcome this obstacle by pointing towards some unique and yet tangible features of action learning, encompassing most particularly the balance between problem solving and management development.

The City consortium

The problem with our own action learning-based consortium, at least insofar as City University and the Borough of Ealing are concerned, is that problem solving in the context of our 'business' projects, and management development in association with our personal 'projects', have never been fully integrated. I guess the same applies for most of the consortium members. Revans's notion of building a social process of learning into the institution as a whole, though it is intrinsic to the development of an enabling organization, is still alien to our bureaucratic and/or market-oriented culture.

Know–care–do

To cope with the various problems of implementation which accompany action learning, Revans has developed a formula for the ALP Consortium:

> A decision has to be designed and then negotiated; the problem or the opportunity has first to be diagnosed and then treated. All our work suggests that the guile of realistic diagnosis – what are we after? What stops us? What can we do? – demands just less than 50% of our total effect, and the artfulness of effective negotiation – *who KNOWS? who CARES? who CAN?* – most of the remainder. Knowing goes with Thinking and Cognition: Caring goes with Feeling and Affective Processes: Doing (being able to) goes with Behaviour. In tapping the Whole Man, we tap the Whole Organisation. In tapping the Whole Organisation, we tap the Whole Man.

Action learning programmes, then, aim to help managers and organizations develop the skills and capacities required to deal with a changing environment. To achieve this, the primary resources are management time and organizational co-operation; secondary resources are people, finance, facilities. The risk is that the individual's 'predisposing mental set' or the organization's 'prevailing culture' will collapse and there will be no one capable of putting all the pieces together again. The expected economic return manifests itself as profits or productivity. The expected psychological return becomes an enhanced ability to cope with change. The unexpected spiritual return emerges as a resolution of inner conflicts and a gaining or moral conviction. The expected societal return realizes itself as Toynbee's process of etherealization and as the healing of Mant's schizoid split in the nation.

How action learning is facilitated

The process: action learning

For Revans:

> The theory of learning, whose inner logic is that of System Beta, suggests that the recognition of one's own need to learn, the search for new knowledge, the test of that new knowledge in practical action, the critical evaluation of the results of that test, and the consolidation of the whole exercise in memory, are all essential to complete learning.

Cycles of learning

For Revans, as for Francis Bacon before him, the cycle of learning involves an iter-ation between *action and reflection*. The actor changes the system; the reflector changes the self. Neither can operate effectively in isolation of the other. You can only learn from experience if you reflect on it. Unless you have experience, you have no foundation on which to base your learning.

        Action   Reflection

If we go a stage further, our polarity becomes a triangle:

                                Understanding

        Action   Reflection

The model of the learning process that Revans puts forward is a particular appli-cation of general scientific method. Faced with a problem, managers use their general understanding of the situation in order to decide on a strategy and means of implementing it. They enter an action phase when they try to put their ideas into practice. This is followed by a stage of reflection in which expected and actual results are compared. In fact, David Kolb's well-known learning cycle (see Figure 4.1) is an adaptation, consciously or otherwise of that of Revans. Kolb, an organizational psychologist based at MIT, speaks of reflective observation, abstract conceptualization, active experimentation and concrete experience. Revans alludes to *survey*, *hypothesis*, *test* and *audit*.

This constitutes Revan's System Beta, the sequential cycle of learning that closely corresponds with scientific method. The *survey* activity involves observing, col-lecting data, investigating, fact finding, becoming aware. *Hypothesis* making involves speculating, conjecturing, theorizing, design, invention, pattern formation. *Testing* involves trial and experimentation. *Audit* involves inquiry, inspection scrutiny, verification. Finally, there is an integrating *control* phase where an attempt is made to improve general methods following the particular experiment.

Learning to perform

> In the spring of 1992 I was given the opportunity to completely overhaul our performance-appraisal system. As far as management were concerned, within Social Services, my task was to build more explicitly into our appraisal system a set of core professional competencies. As far as I was concerned this offered me the golden opportunity of integrating performance with learning, in a purposeful way. In fact I took up Kolb's learning cycle – inclusive of active experimentation and reflective observation, abstract conceptualization and concrete experience – and developed a performance-appraisal approach that incorporated all of these elements. While my

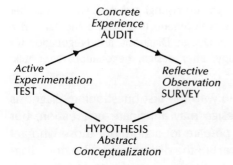

Figure 4.1 Kolb's Learning Cycle

pilot group became altogether enthused by the new approach, senior management were initially somewhat bemused by the whole thing, though the idea has more recently begun to grow on them.

Self and system

It doesn't stop here. Revans is quick to point out that action learning is not founded on scientific method and rationally based decision making alone. It is equally dependent upon the exchange between people, plus the learning of new behaviour. For Botkin *et al.*:

> Whereas anticipation encourages solidarity in time, participation creates solidarity in space. Anticipation is temporal, while participation is spatial. Where anticipation is a *mental* activity, participation is a *social* one.

For Revans, learning is also just as much a social as a physical and intellectual process. As Casey says in his article in the *Journal of European Training*:

1. There is a great power in an intelligent interloper asking idiot questions, i.e. the power of original *thought*.

2. Comrades in adversity learn best with and from each other, i.e. through people with whom they *feel* identified.

3. To get things *done* in an organization, one needs to find out who cares, who knows, and who can.

These three psychological attributes, finally, are also found in what is perhaps the most significant of all Revans's statements.

> One cannot change the system of which one is in command (at least in any new sense) unless one is oneself changed in the process, since the logical structure of both are in correspondence. The change in the system we call action (behaviourial); that in the self we call learning (cognitive). Such learning consists much more in the reorganization of what was already (feels) familiar than it consists in acquiring fresh knowledge. The Learning Process as described, moreover, contains sequential

(though interactive) complementary (though contrasting) activities, which together make up Individual and Organisational Development. It is both a Mental and a Social Process. It also involves a mixture of Design, Diagnosis, and Negotiation (or implementation). After diagnosis, therapy; after design, negotiation, after talk, action.

The dichotomy is false: therapy has started with the first questioning; diagnosis continues until the end of treatment; design may anticipate negotiation, but negotiation may modify design; talk may prepare for action, but those who act learn to talk in a different tone for the future. But the dichotomy is also true: diagnosis, design and talk call only for intelligence; therapy, negotiation and to act call for courage, belief and commitment.

Design and negotiation

In many ways designing the new performance appraisal was the easy bit. Okay, it took me some time to come up with a core set of social work competencies that were applicable to the range of fields which we covered, but it was not too difficult for me to rise to that occasion. The real tricky part was convincing particularly my superiors on the management committee that learning and performance were inextricably intertwined, and evaluation was only one part of a much more important learning-based whole. I'm glad to be able to say now, that after several formal meetings and innumerable discussions on each side, I have won over even some of the greatest sceptics.

Interaction: the learning 'set' and the 'set' advisor

According to Glyn Trollope, Group Personnel Manager, GEC:

Action learning gives participants reasonable opportunities to think and take stock through the eyes of others. Inevitably some participants have limitations which cannot be remedied. And it is counterproductive to highlight characteristics which a participant cannot control or improve. But most individual talents and characteristics can be developed. So within a project set, in the process of seeking solutions to problems, we tried to improve our abilities to listen, analyse and learn, and to recognise and improve various personal inadequacies which impede effective management.

Interactive learning
The 'learning set' is both route map and resting place for the action learner, even if the 'project' is the actual learning vehicle. It is a source of challenge and support, a focal point for reflection upon action. It is through the 'set' that the learning cycle is channelled. As we have indicated, action learning for Revans is a social process, a place of social and psychological as well as commercial exchange.

Managers learn with and from each other by supportive attacks upon real and menacing problems. A 'set' consists of some four to seven individuals, and is convened by a 'set advisor'. In the course of up to a day's meeting, arranged perhaps monthly over a period of some six months, there will be:

- An exchange of *information* – ideas, advice, contacts, hunches, concepts.
- *Interaction* between set members, offering each other support and encouragement as well as challenge and critical appraisal.
- *Behavioural* change resulting more often from the re-interpretation of the past experiences than from the acquisition of fresh knowledge.

With the 'set', learning takes place through the interplay of *thought* (information), *feeling* (interaction) and *action* (behaviour). Production managers, for example, who 'thought' that marketing was about 'bribery and lunches' would never be able to absorp fresh information about it until they came to 'feel' differently about the subject. Only when they had re-interpreted their past experiences would the managers be able to think and subsequently 'act' differently. According to Burgoyne and Cunningham, many people who have thought about the 'learning set' highlight:

- What is going on inside the person
- What is going on between people, and
- What is going on in terms of group phenomena

From project team to learning 'set'

Over the course of the last year, in particular, I have made a concerted attempt to convert my project team into something resembling a learning 'set'. We now much more consciously devote time and attention to assessing what is going on not only within our group as a whole, but also within and between its different members. Moreover, we are now as much concerned with the development of our professional knowledge, skills and character as we are with completing the everyday task at hand. What has been involved, therefore, is an entire culture change, wholly within our team, and to some extent within the department around us. Individual, if not also organizational, learning has become our ultimate reason for being at work, thereby stimulating the development of an enabling organization.

This kind of developmental orientation is exemplified by the comments of Barry Scott, a technical manager at GEC:

The project set quickly established a high degree of *group* cohesion. Within the framework of support a high level of *personal integrity* developed, and support was counterbalanced by criticism. Eventually, however, the persistent pressure of the set on *each other* was effective in creating a definite awareness of personal shortcomings.

The 'set' advisor

Burgoyne and Cunningham refer to the general characteristics of group leader effectiveness as providing feedback, questioning participants, providing a behaviour model, giving a psychological support, creating structured exercises and providing conceptual frameworks. David Casey adds, more specifically, tolerance for ambiguity, openness and frankness, patience, a desire to see others learn, and the ability to empathize as required 'set advisor' characteristics. In contrast, if we take a more pragmatic look at 'group meetings' we see the following:

1. Meetings provide an opportunity for members to *seek each other's help* in carrying out the project.

2. Meetings serve as an external *source of pressure* upon members to keep their individual work moving.

3. They are a source of *progress planning and review*.

4. Sessions can lead to the provision of formal *inputs*.

5. Reflection leads to the gaining of *insights*.

6. Meetings can provide for mutual encouragement and *support*.

Action learners need to purposefully decide upon the orientation of their meetings. In this pragmatic approach we see a balance of cognitive, affective and behaviourial influences and outcomes. This is borne out by Casey, when he alludes to required set advisor skills:

1. Skill in *timing interventions*: too early and the intervention is not understood, too late and the opportunity has passed.

2. Skill in *asking good questions*, which make people think, but at the same time feel challenged and supported – not criticized.

3. Skill in using the language of *managers* avoiding speaking down and intellectualizing.

4. Skill in selecting and applying the *appropriate model* to reflect *processes* taking place at a particular time.

5. Skill in hearing two or three processes *simultaneously*.

6. Skill in *making statements truthfully*, while structuring them to be of maximum use.

Becoming a 'set' advisor

> I have had to become much more conscious of my role, of late, not only as a project manager but also as a set advisor. In that context, again, the division between 'work' and 'education' becomes much more blurred than it was before. I no longer feel, moreover, that I have taken time out to 'do' a programme of management education. My management and my education have become as one. Team leadership and group facilitation have become wholly intertwined. When I spring up to the flip chart and introduce a management concept to the team, or put a diagram to reflect

our group interactions, I am playing my natural part both as a manager and as an educator. Having said all that, of course, there are times when I still feel self-conscious about playing that dual role with a team that until recently would never have seen me in this combined light. I am trying, therefore, to gradually spread the facilitating role among other members of my group, particularly involving those who are naturally reflective.

Given the range of required skills, the 'set advisor' role can be viewed from a number of perspectives. Burgoyne and Cunningham, in effect, see the role changing over the lifetime of the 'set'. They first identify five kinds of task, and the accompanying role requirements of 'set advisor'.

Table 4.1 The evolving role of set advisor

Process	Role
The task project	Expert consultant
The task process	Expert teacher/educator
Interpersonal processes consultant	Interpersonal process
The learning process	Learning process manager
Learning to learn process	Self-development facilitator

As the life of the 'Set' evolves, so the 'advisor' moves down Table 4.1, from expert consultant to facilitator. At the outset the 'advisor' moves away from helping with knowledge acquisition towards the development of skills, and finally, to facilitating personality change. Yet, as Casey suggests, the development of the role is unlikely to be as clear-cut as that. A good facilitator is sowing seeds for personality change at the outset and demonstrating expertise even towards the end.

The learning 'set'
What about the 'set' members themselves? Where do they come from? How do they learn? Where do they go to? Each individual is engaged on a single project which involves design and implementation.

A task group as a learning 'set'

Since having become wholeheartedly committed to action learning, I have tried to set up, with each of my team members, individual projects that serve to develop the person as a professional, as well as the work of the team. For example, one of our group has taken on a project – over the course of 1992 – which requires her to investigate the way in which similar project teams function in other London boroughs, with a view to improving the functioning of her own. In the process she is expected to improve her own knowledge of group dynamics, her skills as a social researcher, and herself as an analytical manager.

The 'set' is likely to be composed of people with very diverse project interests but of roughly equal standing to each other. Earlier we referred to Revans's System Gamma and to each individual's predisposing mental set: For Revans:

> All managers are branded (some for life) by their past experiences, particularly by those that seemed successful or disastrous at the time; in consequence, managers are often unable to see more in the present than still further confirmation of the unforgettable past; their vision of today's truth is obscured by the mists of yesterday's ghosts.

Revans goes on to describe four typical responses to tasks that get in the way of learning:

1. The idealization of past experience.

2. The charismatic influence of successful managers.

3. Impulsion to instant activity.

4. Belittlement of subordinates.

By implication, the 'set' needs to deal with these blocks to learning. This is where re-interpretation of past experience, stimulated by other members' critical challenges and warm support, is important. This alternating current provides the action learning dynamic. The actual way in which the current flows is very much open to interpretation.

Action: the mission of action learning

According to Revans:

> The fundamental of this educational method is action, as the essential task of the manager. Experts and analysts may advise, forecast, recommend and so forth, but it is the manager's characteristic responsibility that, having listened to his advisors and perhaps debated their advice, he must do something. To help him carry this singular burden is one mission of action learning; a second is to help him learn from the carrying out of it.

The project

There is an essential paradox contained within action learning. As David Casey has pointed out, the project is the vehicle for learning and, as such, it must be seen to be exciting and worthwhile. Yet, at the same time, by virtue of being a vehicle it is taking a manager somewhere else. It is a means rather than an end. The 'project' is of some 6–9 months' duration. It needs to involve design and negotiation, problem definition and solution, survey and test, hypothesis and verification:

- It is concerned with taking specific action as well as with talking about taking some general class of action.
- Because specific action must be taken by specific persons, those engaged in action learning gain insight into not only their problems but also their individual perceptions of and personal responses to such problems.
- The majority of time is given both to diagnosing in the field what the problem may be (so challenging the value systems of those caught up in it) and to applying any solutions to the problem that may be suggested.
- It is vitally concerned with the posing of effective questions in working conditions of ignorance, confusion and uncertainty.

But the picture is fuzzy, too general in outline. Let's take another look at what Revans has to say:

- Learning implies the acquisition of the power to perform the action as well as to specify it.
- People learn, or change their behaviour, of their own volition and not at the will of others.
- In learning such new behaviour people must attack real problems, so as to be aware of their progress.
- These attacks must carry significant risk of penalty for failure.
- Continuous comparison between prediction of outcome and results will show the person the nature of their learning processes and the factors upon which they depend.
- The deliberate analysis and modification of a real-life problem uses scientific method and thus reflects the learning process of those who take part.

It is helpful, at this point, to give some example of actual dialogues of managers engaged in the process of learning.

Learning to deal with information

Each month participants in a learning set are urged to set objectives and to review progress:

R   Your project? What have you done so far? Where do you go from here?
J   (*Looks down the list of typed objectives from last week*) I've been too busy to find a new source of supply, I'm working on my priorities. I've checked out the legal side – falling asleep, Brian?
B   What you need to set up is an agency arrangement with your supplier of drinks dispensers.
J   It needs delicate wording. Found out I needed a tailormade contract.
R   What do we feel about Joe's progress?
M   For me, Joe is back to the beginning. I don't see much.

B Can't you learn about administration as you sell?

J Advice from the group is OK, but it's up to me to make the final decision.

This particular dialogue is rich with information exchange and with a testing of the different ways of processing it: asking relevant questions, seeking appropriate advisors, giving and taking advice to and from the group. Joe and the 'set' are also checking together which of his objectives or achievements are more realistic. In the final analysis, Joe learns what he wants and ultimately asserts his control over his own destiny.

Learning from and through others

The following excerpt from a second set meeting gives an indication of how learning through others takes place:

M One problem is when I answer the phone, trying to arrange for a demonstration, and they say 'Who are you?' I fall to the bottom of the priority list. I have no credentials.

O This raises the question of credibility that comes up with all of us. How much are you prepared to kite-fly?

R What do you think, Dave?

D You've got to incorporate a bit of duplicity. People like to deal with something.

M I can convince, on the academic side.

S You've no need to apologize. You're a potential ally.

G I shall say I have been authorized to review the authority's structures and systems in general.

In this excerpt, Mary, whose project is at a very early stage, is drawing from Dave's opinions as a man of experience, Simon's as a politically astute operator, and Oliver's as somebody at the same stage of development as herself. She combines their advice to come up with her own solution – integrating her academic bent with their selling/hustling approach. In the process of so doing, moreover, she is also acknowledging her dependence on others, and is learning to respect their different values and viewpoints. Furthermore, she is *taking advice* – even *criticism* – and assimilating it. Having moved from vision through to action, it is now time for us to conclude.

Conclusion

Action learning, in the context of management and organizational development at large, gets caught between three stools. On the one stool sits Mr Commonsense. He says he does it anyway, so what's all the fuss about? On the second stool sits Mr Conservative. He says that it all sounds like good stuff, but why should he rock his steady boat? On the third stool sits Mr Social Skills. He says that action learning is just one kind of interpersonal process. It has its merits, but so do a whole lot of other approaches. Our object has been to explore the spaces between the stools as well as the responses to the three caricatures sitting upon them. There is much more to action learning than common sense, effective organization and appropriate social interaction.

The *vision* of action learning has even bypassed some of its disciples. Revans is passionately concerned that we be 'doers of the word and not hearers only'. His numerous quotes from the Bible reveal an almost religious devotion to grounded learning, and to the 'spiritual barter' that fellow-learners undergo in the process. In reflecting upon action, people face up to themselves, and in taking appropriate action, have the courage to do something about it.

Because the pragmatist focuses only on the company, and the organization development people on the individual and group, *society at large* is left out in the cold. Yet Revans believes that learning must be greater than the rate of change in society. He also deplores the split between 'artisan' and 'scribe'. Like Alistair Mant, he declares that Britain's particular schizoid tendencies, to divorce head from hand, lie at the root of its economic and social problems. The dual need, therefore, is to bring together thought and action within the person, and scribe and artisan within society. The internal issue is totally intertwined with the external one.

Underlying, if not central to, action learning is *concept of management* developed by Revans. This has been relegated to the 'P' corner – Programmed learning – as opposed to the fashionable 'Q' corner – questioning or discovery learning. In fact, the subjective manager and the objective management technique can never be completely separated. The stuff of management in Revans's terms – values, systems, information, decisions, uncertainty and learning – lend themselves to both subjective inference and objective analysis. By separating P from Q too rigidly, management science has become divorced from social science. This has served to reinforce the case of the pragmatic and human relations experts and detracted from the more rigorous, scientific analysts.

The 'politics' of organizations have loomed large for action learning. Because of the radical implications of the technique, companies have had to be approached with due care and not a little guile. The 'Three Wise Men' of Revans's organization world – *those who 'know', those who 'care', and those who 'do'* – need to be involved in any development programme. The political activity required to generate that commitment has been dealt with at length in the action learning literature. Strategies for infiltrating conservative and pragmatic as well as socially aware institutions have been developed.

At the core of action learning is a sequential process that Revans has termed System Beta, involving 'survey', 'hypothesis', 'test' and 'audit'. David Kolb has used the more academic language of 'reflective observation', 'abstract conceptualization', 'active experimentation' and 'concrete experience.' This is, in fact, scientific method in action. It is the renowned learning cycle. What it does not allow for is the interactive process surrounding it, the comrades in adversity learning from and through each other. For this reason, we have developed an extended, three-dimensional cycle that incorporates feeling together with thinking and doing.

The 'learning set' truly introduces the social dimension. It has been thoroughly analysed by practitioners in organizational development. At the same time, it has been scorned by the commonsense traditionalists, who say it involves the blind leading the blind. In effect, the combined elements of warm support and critical challenge create an alternating current, which in turn generates a very powerful dynamic. The continual feedback and feedforward between the person and the project ensure that both self and system are ripe for change.

Action learning projects incorporate elements of both *design and implementation*. It is the process of questioning and the negotiation of the 'means whereby' that both count. Action and learning, in the final analysis, reinforce each other. This is borne out by Mary Coles, who, as a social worker turned manager, has applied both Revans's action learning approach and our own spectral theory to her department. For, as a project manager within the Borough of Ealing's Social Services, she has felt the need, as she herself has changed, to change the system around her. This has, moreover, not only become an inner imperative but also, because of the rate of change within local government, an outer one. In effect, the government has been encouraging local authorities to turn from bureaucratic organizations into enabling enterprises.

REFERENCES

ALP Consortium, *The Self Developing Manager*.

Boddy, N., 'Some Issues in the Design of Action Learning', Newsletter of The Action Learning Society, 9; p. 6.

Botkin, J. et al., *The Limits of Learning*, Pergamon (1985).

Casey, D., 'The Emerging Role of the Set Advisor', *Journal of European Training*, Vol. 5, No. 3, page 3 (1976).

Casey, D., 'Transfer of Learning', in J. Beck and C. Cox (eds), *Advances in Management Education*, Wiley (1980).

Casey, D. and D. Pearce (eds), *More than Management Development*, Gower (1977).

Kolb, D., *Organisational Psychology*, Prentice-Hall (1973).

Mant, A., *The Rise and Fall of the British Manager*, Pan (1979).

Morris, J., 'Book Review of Action Learning', *Management Today* (October 1980).

Powell, R., *Initiating Action Learning Programmes*, Training Services (1980).

Revans, R., *Developing Effective Managers*, Longmans (1971).
Revans, R., *The Theory and Practice of Management*, Macdonald (1974).
Revans, R., in *Management Education and Development*, page 10 (1975).
Revans, R., *The ABC of Action Learning*, Revans (1978).
Revans, R., *Action Learning*, Blond and Briggs (1980).
Toynbee, A., *A Study of History*, Thames & Hudson (1985).

5

Managing complexity – organizational learning and development

Context

Lecroy Geneva: High-tech instrument manufacturer

Lecroy Corporation was founded in the New York area in 1964. The founder, Walter Lecroy, is still active in the company, and is Chairman of the Board. Corporate headquarters are in suburban New York, although the company has subsidiaries worldwide, including a major manufacturing division in Geneva, Switzerland. It is with this division that we are concerned here.

Lecroy's initial product offering was a line of instrumentation for physics research. As such, it was engaged in the measurement of complex physical phenomena. Walter Lecroy is himself a physicist, and began by making instruments for his own experiments. Demand for these instruments soon grew, and Walter started manufacturing his designs commercially. Such is the action-centred American way. This product line, and its successors, are a significant part of the company's business today. Customers for these include all the major national and international laboratories, including CERN in Europe, JET in the UK and Brookhaven and Fermi Laboratories in the USA. To reach and satisfy such a far-flung customer base, Lecroy has had to develop a sales and marketing capability. That is why, in the summer of 1991, Conrad Fernandez was invited to join Lecroy's European division, based in Geneva.

Conrad Fernandez: European marketing manager

Conrad Fernandez, half-Indian and half-Irish, was an unusual marketing manager. From his Indian and philosophical heritage he had an analytical turn of mind, and from his Irish stock he had inherited the gift of the gab. Not surprisingly, therefore, he had been trained as an electronics engineer, and had developed a role for himself in sales and marketing.

When Conrad joined Lecroy in Geneva, having previously worked for another American instrumentation company in Britain, he was immediately struck by the formality. The move from Anglo-Saxon England to a Gallic part of Switzerland came as something of a culture shock. His sales and marketing team, moreover, included French–Swiss, Italian and American representatives, each with their different cultural and personal orientations.

Conrad's initial response therefore – having been exposed to the idea of a learning organization – was to try to build a learning orientation into his team. In fact, having gauged their learning styles through instrumentation of the personalized kind, he set out to bring about a more balanced approach among them. However, and at the same time, Conrad became increasingly aware of the overriding impact of the French–Swiss culture on the organization as a whole. Whereas he himself was prone to an action learning approach, in a way that was not dissimilar to that of Walter Lecroy, he realized that the kind of organizational stratification that existed in Geneva was somewhat alien to such. Yet the stratification seemed to work, in fact remarkably well. So much so that the Americans let the Swiss get on and do it, very much their way. They seemed to be skilled in managing complexity. So Conrad set out to learn more about it, and Elliot Jaques's ideas proved very helpful in that respect.

Introduction

The roots of cognitive learning

While Anglo-Saxon Reg Revans insisted that we become doers of the word, and not hearers only, for the European generally to believe in an idea, according to the Spanish social philosopher Salvador de Madariaga, it must first have passed through the filter of intellect. The ideal of the European, for de Madariaga, 'is a conscious and self-possessed unit of life, advancing in the state of knowledge in a state of Socratic doubt, but in the realms of action, resolutely, in a spirit of Christian love'.

Planning and love

> The philosophical side of me, perhaps drawn as much from my Indian as from my European heritage, has always been fascinated by the complexity, initially of the physical world and subsequently of the organizational and managerial world. At the same time, and I suppose this is the Irish and the Catholic in me, I have always warmed to people. I suppose such a combination of what you might call planning and love led to my immediate interest in the dynamics of a learning community.

Salvador de Madariaga, Spanish *ambassador-extraordinaire* in the first half of the twentieth century, characterized the English as men of action and the French as archetypal thinkers. Interestingly enough, perhaps subconsciously alluding to Reg Revans, he likened action, in a European context, to a religious source. Thought, on the other hand, he related back to the ancient Greeks, to Socrates.

The second of our seminal approaches to the learning organization was developed in the fifties and sixties by Elliot Jaques, a Canadian who has made his name in Britain as an organizational psychologist. In a noted partnership with British industrialist, Wilfred Brown, over twenty years Jaques attempted to introduce a 'requisite' form of bureaucracy into Glacier Metals. The argument that Jaques has pursued is that, contrary to general opinion, bureaucracies *per se* are neither centralizing nor localizing powers, neither humanizing nor dehumanizing. They are dependent institutions, social instruments, taking their initial objecties and characteristics from the associations which employ them. The bureaucracies that dehumanize are those which have outgrown their organization structure or have never had an adequate structure.

'Requisite' Lecroy

> When I first came to Lecroy I was awestruck by the bureaucracy. Heavily under the influence of such modern-day management 'gurus' as Peters and Moss Kantor I was highly sceptical. Moreover, my Anglo-American working experience had led me to spurn much of the so-called benefit of rationality. It was interesting then, helped along by the precision of Elliot Jaques's mind and the clarity of thought of some of my Gallic colleagues, that I began to see formal organization in a potentially 'requisite' light. Organizational stratification, I began to see, was a necessary part of managing complexity.

Some types of bureaucratic structure facilitate normal relationships between individuals, make it easy for them to link into immediate social relationships and through these into the larger network of institutions which lie beyond, with feelings of trust and confidence. Jaques calls such structures 'requisite' or socially connecting: requisite in the sense of being called for in the nature of things, including a person's nature; and socially connecting in the sense of linking people to their society and giving them a hold upon it. Other types of structure make it difficult or impossible for individuals to have normal relationships of confidence or trust. They force social interactions into a mould, calling for forms of behaviour which arouse suspicion, envy, hostile rivalry and anxiety, and constrain social relationships. Mutually antagonistic groups and societies form. Jaques calls such institutions anti-requisite or alienating. They run counter to a person's normal nature, and split individuals off from their society.

Requisite marketing

> Three months into my job I found myself grappling with the problem of 'requisite' organization within my own sales and marketing division. For, on the one hand, sales *per se* is very much influenced by the American approach – which was duly re-inforced by my previous working experience and natural gift of the gab. On the other hand, I sensed that some of the European members of my team, and certainly the overriding Swiss culture, was antithetical to this informal, freewheeling approach. So I set about looking for some organization that was 'requisite', in the sense of

being called for, in the nature of the people and the culture that surrounded them. In fact, in order to get closer to the French–Swiss culture of formality, I 'apprenticed' himself to my boss, who was a native Genevois.

The particular significance of bureaucracy as the central workplace, for Jaques, derives from the psychological importance of work itself. It is through work that a person maintains a primary sense of reality. Work is the prime contact with the external world and, more particularly, Jaques argues, *mediates between a person's own mental processes and the external world*.

The idea of rationalism

In fact Jaques's approach, originally drawing from the Socratic tradition, is more recently rooted in cognitive rather than behavioural psychology, in the organization more than the individual, and in a rationally as opposed to empirically based philosophy. The philosopher, René Descartes ('I think, therefore I am'), may be considered his high priest, and the Swiss psychologist, Jean Piaget, a formative influence.

Descartes, like his counterpart in England, Francis Bacon, believed that science should divest the world of mystery, and should fill the gaps in our understanding with real knowledge. However, where Descartes parted company from Bacon, thereby feeling that empiricism was not to be trusted, was in his view that the existence of the material world is not self-evident on the basis of direct perception. According to Descartes, therefore, fundamental laws of the universe could be discovered independently of experience, by careful analysis. Man, in his thinking nature, as a 'manager', stood apart from the world, in its physical nature, as a 'business'. In the same way as mind and body were for him things apart, so experience based on the physical senses – sensing – stood apart from thinking. Experientially based perceptions, of oneself or of one's world, were to be mistrusted.

Sense and thought

It's strange the way we compartmentalize our thinking. On the one hand, any physicist or engineer worth his salt would recognize the limits of the human senses. After all, the only reason we, at Lecroy, are in business with our instrumentation products is because of man's physical limitations when it comes to investigating worldly phenomena. Yet, when it comes to management, we fall for Tom Peters's philosophy of 'MBWA' – managing by walking about, as if our physical senses alone could reveal what is managerially going on.

Toward a providential economic order

France's eighteenth-century physiocrats brought to the economic order the same rational outlook that Descartes gave to the natural one. For example, both the physiocrats and the Scottish empiricist Adam Smith are attached to economic

individualism and liberalism. However, the philosophies on which their attachment was based were entirely different. The views of the physiocrats postulated a
providential order of the world, harmonious, immutable and beneficial. For
Smith, the point of departure was the nature of man – through his propensity to
truck, barter and exchange – rather than in the nature of the world. The
physiocrats were rationalists who set out to find self-evident truths in the light of
reason rather than with the help of experience. They maintained that in Adam
Smith's marketplace the free play of individual forces would in fact be frustrated.
In their rational order, they believed, harmonious individualism would reach its
full flowering.

Group dynamics

> When I took over as sales and marketing manager, at Lecroy, I had to decide
> whether to give every individual their head, as Adam Smith would perhaps have
> advocated, or whether to create a structure within which individualism, supposedly,
> might reach its full flowering. Whereas my Anglo-Saxon background led me towards
> the former, my boss's Gallic upbringing, perhaps, led him in the latter direction.

Structuralism – Piaget's quest for mind

Following in the footsteps of Descartes, if not also of the physiocrats, was the
structurally based Genevois child-psychologist, Jean Piaget. Accompanying his
quest for psychological understanding has been a belief in the uniqueness of a
person's cognitive processes. For many years the image of humans as struggling bio-
logical organisms with strong drives which govern their behaviour has predominated
in Anglo-American social sciences. According to Gardner, 'Structuralism threatens
this outlook, for it attributes to the individual more innate mental structuring and
functioning'.

Structuralism exhibits both a general strategy and also specific formalities. The
strategy is to focus upon the deep structure of a realm, rather than upon its super-
ficial aspects; to look at the relationship between elements (organization structure) rather than at the elements *per se* (personality traits); to search for an organized
system governed by general laws. Once the elements of a structure have been
isolated, the aim is to formalize all relationships through some sort of logical
model or system.

Piaget reasoned that an organism's intelligence was embodied in a series of
structures with latent tendencies for development. These could be brought out
by appropriate interaction with the environment. The organism was not a passive
reflector but rather possessed active potentialities which could unfold to a
greater or lesser extent, depending upon the nature of the interaction with the
environment. He, thereby – like Revans – tied thought to action, and saw the
level of thought as a direct reflection of the actions of which the person is capable.

His guiding picture of the individual attaining knowledge depicts a seeking, exploring individual, continually acting and coordinating actions until they eventually coalesce into structures.

Growth and development

> The reason that Lecroy now has a flourishing European subsidiary, which has in turn evolved to the point where it requires a sales and marketing manager, is because its American founder – Walter Lecroy – was able to outgrow his individualistic, entrepreneurial personality, so that a structured organization could be created around and beyond him. The structures that we shall be creating here in Geneva, particularly given the rationally based Swiss environment, should enable the company to transcend its origins yet again, and develop into an even larger and more complex entity. Thereby it would become a continually learning organization.

For Piaget, however, unlike for Revans, activity, while linked with thought, is subordinate to it. Hence the organization, as a structure, needs to be 'requisite' for the task, and for the individual who is to carry it out. In Jaques's own words, 'the well or ill functioning of an institution is not just a matter of "personalities". Its primary source lies buried in the structure of the organization itself'.

Test and Measurement

> In 1984, Lecroy entered the Test and Measurement (T&M) market. It now offers a broad range of T&M instrumentation. While these use many of the technologies developed for the physics research products, they address a very different market: commercial electronics companies in the telecom, consumer products and computer industries. Now a major player in this market – ranked number three in digital oscilloscopes – the company has had to grow and change, in strategy and structure – rapidly, in order to maintain leadership.

> The digital oscilloscope business was pioneered by Lecroy's ITI (Interactive Test Instruments) Geneva Division, staffed and managed predominantly by Swiss and other Europeans. While having adopted some of the American operating procedures and practices, ITI ultimately maintains a distinctively Swiss approach, embodied in its operating strategies a well as its products. In fact Europe's greatest watchmakers are well attuned to this kind of instrumentation business.

Piaget, in the final analysis, focuses particularly on a person as a constructive organism, with generative capacities, who nonetheless is preordained to follow certain paths in his or her intellectual development, and achievement. This arises because of the structure of the human brain and the regulating forces in the human environment. These paths of intellectual construction, for our purposes, constitute the organizational strata of the learning organization.

Managing complexity

Hierarchies of complexity

Hierarchical layering

Central to managerial organizations, for Jaques, is the meaning and structure of the hierarchical layering, since that is what these organizations are fundamentally about. This method of layering is a true human discovery, like fire or the wheel, which originated in China some three thousand years ago. It was a major event in the transition from the family/tribal society to the more dispersed type which we take for granted.

How many layers should any organization have? Layering should be such as to encompass successive categories of task complexity and cognitive complexity within each stratum of organization. Seven categories of task complexity are used in managerial hierarchies. Equivalent firm boundaries of real managerial layers have been found by Jaques to exist at time spans of 1 day, 3 months, 1 year, 2 years, 5 years, 10 years and 20 years. The prime act of managerial leadership in any organization, therefore, is to establish an effective and efficient work organization where the work gets done by competent individuals, at just the right organizational strata, to deal with the inherent complexity of the work itself.

The right strata

The dilemma I was presented with from the outset, as someone attempting to develop a learning organization, was where to position sales and marketing division in terms of strata. What time span of discretion was it appropriate for me to allocate to myself, and what were the expectations of my superiors? Was I to focus 3 months ahead, 3 years, or even 10? What discretionary time spans, moreover, should I allocate to each of my team members? How much did I need to take into account their cognitive capacities, and how much the complexity of the tasks they were undertaking? What work, in the final analysis, were we primarily there to tackle?

Levels of work

Work is defined by Jaques as that plane of human activity in which the individual exercises discretion, makes decisions and acts in seeking to transform the external world in accord with a predetermined goal. Bureaucratic systems are social systems which call upon individuals to work in a setting in which the goals of the activity are set by the employing institution through its managers in the form of assigned tasks, rather than by the individual.

Bureaucracies, moreover, are hierarchical systems. They contain a range of different levels, reflected in different levels of work. Jaques's definition of level of work is given in the form of a measuring instrument based upon the maximum of time spans during which people are required to exercise discretion. He suggests, as a first proposition, that there is a universally distributed depth structure of levels of bureaucratic organization, of natural lines of stratification. The second proposition is that the existence of the stratified depth structure of bureaucratic hierarchies is the reflection in social organization of the existence of discontinuity and stratification in the nature of human capacity. The capacity is referred to as work capacity, which is further analysed in terms of a person's level of abstraction. A multi-modal distribution of capacity is postulated.

The third proposition is that the rate of growth of the work capacity of individuals follows predictable paths. Maturational shifts in the quality of an individual's capacity occur as a person moves across the boundary from one level of abstraction to another. This finding that measured time span, or measured distance of goals into the future, corresponds to subjective feelings of levels of work, is like the finding that the measured length of a column of mercury in a thermometer corresponds to subjective feelings of warmth. This leads Jaques onto the keystone of his argument, relating to cognitive processes.

Cognitive processes

Making information available for work
The concept of cognitive processing, for Jaques, lies at the heart of any possibility of understanding the nature of competence at work. Cognitive processes are the mental processes by means of which a person is able to organize information to make it available for doing work. This processing enables the individual to deal with information complexity. When a person's cognitive processing is up to the complexity, he or she is comfortable. Cognitive power is the potential strength of cognitive processes in a person, and is therefore the maximum level of task complexity that someone can handle at any given point in his or her development. Just as we find that the greater a person's cognitive power, the larger is the mass of information that can be coped with, so we find that the greater the person's cognitive power, the longer is that person's time horizon.

The dynamics of organizational learning

As I immersed myself in Elliot Jaques's work, as part of my own knowledge development, I began to realize that the path to our organizational learning, at Lecroy, lay within our management of ever greater layers of technological, economic and cultural complexity. This, in turn, was dependent upon our ability to match the cognitive capacities of our organizational members with the respective levels of complexity of the tasks to be undertaken. That now appeared to me to be a necessary part of the development project I was undertaking. The question that remained was, did my company recognize this, and indeed did the business school with which I was associated?

Levels of mental processing
Cognitive processes are the mental processes by means of which a person is able

to organize information to make it available for doing work. Not only do cognitive processes come in greater or lesser degrees of complexity, they proceed in discontinuous jumps. Each of these steps is characterized by a change in the nature of the cognitive process, just as some substances change in state from crystalline to vapour when they are heated. For Jaques, there are four types of cognitive processes:

- First-level *assertive* processing organizes information and pulls it together in a form that is directly relevant to the immediate situation.
- Second-level *cumulative* processing reasons by accumulating possibly significant pieces of information and organizing them in relation to each other so as to be able to combine them into a decision.
- Third-level *serial* processing reasons by putting information together in some logical sequence – a progressive story, an algorithm or a decision tree.
- Fourth-level *parallel* processing reasons by organizing information into a number of separate trial processes, and then deals with the information in each of these processes in parallel, showing how they impact upon each other.

A fundamental point is that as we mature, we progress through developmental stages, moving from one type of cognitive processing to the next more complex type. But there is more to management, for Jaques, than cognition. Such layers of mental processing, in the person, are therefore interspersed with layers of complexity in the task environment.

Mental processing in marketing

1. Assertive processing
The base level of sales activity is known in Lecroy as 'prospecting'. Much as the gold-digger sifted through tons of sand to find little nuggets of gold, so the salesman sorts through raw information – personal contacts, company reports, technical journals, etc. This occasionally yields 'pay dirt', or the names of people or organizations who may need our products. This lead-generation activity requires the organization of small nuggets of information, and immediate follow-up.

2. Cumulative processing
Once a prospect has been identified, the salesman moves to the 'qualifying' stage. This involves gathering disparate data, and organizing them to provide an overall picture of the situation. Typically a situation would be summed up as follows: 'XYZ company needs a digital oscilloscope for production testing. We have demonstrated an acceptable solution, and the customer is convinced. No competition exists, because our product has several unique capabilities. The instrument will fit into next quarter's budget, but we haven't yet met the production manager, who has the buying authority. Potential here for $10 000 in three months at 75% probability'.

3. Serial processing
A sales manager will regularly receive 'situation reports' like the one above from his salesmen. He combines them into an overall business forecast. This will show

expected sales over the next one, three and twelve months. In addition, he receives information from the product divisions on their plans for new products and markets. Using this knowledge of the marketplace he develops various sales strategies appropriate to local conditions. These alternative strategies are reviewed with the division's marketing staff, and the most attractive ones are implemented as one- to three-year plans, duly addressing pricing, promotion, distribution and the product itself.

4. Parallel processing
A product division will need to constantly monitor global trends in the markets it addresses. These trends will impact upon competitors and suppliers, customers and potential new entrants – all contributing to industry profitability. Intelligence on customers and competitors will typically come from the marketers, while other business functions will be tuned into other industry changes. A business like Lecroy must somehow bring together these diverse strands into a business strategy for the next three to five years.

Cognitive processes – the worlds in which people manage

In the same way as there are layers of ever-greater complexity within our managerial heads, so there are such layers of progressively increasing complexity in the world in which we manage. Such increasingly complex groups of data in the external world we must assimilate and use to inform our cognitive processing in our internal world to solve problems. There are, according to Jaques, four orders of complexity of information:

1. First order *concrete* things, that is, specific things that can be pointed to. The variables are clear and unambiguous ('use this tool'; 'employ him, not her'), they are not tangled together, and they are relatively unchanging.

2. Second order *verbal* abstraction, through which we are able to discuss our work and to issue instructions to others in a manner that makes it possible to run factories, to design new products, to discuss orders with customers, to record data and produce financial accounts, to maintain information systems and generally carry out the activities necessary to manage a business unit. Concrete variables have to be grouped into useful categories in order to see the woods and not get lost in the trees.

3. Third-order *conceptual* abstraction, whereby, for example, balance sheet values serve to bring together a wide range of accounting categories, which can in turn be translated into a large array of items of revenue and expenditure, assets and liabilities. The factors, such as financial policies and political circumstances, are very ambiguous, continually changing and inextricably entangled together.

4. Fourth-order *universal* abstraction, whereby concepts are grouped together into the universal ideas that are required for handling the problems of whole societies.

Cognitive processes in the instrumentation business

1. *Concrete things* are encountered regularly in selling products to technical buyers. Questions like 'how big is it?' and 'how hot does it get' require immediate answers.

2. *Verbal abstraction* is home ground to the designer or scientist. Concepts like bandwidth, frequency and risetime can only be discussed and measured if there is an appreciation of the theory underlying each.

3. *Conceptual abstraction* becomes part and parcel of work with the client organization. 'Preferred–Vendor Policies' or 'Ethical Purchasing Policies' are likely to change with world events. While the individual salesperson may seldom encounter such concepts, they are an essential part of marketing as a whole.

4. *Universal abstraction* in the sales and marketing context, at Lecroy, seldom impinge on the business, and are usually broken down and addressed as lower-order abstractions.

Categories of potential

Layers within layers

As we mature, we move not only from less to more complex cognitive processes but also rise in the orders of information complexity that we can handle. We obtain a series of recursions of the four cognitive processes in each of the four worlds of information complexity. Different individuals will mature to different levels of complexity at different stages of their lives. Jaques refers to a category of potential capability (CPC) as a particular cognitive process within a given order of information complexity. Whereas the first order of complexity, A, is clear-cut, the second and third orders, B and C, each have layers to them. Finally, category D, like A, is equally definitive but now at the highest order of complexity.

Second-order cognitive process (B)

Verbal abstractions, then, unlike the definitive nature of concrete things, can range from unsupported assertions – 'I can't stand my boss' – to arguments supported by logic – 'my boss is a difficult person because . . .'. More specifically, there are:

B1. Unsupported verbal *assertions*, through which people argue with unconnected strings of assertions – 'Well, it's wrong, isn't it?' or 'You don't know what you're talking about' or 'I disagree with you'.

B2. *Arguments* supported by data, whereby people support their views with accumulated information to justify them 'We're selling the wrong product; look at the declining sales figures over the past six months' or 'He's the right man for the job' look at the high-powered positions he's held over the past ten years'.

B3. *Arguments* supported by logic, whereby an argument is organized in sequence, in which one thing leads to another, or may have been led on, one from another, in the past. 'My experience has been that such an approach to promoting our cars is a bad idea. I've worked in Germany and I have found that the Germans there are not receptive to a brash line of advertising approach. And they have good reasons to react against it. Their whole educational background is oriented, especially when it comes to matters of *technik*, to quality rather than quantity'.

B4. Parallel processing of several *lines of argument*, whereby two or more arguments are pursued and aspects from each related to one another. 'When I think about it, neither promotion from within nor selection from without is exclusively right. Let me outline the pros and cons of each, and then make my intermediate case.' We now move on from second-order to third-order categories of processing potential, again identifying four layers of possibility.

Third-order cognitive process (C)

C1. Conceptually formulated *assertions*, whereby statements of principle are grounded in practical examples – 'Look, let me get back to the principle I was putting forward' – without being able to articulate it, support it with data or relate principles.

C2. *Arguments* supported by related concepts, whereby mutually reinforcing concepts are interrelated (say, of salesmanship and of consumer motivation). 'Salesmanship, as a matter of arousing attention, interest, desire and action (AIDA) – in that order – can be related to Maslow's hierarchy of personal motivation.'

C3. Serial conceptual *arguments*, whereby the values pursued are linked to progressively higher-order issues, such as profitable sales being associated with the advancement of individual learning, or the betterment of social welfare. There is an overall difference, finally, between what Jaques terms 'hollow' language, mere words or academic arguments, and solid language, based upon real, personal experience.

We now turn from the individual and managerial to the institutional and organizational, albeit still within a cognitively based analytical as well as hierarchical framework.

Role complexity and task complexity

Layers of complexity
What Jaques postulates, as we have now seen, is the existence of a universal bureaucratic depth structure, composed of organizational strata with boundaries

at levels of work represented by time spans of 3 months to 20 years. These strata are real in the geological sense, with observable boundaries and discontinuity. They are not mere shadings and gradations. Requisite organization of bureaucracy must be designed accordingly.

In other words, strata of organization need to built up that are 'requisite' for the complexity of the task at hand. The complexity of a task lies in the number, variety, rate of change and degree of interweaving of the variables involved in it. Jaques identifies seven such levels, or strata, of organization, drawn from a combination of categories of inner and outer complexity, of the first and second order.

Management spectrum and organizational stratification

It is probably no accident that the spectrum of management and learning, which is generic to this particular book on 'business as a learning community', is also a fundamental part of Jaques's approach to organizational stratification. In fact, and as I understand it, whereas the spectral approach draws on Indian philosophy – from what we call the *chakras* or human energy centres – Jaques draws on the work of Jean Piaget. It seems to be the case that great minds think alike, even when they are separated by continents and centuries!

Whereas first-order complexity – that is, the concrete world – stands prior to organization, the fourth order, universal world – for Jaques – lies beyond it. The work of a single craftsman, on the one hand, and of an individual 'guru', on the other, lies outside the realms of Jaques's organization.

Strata of organization

Second-order complexity
Stratum 1: Direct action (B1)
These are shopfloor- or office-level activities, requiring a person to proceed along a prescribed linear path, getting continual feedback in order to do so – drilling holes with a jack hammer, typing a letter.

Stratum 2: Diagnostic accumulation (B2)
These kinds of task are found at first-line managerial level; the individual must anticipate potential problems through accumulating significant data – designing a new jig for a machining process, working out the design as the job proceeds.

Stratum 3: Alternative serial plans (B3)
Increasingly complex situations require alternative plans to be constructed before starting out, one to be chosen and serially progressed to completion – heading a project team to create a new software program, having initially to select between alternatives with varying times, costs, specifications.

Stratum 4: Mutually interactive programmes (B4)
These comprise a number of interacting programmes which need to be planned and progressed in relation to each other. Trade-offs must be made between tasks to make progress along the composite route – new venturing requires a combination of overlapping product development, market analysis, product engineering and commercial assessment, with mutual adjustment along the way.

Third-order complexity
Stratum 5: Business-strategy formulation (C1)
These are the kinds of tasks faced by presidents of strategic business units in large corporations. Practical on-the-spot judgements must be used to deal with a field of ambiguous conceptual variables, and to make decisions envisaging second- and third-order consequences – setting half a dozen critical tasks to achieve a seven-year plan, continually picking up important areas of impact and likely consequences of change, keeping profitability at a reasonable level while maintaining customer goodwill, high employee morale and a growing asset base.

Stratum 6: Developing a supportive business environment (C2)
At this level executives must build up a picture of likely critical events worldwide, using international networking to accumulate information about potentially significant developments that could affect the business and its units, forestalling adverse events and sustaining a friendly environment for corporate trade.

Stratum 7: Envisioning the future (C3)
At this ultimate point CEOs work out strategic alternatives for worldwide operation, using complex conceptual information concerned with culture, with values and with the business of nations and international trade well into the twenty-first century.

Because, in the final analysis, each category of task complexity has a corresponding category of cognitive complexity in human beings, complexity in work can be matched with complexity in people in the same organizational layer.

Organizational strata in marketing

Stratum 1: Direct action
Much of the sales process in Lecroy's business is customer driven. It is also intensely competitive. Customers who express an interest in our scientific instruments must be responded to while the interest is still fresh. Literature coordinators, telemarketers and customer service representatives all play a role at this level. The main requirement is that appropriate action is taken, with zero delay.

Stratum 2: Direct sales
As well as making individual sales, the Lecroy salesman is responsible for maintaining an ongoing relationship with the customer. Since the company's products are highly complex he will spend a lot of time showing the customer how the product's

capabilities address a specific requirement. This highly technical 'consultative sell' has become a trademark of our approach to customers.

Stratum 3: Product/market coordination
As sales manager I coordinate the various 'situation reports' received from individual salesmen, and feed appropriate information through to the product divisions. I also work with salesmen to ensure that they are taking a long-term view of their customer, as well as pursuing the current opportunity. In addition to this steady-state function, I form a bridge between the field and the factory, often steering the product manager towards specific applications.

Stratum 4: Marketing management
The marketing manager is typically responsible for the work of several product managers. The key difference between their work and his is the longer time window he adopts. He will characteristically be responsible for marketing operations (order processing and fulfilment), new-product strategies, new market plans, and overall promotion, pricing and distribution.

Stratum 5: Division management
With particular respect to my marketing and sales function, the Divisional Manager at Lecroy is responsible for defining the markets that we will address; ensuring that the resources are available to exploit these markets; developing growth targets for the business, and translating these into marketing objectives; ensuring that the marketing function develops and grows in line with the needs of the business.

Strata 6 and 7, finally, are not specifically addressed in the company, certainly not in relation to the marketing function. Prospectively, therefore, the organization's learning is falling short at these high levels of environmental analysis and envisioning of the future.

These propositions can be applied not only to the design of organizational structure for bureaucracies but also to coping with changes in these systems induced by the developing capacities of their employees. If the propositions are valid and reliable, Jaques argues, they will show that the relationship between bureaucracy and individuality is not an unresolvable conflict to be softened by uncomfortable compromise. Rather, it is a dilemma which can be dealt with by creative interaction between social institution and individual.

Levels of abstraction
The functionalist type of argument, Jaques maintains, that bureaucratic systems are economically efficient in themselves, and that these systems were established in order to get the necessary work done, is, at best, incomplete. Social systems cannot endure if they are not closely attuned to a person's nature. If, for example, all people were equal in work capacity, the bureaucratic hierarchy would be an impossible social system. Employees would have worked together in leaderless groups, but a bureaucratic hierarchy, Jaques asserts, never!

Nor can the nature of tasks readily explain the phenomenon. For tasks are artificial things. They are products of human desire and aspiration, created by human imagination of the objects to be produced as the output of the task. According to Jaques, any evidence that there might be not only an hierarchy of tasks but also an inherent discontinuous stratification of tasks would therefore point to stratification of populations with respect to the mental functioning of its members. Each of the discrete levels described is a level of abstraction. These levels, or strata, of cognitive complexity are central to Jaques's notion of 'requisite' management and leadership.

We now turn from this richly laden perspective on cognitively based learning and development to Jaques's more limited affective and behavioural orientation, where in fact Senge, as we shall see, and Revans are more at home.

Managerial leadership

Effective leadership
Effective leadership, for rationally minded Jaques, is indistinguishable from 'requisite' management. It demands four straightforward and basic conditions. First, a person must have the necessary competence to carry the particular role, including strongly valuing it. Second, that person must be free from any severely debilitating psychological characteristics that interfere with interpersonal relationships. Third, the organizational conditions must be requisite, that is, conforming to the properties of hierarchical organizations and human nature. Fourth, each person must be encouraged to use their natural style, namely, to allow the full and free expression of their natural self.

Horses for courses

> What fascinated me, when I joined Lecroy (Geneva) was to discover how incredibly different the style of leadership was from what I had experienced at Tektronix in England. It was much more formal, more subtle, and technologically oriented in the Swiss case than in the British one. Yet both worked in their own way, and in their own time. It was interesting to note, moreover, that whereas the Americans felt pretty much at home in Britain, as was the Tektronix case, they were much less inclined to take a hands-on approach in Geneva. Switzerland, in culture and style, was much more like foreign territory to them, and it wasn't only the language!

Cognition and capacity
Central to Jaques's concept of 'requisite' management, as we have now seen, is the manager's powers of cognition. In that sense, Jaques is a direct disciple of Piaget. However, he is also concerned with values, knowledge and skills, wisdom and temperament. Ever inclined to use mathematical formulae, Jaques describes:

Current actual capacity (CAC) = $fCP.V.K/S.Wi. (-T)$
where

CP = cognitive capacity (that is, mastery of complexity),
V = values, interests, priorities,
K/S = skilled use of relevant knowledge,
Wi = wisdom about people and things, and
$(-T)$ = the absence of serious personality/temperament defects.

A sales manager's CAC

As I see myself, at this point of time, I have no serious personality defects – thank God – and have the cognitive capacity to master the complexity inherent in my job. Having said that, I have had more experience in coping with technical and commercial complexity than with handling managerial complexity. As a result, I am currently engaged in acquiring relevant knowledge of management, as well as marketing, and of developing my interests and values in matters managerial, and organizational. Accumulating wisdom about people, as well as things, of course, is a lifetime's endeavour.

Current potential capacity (CPC), moreover, is the maximum level at which a person could currently work, given optimum opportunities and conditions, provided that the work is of deep inherent value for the person, even though he or she has not had past opportunity to acquire the necessary skilled knowledge. A person's CPC is determined by his or her cognitive power alone. Such cognitive power determines the level at which he or she should be employed. Future potential capacity, finally, is the maximum level at which a person will be capable of working, say, at 5, 10, or 15 years into the future.

Values – knowledge – wisdom – temperament

Values and motivations
Jaques's experience is that everyone will put their best effort into doing what they value. People, he says, are spontaneously energetic with respect to things that interest them. The issue is not to encourage output by incentives but to provide conditions in which the work itself has its inherent value and allows the individual to release and direct his or her energy and imagination into the work.

The core of motivation, then, lies in valuing something. If we value something we will try to attain it. Values range from generic to specific. Generic values are usually referred to as our philosophical or ethical position. Specific values are the things we currently give priority to, or spend our energy pursuing. To be an effective managerial leader a person must really value the opportunity to work with subordinates and value being able to unleash their enthusiastic and effective collaboration. Get the values right, Jaques argues, and such factors as style and personality will fall in line.

Valuing management development

> I recognized, almost from the moment I embarked on a programme of conscious management development, that I would only put my all into it if I really valued what I was going to get out of it. If I look back on the process now, what I have most valued is 'learning how to learn', both for myself and in order to instil such learning in other individuals and organizations.

Knowledge and skills

We learn from our experience, from teaching and from practice. We store our learning in the forms of knowledge and skill in the use and application of that knowledge. By knowledge, we refer to objective facts, including procedures, which can be stated in words, formulae, models or other symbols that one can learn. By skill, Jaques refers to the application of facts and procedures that have been learnt through practice to the point that they can be used without thinking.

The key issue, for Jaques, is not that leadership capacities, such as communication or listening skills, can be taught but that the necessary conditions for effective managerial work must be set. It is specifically necessary to have a requisite organizational structure, with layers sufficiently wide and few to call for managers who are one category in cognitive complexity above their immediate subordinates, and who are working at a level of task complexity that is also one category higher. It is also necessary to have established a range of requisite managerial practices for managers to carry out, which can be taught and which managers can, with practice, learn to use without having to think about them.

Thus education in managerial leadership, according to Jaques, should be approached not in terms of the inevitable vagaries of 'leadership skills' but, instead, by learning standard practices that have been formulated for clear understanding and teaching. Our knowledge provides the verbal framework within which we organize and set contexts for our work. It enables us to set contexts for subordinates as the prime act in managerial leadership. Knowledge and its appropriate skilled use enable us to organize our field of work so that our non-verbal cognitive process can handle the complexity of the field more readily.

Wisdom and temperament

Action without sound theory, Jaques believes, can be counterproductive. Unsound theories distort our experience, narrow our vision and leave us none the wiser about the effects of our actions on others. Wisdom can be developed in people, especially by good mentoring by a more senior person. For rationally minded Jaques, though, in the final analysis, focus upon personality traits is misguided. Emotional make-up has little effect upon the person's in-role leadership work, unless these qualities are at unacceptable or abnormal extremes, and the person lacks the self-control to keep from disturbing his or her work relationships.

In the English language, Jaques maintains, there are over 2500 personality variables which are possessed to a greater or lesser extent by everyone. This large range of commonly occurring characteristics combines in infinitely varied patterns to give the great richness in personality make-up, all of which may be consistent with effective managerial leadership, and none of which is likely to be better or worse. For Jaques, 'Our argument is that the personality variable figures in managerial leadership in a negative rather than a positive way'.

Many people would argue that it is precisely by understanding and attending to the special emotional needs and personality styles of each individual that a 'leader' can best motivate a follower. But that can result in the 'difficult' personalities getting special attention as compared with their more collaborative colleagues. This is not what managerial hierarchies should be about. Managerial hierarchies are not seller–buyer situations, nor families. It is simple not acceptable, Jaques argues, for individuals to behave in ways that are disruptive of working relationships. How, for Jaques, are people developed?

Fostering the development of individuals

Mentoring and coaching
The art of the development of individuals, first, is to take note of the rate of growth of their potential and try to provide work opportunities consistent with it. Second, and in addition, they should be given the opportunity to consider their values, gain the necessary skilled knowledge, fortify their wisdom and take the necessary steps to get rid of any seriously abnormal personality quirks they may have.

Mentoring, in relation to the former, is the process whereby a manager-once-removed (MoR) helps the individual to understand his or her potential and how it might be applied to achieve full career and organizational growth. There are three major approaches to the latter. Coaching is the process through which a manager helps subordinates to understand the full range of their roles and then points out the subordinate's strengths and weaknesses.

Teaching and training
Teaching is the imparting of knowledge to individuals by lectures, discussion and practice. Training is a process of helping individuals to develop or enhance their skill in the use of knowledge through practice, either on the job or in a learning simulation. Skill enables individuals to use their knowledge in problem-solving activities without having to think, thus freeing up discretion and judgement.

Career progress and level of aspiration
Whereas an individual's aspiration towards equilibrium between work capacity and level of work is absolute, that between level of work and payment is relative. In the case of pay, Jaques argues, each person's aspirations appear to be geared

to a sense of fairness of economic reward relative to others. In the case of work, however, each person's level of aspiration is geared to his or her deepest feelings of reality and freedom.

The construction of adequate grading and progression systems, therefore, is an essential mechanism for making individual freedom real. For if their levels of work in time-span terms are shorter than their time-span capacity, individuals will be deprived of the opportunity to test their capacity at full stretch, that is, to maintain their relationships with reality over as wide a spectrum as possible. Conversely, if their levels of work are longer than their current work capacity, their freedom will be destroyed in that their relationship to reality will be disorganized and their deepest anxieties aroused. Whereas, Jaques believes, all employees should be entitled to receive periodic assessments of the adequacy of their performance from their immediate managers, managers-once-removed should be responsible. Such judgements need to be made at least from the next higher level of abstraction, Jaques says, if they are to be genuinely detached.

Management and career development

I can see how, over the course of the past few years, I have undertaken a purposeful course of training and education, and received considerable coaching if not also mentorship in management. What has been significantly lacking, though, is an orchestrated approach to career progression that takes explicit account of my growing cognitive capacity, alongside the accelerating task complexity with which I am faced. It seems to me that organizations, be they Tektronix or Lecroy, City University Business School or our Development Consortium, need to become much more strongly keyed into notions of cognitive capacity and organizational stratification if we are collectively to learn and develop, as individual managers and as managed organizations.

Conclusion

Growth of bureaucratic systems

Bureaucratic systems, for Jaques, are internally live and changing, as the occupants of the systems join, develop, change and leave. There is a continual ebb and flow, with stable periods and critical change periods. At the same time, different parts of the system change at different rates, as do the individual members of these parts of the system.

New technology-led growth at Lecroy

New technology-led growth occurs when the company offers radically new products to both new and existing customers. Lecroy has done this in the past, as, for example, in 1985 when it introduced a new and highly successful range of digital oscilloscopes. More recent examples include function generators and pulse generators. In each of these cases the products have offered new capabilities or price–performance to the customer as a result of new technologies that the company was able to exploit. Following its experience in data acquisition for the high-energy physics market, moreover, Lecroy has become a specialist in certain data-acquisition technologies. Many of these technologies could be applied to the more general test and measurement market, but such a strategy would carry with it significant risks. There are various ways of minimizing the technological risk; for example, by partnering with companies (or research institutions), which can provide experience of the unfamiliar technologies without the need for a full ground-up investment. Lecroy has used this approach successfully in the past, in partnering with both research institutes and commercial electronics firms to produce new devices.

Lecroy's design team, moreover, and particularly the Geneva-based group, has worked together for longer than is typical (before joining Lecroy several key players worked together at the University of Geneva) and have developed a cohesiveness, notwithstanding their individual differences, which allows designs to be implemented with unusual speed.

It is precisely by identifying such differences in individuals that a society can accomplish two important social ends: first, it can arrange social procedures to make it possible for everyone to gain a level of work and career consistent with his or her work capacity; second, it can bring political power and legislative control to bear to ensure that bureaucracy is managed in a manner consistent with the political outlook of the society. Thus whether or not bureaucratic organization would lead to economic elitism would be a political decision.

Size of organization, Jaques maintains, tends commonly to be regarded as a function of size of market, the nature of the economy, the type of technology and other such external factors. They are necessary but not sufficient. For Jaques, ultimately, the distribution of sizes of bureaucracy will be determined by the distribution in level of work capacity of those available to manage the bureaucracies.

There is a kind of Archimedes' principle at work, whereby bureaucratic systems grow to the level of work capacity of their chief executives; conversely, chief executives stimulate bureaucratic systems to grow to the level consistent with their work capacity. In posing, in fact, the existence of up to seven strata of organization, preconditioned by executive work capacity, Jaques is following in the structural footsteps of Jean Piaget.

Progressive abstraction

According to Jaques, as the strata of operation ascend, from the practicality of the operational world to the abstraction of general management:

> the total field is available now to the manager only in conceptual form, in histograms of performance, drawings of product families and other such conceptual models. He

must have that sense of security in his abilities to let go to some extent of the concrete outside world, and to rely upon an interplay between data of immediate experience and data culled from mental constructs. The manager or administrator must learn how to work from an office, not in complete detachment but with sufficiently frequent contact with the various parts of his domain to keep lively examples in mind of the activity of the situation he is dealing with *in abstracto*.

Progressive managerial abstraction

The irony is, and here's my parting shot at the learning organization, that whereas we are inherently familiar with progressively increased layers of abstraction, within the field of electronics, we are comparative ignoramuses when it comes to management. I guess this is the major challenge that I face, when I advance as an engineering manager, as opposed to being a research engineer. When the time comes that I am able to handle time spans of discretion ten to twenty years out, and can design and manage organizations with the same capacity, I shall be a happy man. Moreover, until we are able to orchestrate our management and institutional development in that sort of direction, organizational learning will be left on the back burner.

Insofar as managers are able to deal with progressively higher degrees of abstraction, so they will have satisfied one of Reich's four requirements of the symbolic analyst. In so doing, they will also be helping their institutions to evolve through their organizational strata. At the same time, to the extent that any organization is 'requisitely organized' so it will enable its members not only to manage appropriate levels of complexity but also to learn and develop as they mature. Managerial learning, for Jaques, is reflected in an individual's ability to cope with progressively higher levels of complexity, as he or she matures. Organizational learning and development takes place, moreover, when there is a good match between organizational strata and cognitive capacities. Such development, finally, is individually preordained and organizationally orchestrated.

Now we need to turn from abstraction, which came so naturally to Elliot Jaques, and from experimentation, with which Reg Revans was so at ease, to systems thinking, where Peter Senge feels most at home.

REFERENCES

De Madariaga, S., *Portrait of Europe*, Hollis & Carter (1968).
Gardner, H., *Quest for Mind*, Wiley (1974).
Jaques, E., *A General Theory of Bureaucracy*, Heinemann (1976).
Jaques, E., *Requisite Organization*, Cassell (1989).
Jaques, E., *Executive Leadership*, Blackwell (1991).
Revans, R., *Action Learning*, Blond and Briggs (1980).

6.
The fifth discipline: systemic learning and development

Context

The Norwich Union

In nineteenth-century Britain, while the Industrial Revolution was proceeding apace spearheaded by individualistic entrepreneurs, a parallel phenomenon was making itself apparent. In financial services, particularly within insurance, a mutual tradition was being established alongside the more prevalent private enterprises. Specifically, and again particularly within the field of insurance, friendly societies and organizational 'unions' were being created. These were founded upon the dual basis of individual enterprise and mutual organization, thereby combining personal mastery with a recognition of systemic interdependence. In that context an entrepreneur such as Thomas Bignold, who founded what was to become the Norwich Union, predated Peter Senge's contemporary business leader.

In company folklore, Norwich Union, one of Britain's larger insurance groups, portrays its founder as a rugged merchant adventurer. Having failed in 1797 to arrange insurance protection against the loss of possessions by highwaymen – he had intended to journey from the hopfields of Kent to the quiet pastures of Norfolk – Bignold allegedly decided to take remedial business action. Realizing that there was an unfulfilled need for insurance, he persuaded twenty-seven of his fellow businessmen to join him in the formation of both a fire insurance company and subsequently also a life insurance enterprise. Both were based upon mutual foundations.

In fact, what is missing from the Norwich's folklore is Thomas Bignold's manifest awareness of the interdependent nature of the insurance business. For the very basis of insurance in his eyes was a cooperative one. Financial requirements, at a time of need, was met much less by the individual and much more by the multiple contributions of others. Unfortunately, today, whereas most insurance companies in Britain – like the Norwich Union or the Commercial Union – remain a union, or a mutual enterprise in name and financial structure, they have lost their mutual essence. Brian Johns, Head of Pensions Actuarial Services at the Norwich, has spent the last few years attempting to renew this spirit of mutuality, albeit in modern guise. As such, he has inevitably been drawn towards Senge's systemic approach to the learning organization, encapsulated in the 'fifth discipline'.

An actuary with a difference

Few actuaries today, for all their years of intensive training in quantitative methods, are aware of the qualitative origins of their discipline. In fact, *Familiar Observations on Life Insurance* by Robert Morgan, one of the first actuaries at the Norwich Union Life Insurance Society, set the mid-nineteenth-century scene. In this pioneering document Morgan attempted to 'give a succinct account of the science of Life Assurance, its connection with many parts of philosophy and politcal economy, and its bearings on everyday business life'.

Not only were the pioneers of actuarial science intrinsically systemic in their outlook, they shared lofty values. 'If the practice of Life Insurance,' Morgan maintained, 'could be made general, so as to embrace the great mass of the community, the evils of poverty would be little known.'

Brian Johns, a committed Christian as well as a loyal member of the Norwich Union, has introduced mutual principles into his own department of thirty people, in a notable way. He has played something of the role of a 'priest', in Deal and Kennedy's corporate cultural terms, in representing the mutual values of the Norwich. Ironically, currently, the company as a whole has been much more dedicated to fostering the self-development of its individual employees than to the mutual development of its Norwich Union, as an interdependent system. It is with the latter goal in mind that Brian Johns has associated himself with Peter Senge's work, attempting to review his department as a learning system.

Introduction

The roots of systemic learning

A discipline for seeing wholes

The third of our approaches to the learning organization is systemically based on the work of Peter Senge, who was a Professor of Organizational Learning at MIT before he became independent. He has been responsible, perhaps more than anyone else, for putting the notion of a learning organization onto the business map. Moreover, as a systems thinker operating out of America, he has constructed bridges between Anglo-Saxon and Germanic, Western and Eastern streams of management thought. Wherein, then, lie the origins of such a systemic approach?

The origins of systems thinking

The evolution and development of systems theory, according to the contemporary German management theorist Helmut Lehmann, can be traced back to the beginnings of Western civilization, thereby being linked to Plato and Aristotle. In more recent times systems thinking has taken on new forms – for example, in biology (neo-vitalism) and in psychology (*gestalt*). Modern systems thinking can be traced back to the twenties. In that decade a number of scientists in the English- and German-speaking worlds – Wiener, Bertalanffy, Kohler, Lotka – provided the foundations of systems theory in its two modern forms. In its more Anglo-Saxon form it has close links with cybernetics and control engineering; the more Germanic approach came about through the extension of holistic thinking to the social sciences. In the context of business the subject matter of systems theory embraces material, goal-oriented or teleological systems designed by people, usually socio-technical systems, whose elements are linked to each other by a complex set of material and informational relationships. These intricate relationships manifest themselves in space, linked interdependently, and over time, unfolding developmentally.

An interdependent union

> The Norwich Union was founded in 1797 by Thomas Bignold. Over the ensuing two centuries the life and fire societies have greatly expanded. They have assimilated other companies, notably the Scottish Union, to become an interdependent union, or group of companies, as well as of policyholders. The 1991 Report and Accounts shows over £20 billion worth of assets, with over £4 billion worth of premium income. The mutual structure remains.

Developmental management

According to Professor Ulrich at the German–Swiss University of St Gallen, management is a process of shaping, that is, designing a model of an institution on the basis of characteristics that are sought after. It involves guiding, that is, of setting goals, determining, promoting and checking on activities in a system with its own specific objectives. It is also a process of development, involving the evolution of social institutions. While leadership theory, with its individual and empirical orientation, has generally followed behaviourist approaches, 'wholist' management theory stands first and foremost under the influence of systems-oriented ones. Ulrich maintains that managers, in fact, are located at the point which links the intellectual sphere of ideas, values and goals to the material sphere of this world; they are the people who transform ideas into deeds and goals into action. Such 'wholistic' managers see themselves as part of a wider *gestalt*, a subsystem of a larger system, both here and now and extending into the future. In other words, they think systemically.

Bernard Lievegoed, the leading Dutch management thinker, has adopted a notably systemic perspective in his work on developing organizations, with his biologically based 'laws of development'. The term 'development' for Lievegoed incorporates the following phenomenon: growth continues within a certain structure until a limit is reached. Beyond this limit the existing structure or model can no longer impose order on the larger mass. The consequence is either disintegration or a step up to a higher level of order. We have here, as we shall now see, a developmental approach that goes back to Hegel and Marx! Lievegoed, in fact, discerns the following developmental laws:

- Development is principally discontinuous.
- Within each advancing stage a new subsystem appears which has a structure characteristic of that stage.
- The new stage has a dominant subsystem; this does not lead to a process of addition but to a shifting of all the relationships within the system.
- In a following stage, should the system evolve, the structure differs from the previous one in that it has a higher degree of complexity and differentiation.
- Development is irreversible – youth does not return.

The developing Norwich Union organization

> Norwich Union had until recently been very much settled into a traditional rational mode, dominated by mathematically trained actuaries. The structure was that of a pyramid-shaped hierarchy, with the top sixty or so designated as the Executive with their own plush luncheon room (recently abolished together with the title Executive) and other privileges. Management was by laid-down, rather dictatorial, objectives, and the approach to most isues appeared to be painstakingly detailed, methodical and somewhat cumbersome. Nowadays, with the very fast pace of change and the many and varied technical, commercial and cultural issues to resolve, all this becomes less appropriate. A learning organization requires horizontal as well as vertical structures, networks as well as hierarchies.

In becoming familiar with the laws of development, Lievegoed argues, it is necessary to free ourselves from the actual situation of one's organization, and to learn to think in terms of evolving systems, or progressively more interrelated wholes. Such a wholistic, or 'idealistic', orientation stems from a typically Germanic, as opposed to a characteristically Anglo-Saxon (empirical) or French (rational) *weltanschaung* or comprehensive view.

The idea of 'wholism'

Idealism versus realism

For many people 'idealism', from which has come wholism, represents the very antithesis of realism. Yet Germany, where the core of 'idealistic' philosophy has been developed, is currently the most successful of the European economies. Why should that be? Idealism, as we have now seen, is associated with 'wholism' or *gestalt* philosophy, and with a systemic or a developmental *weltanschaung*. From that kind of philosophical source has sprung the social market, economically, the *kereitsu* – the Japanese term for a business constellation or cluster – commercially, and the interdependently minded German *Aufsichstrate*, or supervisory board, managerially. Where did such an idealist philosophy spring from?

The social market

The origins of insurance are pre-eminently social, as well as economic. My predecessor Robert Morgan, one of the first actuaries to be appointed to the Norwich in the mid-nineteenth century, was inspired to do his work because of the horrific waste of human life that he perceived around him. He saw life insurance, then, as a successor to the notorious Poor Law that pervaded England at the time.

Hegel and Goethe

Perhaps the two most formative influences on the development of 'idealism', or 'wholism', were the eighteenth-century philosopher Friedrich Hegel, and his fellow-German playwright and natural scientist, Johann Wolfgang Goethe. Hegel made history a substitute for religion. Goethe derived the forms of development and life of human beings from the observation of nature. Both these early 'systemic' philosophers, moreover, had developmental approaches to the world of work. Whereas they maintained that, originally, work satisfied the immediate needs of the individual, it subsequently became abstract and universal, that is, no one produced what they themselves needed. It therefore became impossible for individuals to satisfy their needs except by collaborating in the total satisfaction of everyone's needs. Need and work, raised to the level of universality, constituted in themselves – for Hegel and Goethe – an immense system of solidarity and mutual dependence.

Stokvels

In my travels across the insurance world I was intrigued to come across the so-called 'stokvels' system to which something like one quarter of South Africa's metropolitan blacks belong. In the indigenous African setting people had a tradition of helping each other. At ploughing time, members of one family would offer their services to their neighbours, who would in turn lend them oxen with which to plough their fields. The 'stokvels' system of insurance is a continuation of that tradition. It is a type of credit union in which a group of people enter into an agreement to contribute regularly a fixed amount of money to a common pool. This money, or a portion, may be drawn on by members either in rotation or at a time of need. Mutual financial assistance is the main purpose of 'stokvels', but they also have valuable social and entertainment functions.

In this process of productive work, moreover, there develops 'culture', theoretical as well as practical. Diverse forms of knowledge evolve, combined with a growing ability to comprehend complicated, universal relationships. Work, for Hegel and Goethe, is culturally educative in that it accustoms people to having regard to the will of others. It teaches objective physical activity and universally applicable skills; it raises an individual to the universal level of spirit. This systemic and developmental world view is a long way from the empiricism of Adam Smith.

The romantic economists
Conventional economic wisdom in Western Europe and the United States of America over the last three hundred years has been moulded by the classical school of empirically based economics, with Adam Smith as its philosopher-king. While his views on the 'invisible economic hand' have been somewhat modified by economists who followed him and by makers of public policy over the subsequent three hundred years, his basic free-enterprise philosophy has remained substantially intact.

Interestingly enough, in eighteenth-century Germany, there was an alternative school of economic philosophy that had more in common with Japanese economic thought today than with Adam Smith's free enterprise then. Adam Müller stressed altruism and religion in opposition to what he regarded as Smith's egoism and materialism. The state, he thought, must be regarded as an organism; the individuals who were the cells could not be thought of as being outside its overall realm. Such a state, moreover, must concern itself not only with tangible things but with the totality of material and non-material goods. The real object of political economy, according to Müller, is a double one: first, the greatest multiplication of all the utility of persons, things and goods; second, the production and intensification of that product of all products, the economic and social union of the great community or the national household.

Morgan's principle of life assurance

> The general principle of life assurance – although the practice is much neglected – is tolerably well known: that a body of shareholders, or of persons mutually guaranteeing each other, engage to pay the representatives of an individual a certain sum in consideration of small annual contributions made by that person to the funds of the company or society.

The factors of production in this national household are not land, labour and capital but nature, man and the past. The last includes all capital – physical and spiritual – which has been built up in the course of time and is now available to help man in production. Economists, says Müller, have tended to ignore spiritual capital, or what we may now term 'intellectual', or in Reich's terms human, capital. The fund of experience which past exertion has made available is put in motion by language, speech and writing; and it is the duty of scholarship to preserve and increase it. All these elements collaborate in all production.

Intellectual capital

> Interestingly enough, Scandia, the largest of the Swedish insurance and financial services groups, have recently appointed a manager of 'intellectual capital'. The

greater the stock of such knowledge capital in their company, at least as they see it, the stronger their asset base. In fact the manager concerned has specific responsibility for maintaining and developing this intellectual asset base within the company, over time.

What makes writers like Müller into a historical school is the overwhelming importance they assign to history in the study of the economic process. Economics had to examine carefully the development of individual peoples and of the human race as a whole. It had to produce an economic history of culture. Economic conditions were constantly changing and developing. Lastly, the historical school stressed the unity of social life, the interconnection of individual social processes and the organic, as against the mechanistic view of society.

In effect, this historical school, despite the fact that it was deeply ingrained within the German national psyche, was assimilated by Adam Smith, on the one hand, and by Karl Marx, on the other. While one was the forerunner of capitalism in the 'West', the other, with his collaborator Engels, foreshadowed Communism in the 'East'. Moreover, because of the dogmatic character of Marxism, most of us have lost sight of its developmental, 'idealist' underpinnings. These we want to focus upon here.

Unionism old and new

The mid-nineteenth century in Britain was a time when little was expected of government but much was expected of individuals; the cults of self-help and self-improvement were well spread, representing the value of achievement over that of birth. Arguably this Victorian era was a forerunner of Thatcherism today. however, and at the same time, in 1860 there were over 200 000 members of mechanics institutes. There were innumerable mutual improvement societies, lyceums and libraries, and adult education took place at most of them. There were 3 million members of friendly and provident societies. This was the original form of unionism in Britain, before an ultimately rationalized form of 'trade unionism' began to eclipse its primal forerunner. Such a 'primal' and spontaneous form of union was indigenous to our particular national culture. Then came Marx!

Marxian dialectics

The first developmental or evolutionary feature of Marx's thinking, which he drew from Hegel, was its dialectical nature. If capitalism was subject to change, what was its motive force? According to Hegel's philsophy of history, it had to be some contradiction inherent in the system. The basic contradiction of capitalism, Marx argued, lay in the increasingly social, cooperative nature of production made necessary by the new productive powers which people possessed, and the individual ownership of the means of production.

In fact, the two poles of an antithesis were as inseparable for Marx as they were opposed, and despite all their polar opposition they mutually interpenetrate. In like manner, cause and effect are conceptions which only hold good in individual cases; as soon as we consider the individual cases in their general connection with the universe as a whole, they run into each other. We have here distinct echoes, as we shall soon see, of Peter Senge's 'fifth discipline' or systemic world view.

Marxian dialectics, in effect, comprehends things and their representations in their essential connection, motion, origin and ending. In this Hegelian system, whose origins lie with Kant, the whole world – natural, historical and intellectual – is represented as a process, that is, as in constant motion, change, development, transformation. Hegel makes a continuous whole of all this movement and development. All successive historical systems, including corporations, are only transitory stages in the endless course of development of human society from the lower to the higher. Each stage is necessary, and therefore justified for the time and conditions to which it owes its origins.

Such was the case, for example, in both America's entrepreneurial and managerial eras. But in the face of new, higher conditions which gradually develop in its own womb, it loses its vitality and justification. The efficiently managed General Motors of Alfred Sloane, in the thirties, becomes the poorly performing GM of Walter Stempel, in the nineties. It must give way to a higher stage, perhaps evolving from mass production to flexible specialization, which will also in its turn decay and perish.

Organizational dialectics

> The Norwich today is evolving dialectically and, to some extent, painfully from what might be termed mass production to flexible specialization, both in its organizational form and in its product portfolio. In such a time of transition our 'union' is bound to be full of internal contradictions, with which we need to come to terms if we are to become attuned to an ongoing process of systemic growth and development. The important point, moreover, is to ultimately conceive of a 'higher form' of union than the primal one which Thomas Bignold and his band of 27 businessmen bestowed upon us. Contained within it will be many more polarities – and indeed mutualities – than those originally imbued within us.

Dialectical philosophy itself is nothing more than the reflection of this outer process within the inner mind. However, the danger is, as with any one philosophical system in isolation, that it turns into dogma.

The social market
Marx had, in effect, replaced one kind of dogmatism, Hegel's idealism, with another, his own brand of dialectical materialism. For that reason, there was a vehement reaction in Germany, after the Second World War, to both Nazism and also Socialism, *per se*. The German social market philosophy and policy that subsequently emerged, as an amalgam of realism and idealism, served to combine economic classicism and romanticism. Its creators were the so-called German

ordo-liberals. In effect, the resultant 'culture clash' between Germanic idealism and Anglo-Saxon realism, as was the case for Japan in 1945, produced an economic blend that was much more effective than its constituent parts, for it served to synthesize the efficiency of the market with social aims. Thus although the market captures an important aspect of freedom it does not of itself constitute a *weltanschaung* (ideology). A social market economy is therefore represented as a sophisticated relationship between economic, legal, social and ethical systems. The individual's economic existence within such a complex social system is seen to depend on the activities of countless other people. Insurance, as we have now seen, is underpinned by such a system.

Such an interconnectedness, moreover, is characteristic of the wholist philosophy that has been embraced, managerially, by Peter Senge, in the context of what he calls his 'fifth discipline'. Were Marx, as opposed to 'Marxists', living today he might well have revised his own utopian conclusions, reviewing Senge's so-called 'learning organization' as a manifestation of his own classless society, one in which old-style leaders and followers, capitalists and workers, wither away! However, whereas the Marxian dialectic builds on a depersonalized polarity, Senge draws upon a diversity of five person-centred disciplines, starting with a systemic shift of mind.

The fifth discipline

Introduction to the learning organization

The presence of a systemic world view
At the heart of Peter Senge's learning organization is a shift of mind, from seeing ourselves as separate from the world to being connected to the world, from seeing problems as caused by someone or something 'out there' to seeing how our actions create the problems we experience. Interestingly enough, and unlike Robert Reich, Senge stops short of viewing managers, organizations and whole societies interconnectedly. No 'enterprise webs' for him. Senge's view remains focused upon the individual manager within the individual organization.

In the absence of a systemic world view

We are our positions
In the absence of a systemic world view managers are trained to be loyal to their jobs, to the extent, Senge maintains, that they confuse them with their own identities. When asked what they do for a living most people describe the tasks they perform every day, not the purpose of their greater enterprise. When people in organizations focus only on their position they have little sense for the results produced when all positions interact.

From Norwich to Sheffield

I see my impending move from Norwich to Sheffield as a symbolic, as well as a physical one. It is as if I am revisiting Bignold's journey from the hopfields of Kent to the quiet pastures of Norfolk, except in my case I am abandoning such quiet East Anglian pastures for the somewhat bleak industrial north. The risk and reward in my case, unlike my illustrious predecessor's, is of national and international, rather than of local, import. For, as we well know in Britain, the capital city with its financial services has become divorced from the provincial cities with their industrial foundations. Sheffield, for example, in the nineteenth century was a leading centre for specialized steel manufactures, across the globe. It is now ripe for renewal, so are we as a company, and so am I as an actuary. Somehow I, in intimate union with other people and institutions, have to find a way of bringing together in powerful combination those three fields of force. That is indeed my ultimate project, as I set out on my developing, managerial way.

The enemy is out there

Out there and in here are usually part of a single system. When people focus only on their position they do not see how their actions extend beyond its boundary. When those actions have consequences that return to hurt people, they misperceive these problems as externally caused. Like people being chased by their own shadows, they cannot seem to shake them off.

The illusion of taking charge

All too often, Senge maintains therefore, 'proactiveness' is reactiveness in disguise. If managers simply become more aggressive fighting 'the enemy out there' they are reacting, regardless of what they call it. True proactiveness comes from seeing how managers contribute to their own problems. It is a product of a way of thinking, not of an emotional state.

Authentic projects

Although I would hardly call myself an existentialist, I can see how such a philosophy applies to my management development in general, and to my development 'project' in particular. For instead of automatically accepting the unity of purpose provided by our founding fathers or by the rules of my 'union', the challenge I face is to create a new union based on reason and choice. Existential philosophers like Heidigger and Sartre, I am told, have recognized this task by calling it a *project*, which is their term for the goal-directed actions that shape and give meaning to an individual's life.

Moreover, such philosophers, I believe, distinguish between authentic and inauthentic projects. The first describes the theme of a person who realizes that choice is free; it does not matter what the choice is, as long as it is an expression of what the person genuinely feels and believes. The second involves projects that a person chooses because they are what everybody else is doing, and therefore there is no alternative. Authentic projects tend to be chosen for what they are worth in themselves; inauthentic ones are set by external forces.

The fixation on events

Conversations in reactive organizations are dominated by events – last month's sales, the new budget cuts, the last quarter's earnings, who got hired or fired.

Focus on events leads to 'event' explanations. Such explanations may be true as far as they go, but they distract people from seeing the longer-term patterns of change that lie behind the events, and from understanding the causes of these patterns. Such a fixation on events is part of our evolutionary programming. What was important for our prehistoric ancestors was to be able to see the sabre-toothed tiger over their shoulders and to react quickly. The irony today is that the primary threats to our survival, both of our organizations and of our societies, come not from sudden events but from slow, gradual processes. Well-known examples are the arms race, environmental decay, the erosion of the education system, increasingly obsolete physical capital, as well as a decline in design or product quality.

Learning must be greater than the rate of change
Learning to see slow, gradual processes requires slowing down your frenetic pace and paying attention to the subtle as well as the dramatic. If you sit and look at the tidal pool on a seashore, initially you won't see much of what's going on. However, if you watch long enough, Senge maintains, after about ten minutes the pool will suddenly come to life. The world of beautiful creatures is always there, but moving rather too slowly to be seen at first. The problem is, people's minds are so locked into one frequency, it is as if they can only see at 78 revolutions per minute; we cannot see anything at 33⅓. We will not avoid the fate of the frog until we learn to slow down and see the gradual processes that often pose the greatest threats.

The delusion of learning from experience
The core learning dilemma that confronts organizations, according to Senge, is that its people learn best from experience but never directly experience the consequences of many of their most important decisions. The most critical decisions made in organizations have systemwide consequences that stretch over years or decades. They also extend far beyond the bounds of one particular organization, economically and technologically, socially and ecologically.

The myth of the management team
In the same way that organizations are lodged within a wider environment, individuals normally work within teams. All too often, teams in business, Senge laments, tend to spend their time fighting for turf, maintaining the appearance of a cohesive team. If there is disagreement it is usually expressed in a manner that lays blame, polarizes opinion, and fails to reveal the underlying differences in assumptions and experience in a way that the team as a whole could learn. People who are skilled in advocating their views are rewarded, as opposed to those who are good at inquiring into complex issues. Such complexity is inherent within the systemic world view.

Cornerstone of the learning organization

For Senge, systems thinking, as we have now gathered, is the cornerstone of the learning organization. He first sets out what he perceives to be 'the laws' of systems thinking – that is, his fifth discipline – insofar as they affect organizational learning, and then reviews their implications.

The laws of the fifth discipline

Today's problems come from yesterday's solutions
Solutions that merely shift problems from one part of a system to another often go undetected because those who 'solved' the first problem are different from those who inherit the new one. In Britain today, Prime Minister John Major may be feeling that way, implicitly rather than explicitly, about the social problems that his predecessor's 'Thatcherite' economic solutions have caused his country.

The harder you push, the harder the system pushes back
When well-intentioned interventions, like those of Margaret Thatcher in the eighties, call forth responses from the system that offset the benefits of intervention we have so-called compensating feedback. The more effort you expend trying to improve matters, the more seems to be required. Pushing harder and harder on familiar solutions, while fundamental problems persist or worsen, is a reliable indicator of non-systemic thinking. Alternating bouts of deflation and reflation in Britain, at a macro-economic level, are typical cases in point. In complex human systems there are many ways to make things look better in the short run. Only eventually does the compensating feedback return to haunt you.

Pushing against recession

As I write my piece, and Chancellor Norman Lamont pushes ever harder against the waves of recession with no apparent results in sight, he and we may be wondering, where is the systemic perspective that Senge talks about? The same might apply to many of our corporations, attempting to push their way out of a recessionary cycle. As systems scientists, duly transcending our more limited actuarial or managerial frames of reference, we need to position ourselves within an overarching system of interdependent technological, economic, cultural and ecological forces. While acknowledging the necessary iteration between stability and change, structure building and structure changing, we need to conceive of a systemic and 'authentic' insurance product that, in itself, alleviates the affects of recession. In other words, we need to become a co-creating part of a system, which is inclusive of cycles of progression and regression, if we are to heighten the former and limit the latter.

The cure can be worse than the disease
Sometimes the easy or familiar solution is not only ineffective; sometimes it is addictive and dangerous. Gradually the cure becomes worse than the disease. The long-term, most insidious consequence of applying non-systemic solutions is increased need for more and more of the solution. Raising interest rates for the

umpteenth time, which in turn leads to thousands of bankruptcies and millions unemployed, is an obvious example of such. Alternating bouts of reorganization within a company, as employees protest 'we've seen it all before', are similar cases in point.

Faster is slower
Virtually all natural systems, from ecosystems to animals to organizations, have intrinsically optimal rates of growth. When growth becomes excessive, as it does in cancer, the system itself will seek to compensate by slowing down. Such was not only the case for the British economy, in the late eighties but also for those innumerable entrepreneurs of the eighties – in America, Australasia and in Britain – who have fallen off their perches in the nineties. Bond, Milliken and Sinclair are some of the better-known examples. In the nineties, then, a learning system needs to replace, though not preclude, the intrapreneurial enterprise.

Cause and effect are not related in time and space
Underlying all of the above problems, for Senge, is a fundamental characteristic of complex human systems. Cause and effect are not close in time and space. By 'effects' Senge means the obvious symptoms that indicate there are problems. By 'cause' he implies the interacting attributes of the underlying system that are most responsible for generating the symptoms and which, if recognized, could lead to changes producing lasting improvement. For Reich, human capital in our day and age, and all the factors affecting its growth and development, has replaced financial capital as the causal keynote of industrial and commercial success.

Small changes can produce large results
Therefore some well-focused actions can sometimes produce significant enduring improvements, if they are in the right place. Senge, in his systems orientation, refers to this principle as 'leverage'. Tackling a difficult problem is often a matter of seeing where the high leverage lies, a change which – with a minimum effort – would lead to lasting significant improvement.

Learning to see underlying structures rather than events is a starting point; thinking in terms of processes of change rather than snapshots is another. Here Senge's approach overlaps with that of Jaques, with respect to underlying structures, and with that of Revans, regarding processes of change. However, Senge retains his distinctively different, systemically based world view.

The fifth discipline's world view

Seeing the world anew
Systems thinking, as has by now become apparent, is a discipline for seeing wholes. It is a framework for seeing interrelations rather than specifics, for seeing patterns of change rather than static 'snapshots'. Systems thinking is the antidote to the sense of helplessness that many feel as they enter the age of interdepend-

ence. It is a discipline for seeing the structures that underlie complex situations, and for discerning high from low leverage.

Seeing underlying structures

> As an actuary I have been trained mathematically, and statistically, to perceive structures that lend themselves to such quantitative analysis. As a developing manager, and actuary, I need to be able to transcend those exclusively quantitative realms, and enter also into qualitative ones that underlie the quality as well as the quantity of life. In so doing, and with a little bit of help from psychology and anthropology, I should be in a position to renew the very nature of our product, with a view to entering new markets. In essence, our pre-emphasis would shift from life assurance, in a numerical and financial sense, to self-actualization, in an emotional and psychological context.

Seeing circles of causality

From the systems perspective, according to Senge, the human actor is part of the feedback process, not standing apart from it. In mastering systems, thoughtful managers give up the assumption that there must be an individual responsible. There is no longer reliance on the one great leader to turn things around, whether in the company or in the country. The feedback perspective suggests that everyone shares responsibility for the problems, or opportunities, generated by a system.

Reinforcing and balancing feedback

There are two distinct types of feedback processes: reinforcing and balancing. Reinforcing or amplifying processes are the engines of growth or decline. Balancing or stabilizing feedback operates whenever there is a goal-oriented behaviour. The state-controlled economy, for Senge, fails because it severs the multiple self-correcting processes that operate in a free-market system. Moreover, when there is resistance to change we can count on there being one or more 'hidden' balancing processes. Aggressive action often produces instability and oscillation instead of moving you more quickly towards your goal.

That is where the free market system, in its turn, can fail. Rather than pushing harder to overcome resistance to change, Senge's artful leaders discern the source of resistance. They focus on the implicit norms and power relationships, rather than upon explicit results. Cultural renewal becomes more critical, as a point of leverage, than a more conventional form of reorganization. Moreover, there are certain recurring patterns, or 'templates', that tend to control events.

Nature's templates – identifying the patterns that control events

Structures of which managers are unaware, Senge maintains, hold them prisoner. That is the essence of his sytems perspective. Conversely, in learning to see structures within which they operate managers begin to free themselves from previously unseen forces, and they ultimately acquire the ability to work with them and change them. Certain patterns or structures – what Senge terms 'systems archetypes' – occur again and again. Within these 'generic structures' lies the key to your learning to see structures in your personal and organizational lives.

If, moreover, reinforcing and balancing feedback and delays are like the nouns and the verbs of systems thinking, then the systems archetypes are analogous to basic sentences or simple stories that are told again and again. Just as in literature there are common themes and recurring plots that are recast with different characters and settings, a relatively small number of these archetypes, for Senge, are common to a very large variety of management situations.

1. *Limits to growth*: in this case there is a reinforcing, or amplifying, process of growth or improvement that operates on its own for a period of time. Then it encounters a balancing – or stabilizing – process, which operates to limit growth. Eventually, growth may slow so much that the reinforcing spiral may turn round and go into reverse. Typically, most people react to limits to growth situations by trying to push hard. But there is another way to deal with these. To change the behaviour of the system, you must identify and change the limiting factor. Leverage lies in the balancing loop, not in the reinforcing one. Not surprisingly, for example, where quality circles have succeeded they have become part of a broader change in manager–employee relationships, rather than a one-dimensional oriented push towards Total Quality Management.

In search of excellence

> Our company has been quick off the mark, in taking on American-style 'customer care' and 'people means excellence' programmes. This has its advantages, as it reinforces our new commitment to the development of people. However, we need to stop and ask ourselves, as the Norwich Union, where does our real, systemic leverage lie? Wherein lie our particular limits to growth? In my view our own limits to growth are contained within not so much our 'market myopia' but within our inhibited union. To the extent that we are able to extend and enrich the concept and application of union – technically, commercially and socially – then we will turn a limiting factor (e.g. market myopia) into a balancing loop (e.g. relationships marketing).

2. *Shifting the burden*: an underlying problem generates symptoms that demand attention. But the problem is difficult for people to address, because it is either obscure or too costly to confront. So people 'shift the burden' of their problem to other solutions, that is, well-intentioned, easy fixes. Unfortunately, the easier solutions only ameliorate the symptoms; they leave the underlying problems unaltered. The underlying problem grows worse, unnoticed because the symptoms apparently clear up, and the system loses whatever abilities it had to solve the underlying problem. Dealing effectively with shifting the burden requires a combination of strengthening the fundamental response and weakening the symptomatic one. Strengthing fundamental responses requires a long-term orientation and a sense of shared vision. None of Britain's or America's

major political parties, for example, appear to have elevated themselves to such a point.

The principle of leverage
The bottom line of systems thinking, for Senge, is leverage that is seeing where actions and changes in structures can lead to significant, enduring improvements. But the leverage in most real-life systems, such as most organizations, is not obvious to most of the actors in those systems. They don't see the structure underlying their actions. The purpose of the systems archetypes, such as 'limits to growth' and 'shifting the burden', is to help see those structures and thus find the leverage, especially amid the pressures and cross-currents of real-life business situations.

For example, in times of recession, real leverage might lie not in shifting the burden onto government by blaming them or onto the workforce by sacking them but rather in a thoroughgoing adaptation of the product line, so as to make it less vulnerable to the economic cycle. Moreover, the one can be an excuse for not doing the other. Compare the British or American motor industries with that of the Japanese!

The art of seeing the wood and the trees
Systems thinking finds, then, its greatest benefits in helping us distinguish high from low leverage changes in very complex situations. In effect, the art of systems thinking is to see through complexity to the underlying structures, not unlike Marx's productive relations, with a view to generating change. Systems thinking does not mean ignoring complexity. Rather, it means organizing complexity into a coherent story that illuminates the causes of the problem and how they can be remedied in enduring ways. This, in its turn, calls upon a certain brand of what Senge terms 'personal mastery'.

The core disciplines – building the learning organization

Personal mastery
The sense of connectedness and compassion characteristic of individuals within high levels of personal mastery naturally leads, according to Senge, to a broader vision. The discipline of seeing interrelationships gradually undermines older attitudes of blame and guilt. We begin to see that all of us are trapped in structures, structures embedded both in our ways of thinking and in the interpersonal and social milieus in which we live. Our knee-jerk tendencies to find fault with one another gradually fade, leaving a much deeper impression of the forces within which we all operate.

This does not simply imply that people are victims of systems that dictate their behaviour. Often, Senge claims, the structures are of our own creation. But this has little meaning until those structures are seen. For most of us, the structures within which we operate are invisible. We are neither victims nor culprits but human beings controlled by forces we have not yet learned how to perceive. We are used to thinking of passion as an emotional state, based on our concern for one another. But is is also grounded in a level of awareness. In Senge's experience, as people see more of the systems within which they operate, and as they understand more clearly the pressures influencing one another, they naturally develop more compassion and empathy. People with a high level of personal mastery, therefore, share several basic characteristics. They have a special sense of purpose that lies behind their visions and goals. For such a person a vision is a calling rather than simply a good idea. They see current reality as an ally, not an enemy. They have learned how to perceive and work with forces of change rather than resist those forces. They are deeply inquisitive, committed to continually seeing reality more and more accurately. They feel connected to others, Senge claims, and to life itself. Yet they sacrifice none of their uniqueness. They feel as if they are part of a larger creative process, which they can influence but cannot unilaterally control. Finally, they make constructive use of mental models.

Destiny and renewal

> The Norwich recently made the strategic decision to shift a significant part of its operations from East Anglia to the north of England. For the company as a whole, the major reason for regionalization was both market and personnel related, thereby being both closer to the northern customer and to a source of unutilized skills.
>
> My own reasons for wanting to go up north were somewhat different. I saw the move as being generic to our corporate renewal. We were returning to this country's industrial heartlands, reconnecting north with south, industry with financial services. I not only wanted to be part of this significant movement of our times, but to reconnect it with our mutualistic heritage. In many ways I saw the decline of adversarially based trade unionism and rise of a harmonically oriented organizational 'unionism' as correlated. I could see myself playing a part in managing the future of not only my own company, but also of this country, and of Europe. In essence, I saw my role of actuary in a new light, resurrecting Robert Morgan's dream of social as well as business renewal.

Mental models

Entrenched mental models will thwart changes that could come from systems thinking. Managers, Senge maintains, must learn to reflect on their current mental models.

Insurance revisited

> In the days of Thomas Bignold insurance had a particular social ring to it, as well as an economic one. Morgan saw it in terms of eliminating the wastage of human life, through poverty if not also through ignorance. Today it is ever more apparent that ignorance leads to poverty. Yet our concept of insurance remains wedded to financial security. We have to evolve such a concept, to take account of Reich's era of human capital. We need to reconceive of our insurance product so that it can contribute to our growth and development, educationally and psychologically as well as physically and financially. We have to raise our product profile up the ladder of Maslow's hierarchy of needs.

Until prevailing assumptions are brought into the open there is no reason to expect mental models to change, and there is little purpose in systems thinking. If managers 'believe' their world views are facts rather than sets of assumptions, they will not be open to challenging those world views. If they lack skills in inquiring into their own and other people's ways of thinking, they will be unable to work truly collaboratively. Moreover, if there is no established philosophy and understanding of mental models in the organization, people will misperceive the purpose of systems thinking as drawing diagrams, or as building elaborate 'models' of the world, not improving their mental models.

Eventually what will accelerate mental models as a practical management discipline will be a library of generic structures used throughout the organization. These 'structures', Senge concludes, will be based on the systems archetypes identified above. But there is more to learning and development, for him, than Jaques's cognitive processes. Organizational learning, for Senge in fact, is dependent upon shared vision.

Shared vision

A shared vision, Senge tells us, is not an idea. It is rather a force in people's hearts, a force of impressive power. It may be inspired by an idea, but once it goes further, if it is compelling enough to acquire the support of more than one person, then it is no longer an abstraction. It is palpable. People begin to see it as if it exists. At its simplest level a shared vision is the answer to the question, 'What do we want to create?' Just as personal visions are pictures or images people carry in their heads and hearts, so too are shared visions pictures that people throughout an organization carry. They create a sense of commonality that permeates the organization, cohering diverse activities.

Mindful of our mutual tradition

> At departmental level I have encouraged closeness to our customers by sending members of my staff out to visit branches. I have also made contact with local brokers in that respect. I have tried to instil in my staff a sense for the end product, whereby – mindful of our mutual tradition – our quotations work contributes to both customer satisfaction and also to the good of society. Profitable business, in the final analysis, is dependent upon satisfied customers.

Shared vision is vital for the learning organization because it provides the energy and focus for learning. While adaptive learning is possible without vision, generative learning occurs only when people are striving to accomplish something that matters deeply to them. Vision becomes a living force only when people truly believe they can shape the future. The simple fact is that most managers, according to Senge, do not experience that they are contributing to creating their current reality. Therefore they don't see how they can contribute to changing that reality. Their problems are created by somebody 'out there' or by 'the system'. But as people in an organization begin to learn how existing policies and actions are creating their current reality, a new, more fertile soil for vision develops. Specifically, a new source of confidence grows, rooted in deeper understanding of the forces shaping current reality, and where there is leverage for influencing them. This new confidence, in its turn, spreads into teamwork.

Team learning

The wisdom of teams

Team learning, for Senge, is the process of aligning and developing the capacity of a team to create the results that its members truly desire. It builds on the discipline of developing shared vision. It also builds on personal mastery, for talented teams are made up of talented individuals. But shared vision and talent are not enough. A great jazz ensemble has talent and a shared vision, but what really matters is that the musicians know how to play together.

Individuals learn all the time and yet there is no organizational learning. But if teams learn, they become a microcosm for learning throughout the organization. Insights gained are put into action. Skills developed can propagate to other individuals and to other teams. The team's accomplishments can set the tone and establish the standard for learning together for the larger organization.

Mutual endeavour

> The Norwich Union, over the course of many years, has been an ardent supporter of 'Endeavour', a charitable educational trust which runs adventure training programmes. Groups of Norwich Union personnel are sent off to rock climb, abseil or traverse ravines. In braving the elements, together with 'comrades in adversity', they acquire teamworking skills of the highest order. Moreover, having engaged in such action-centred learning, groups take time out together to reflect on the experience, alternating between animated discussion and intimate dialogue.

Dimensions of team learning

Shared minds

Within organizations, Senge maintains, team learning has three critical dimensions. First, there is the need to think insightfully about complex issues. Here teams must learn how to tap the potential for many minds to be more intelligent than one. Second, there is need for innovative, coordinated action. Outstanding teams in organizations develop the same sort of relationship, that is, an 'operational trust' where each team member remains conscious of other team members and can be counted on to act in ways that complement each other's actions. Third, there is the role of team members on other teams, that is, inculcating the practices and skills of team learning more broadly. These include a juxtaposition of dialogue and discussion.

Dialogue and discussion

Additionally, for Senge, team learning involves mastering the practices of dialogue and discussion, the two distinct ways that teams converse. In dialogue there is the free and creative exploration of complex and subtle issues, a deep 'listening' to one another and suspension of one's own views. By contrast, in discussion, different views are presented and defended and there is a search for the best view to support decisions that must be made at the time.

The word 'discussion' has the same root as 'concussion' and 'percussion', it smacks of point and counterpoint. By contrast, the word 'dialogue' comes from the Greek *dialogos*. *Dia* means through, *logos* word or, more broadly, meaning. In dialogue a group accesses a larger pool of common meaning. In dialogue people become observers of their own thinking. They also observe the difference between 'thinking', as on ongoing process, as distinct from 'thoughts', the results of the process.

If collective thinking is a flowing stream, 'thoughts' are leaves floating on the surface, according to Senge, that wash up on the banks. We gather up the leaves, which we experience as 'thoughts'. We misperceive the thoughts as our own, because we fail to see the stream of collective thinking from which they arise. In dialogue a 'kind of sensitivity' develops that goes beyond what we normally recognize as thinking. This sensitivity is a 'fine net', capable of gathering in the subtle meanings in the flow of thinking. This kind of sensitivity, for Senge, can be seen to lie at the root of real intelligence. For through dialogue people can help each other to become aware of the incoherence in each other's thoughts, and in this way the collective thought becomes more coherent.

Senge identifies, moreover, three basic conditions necessary for dialogue. All participants must suspend their assumptions, as it were, hanging them in front of them, constantly accessible to questioning and observation; participants must regard each other as colleagues, engaged in a mutual quest for insight and clarity; and there must be a facilitator who holds the context of dialogue. For example, the Quakers enjoined their members to say not simply what popped into their heads but only those thoughts which were compelling, and caused the speaker to 'quake' from the need to speak them.

In team learning, finally, discussion is a necessary counterpart of dialogue. In a discussion different views are presented and defended. In dialogue, different views are presented as a means towards discovering a new view. In a discussion, decisions are made. In a dialogue, complex issues are explored. When they are productive, discussions converge on a conclusion or course of action. On the other hand, dialogues are diverging; they do not seek agreement but a richer grasp of complex issues. A learning team masters movement back and forth between dialogue and discussion, duly by-passing defensive routines.

Conflict and defensive routines

Finally, teams need to avoid engaging, individually or collectively, in defensive routines. Such routines are entrenched habits we use, Senge maintains, to protect ourselves from the embarrassment and threat that come from exposing our thinking. Defensive routines form a sort of protective shell around our deepest assumptions, defending us against pain, but also keeping people from learning about the causes of pain. One of the most useful skills of a learning team would be the ability to recognize when people are not reflecting on their own assumptions, when they are not inquiring into each other's thinking, when they are not exposing their thinking in a way that encourages others to inquire into it.

In effect, defensive routines are like safes within which we 'lock up' energy that could be directed towards collective learning. As defensiveness becomes 'unlocked', that energy and insight are released, becoming available for building shared understanding, and advancing towards what the team members truly want to create. The approach taken by learning teams to defensive routines, therefore, is intrinsically systemic. Rather than seeing the defensiveness in terms of others' behaviour, the leverage lies in recognizing defensive routines as joint creations, and in finding your own role in creating and sustaining them. If you only look for defensive routines 'out there', and fail to see them 'in here', Senge concludes, your efforts to deal with them will just increase defensiveness.

Team learning and the fifth discipline

Without a shared language for dealing with complexity, team learning is limited. If one member of a team sees a problem more systemically than others, that person's insight will be reliably discounted, if for no other reason than the intrinsic biases towards linear views in our everyday language. On the other hand, Senge maintains that the benefits of teams developing fluency in the language of the systems archetypes are enormous, and the difficulties of mastering the language are actually reduced in the team. Language is collective. Learning a new language, by definition, means learning how to converse with another in the language.

While participative openness leads people to speak out, reflective openness leads to people looking inwards. Reflective openness starts with the willingness to challenge our own thinking, to recognize that any certainty we ever have is, at best, a hypothesis about the world. No matter how compelling it may be, no matter how fond we are of 'our idea', it is always subject to test and improvement. It involves not just examining our own ideas but mutually examining others' thinking.

Such is the role, or at least one of them, of an authentic leader. In fact Peter Senge, in concluding his approach towards the learning organization, offers an unconventional line on leadership.

Conclusion

The leader's new work

Old views and new

Our traditional views of leaders, Senge maintains, as special people who set the direction, make the key decisions, and energize the troops are deeply rooted in an individualistic and non-systemic world view. Especially in the West, leaders are heroes, who rise to the fore in times of crisis. At its heart the traditional view of leadership is based on assumptions of people's powerlessness, their lack of personal vision and inability to master the forces of change, deficits which can be remedied only by a few great leaders.

This new view of leadership in learning organizations centres on subtler and more important tasks. In a learning organization leaders are designers, stewards and teachers. They are responsible for building organizations where people continually expand their capacities to understand complexity, clarify vision, and improve mental models, that is, they are responsible for learning.

From actuary to actualization

> I can see my role evolving, in the course of my midlife, from that of an 'actuary', concerned with calculating life expectancy, to that of an actualizer concerned with realizing my life expectations, together with those of others. In that new leadership capacity I can see myself becoming much more of an empowerer than predicter, designer than calculator, life steward rather than security seeker.

Leader as designer

In essence, the leader's task, for Senge, is designing learning procesess. Thereby people throughout the organization can deal productively with the critical issues they face, and develop their mastery in the learning disciplines. Crucial design work for leaders of learning organizations concern integrating vision, values and purpose, systems thinking and mental models.

Leader as steward

Such a leader perceives a deep story and sense of purpose, a pattern of becoming that gives unique meaning to his or her personal aspirations and hopes for the organization. This purpose story, for Senge, is both personal and universal. It is central to an ability to lead. The leader becomes a steward of the vision. The vision is a vehicle for advancing the larger story.

Leader as teacher

The ultimate responsibility of a leader, Senge believes, is to define reality. Leaders can influence people to see reality at four distinct levels: events, patterns of behaviour, systemic structures, and purpose story. Leaders in learning organizations pay attention to all four levels, but focus predominantly on the latter two. At the level of systemic structure, leaders are continually helping people to see the big picture. Moreover, when people throughout an organization come to share in a larger sense of purpose, they are united in a common destiny. Leaders in learning organizations, moreover, have the ability to conceptualize their strategic insights so that they become public knowledge, open to challenge and further improvement. They are masters of creative tension.

Mastering creative tension

> The creative tension that the leadership at Norwich Union ultimately need to resolve is that which plagues this country, in particular, if not Europe in general. How do you reconcile the needs of the individual with that of society? At the present time, economically if not so much politically, Germany's 'social market' seems to offer a much better solution than Britain's or America's free market. Our leaders, at the Norwich, should position ourselves, our products and services in a way which resolves that fundamental tension, taking due account of our own economic and cultural heritage. Product and organization design, stewardship, and dissemination would become an integral part of a development programme that was quintessentially focused on resolving that individual–societal tension. And I can see no better business than that of insurance, especially within a company individually founded upon mutual principles, to take that one on.

Mastering creative tension

In the final analysis, a leader's story, sense of purpose, values and vision establish the organization's direction and target. A relentless commitment to the truth and to inquiry into the forces underlying current reality continually highlights the gaps between reality and vision. Leaders generate and manage the creative tension, not just in themselves but in an entire organization. This is how they energize an organization. That is their basic job. That is why, for Senge, they exist.

Mastering creative tension throughout an organization, Senge claims, leads to a profoundly different view of reality from the norm. People literally start to see more and more aspects of reality as something they, collectively, can influence. This is no hollow belief, which people say in an effort to convince themselves that they are powerful. It is a quiet realization, rooted in understanding that all aspects of current reality – the events, the patterns of change, and even the systemic structures – are subject to being influenced through creative tension. In the words of the great Jewish philosopher, Martin Buber:

> The free man is he who wills without arbitrary self-will. He believes in destiny, and believe that it stands in need of him. It does not keep him in leading strings, it awaits him, he must go to it, yet does not know where it is to be found. But he knows that he must go out with his whole being. The matter will not turn out according to his decision; but what is to come will only come when he decides what he is able to will. He must sacrifice his puny, unfree will, that is controlled by things and instincts,

to his grand will, which is defined for destined being. Then he intervenes no more, but at the same time he does not let things merely happen. He listens to what is emerging from himself, to the course of being in the world; not in order to be supported by it, but to bring it to reality as it desires.

That creative tension, then, between matter and spirit, between bourgeoisie and proletariat, between destiny and free will, between vision and reality, has been accommodated in their turn by Hegel and Marx, Martin Buber and Peter Senge, all in a broad, systemic sweep. Having a natural affinity for contradictions in time and space, these developmental thinkers form a continuing and 'wholistic' line of influence, culminating – for managers – in Senge's approach to learning organization. For Robert Morgan, one of the originators of actuarial science, the creative tension that he sought to resolve encompassed the richness of human potential, on the one hand, and its degradation through poverty and disease, on the other. Insurance was a technical means towards that social end.

At the same time, and unlike, for example, Robert Reich, Senge has oriented his learning orientation towards the individual – as a leader – in his mental models, within a team, managing systemically. To that extent, he has remained truer to his Anglo-Saxon philosophical heritage than to his Germanic one. For that reason, it may be worth promoting a marriage of interest between Reich and Senge, Harvard and MIT. At Harvard, moreover, there is also Shoshana Zuboff, whom we shall now visit.

REFERENCES

Buber, M., *I and Thou*, Charles Scribner & Sons (1970).
Deal T. and A. Kennedy, *Corporate Cultures*, Penguin (1982).
Lehmann, H. (ed.), *Systemtheorie und Betrieb*, Opladen (1974).
Lievegoed, B., *Managing the Developing Organization*, Blackwell (1990).
Morgan, R., *Familiar Observations on Life Insurance*, Josiah Fletcher (1941).
Senge, P., *The Fifth Discipline*, Random Century (1991).
Ulrich, H., *Unternehmungspolitik*, Haupt (1978).

7.
In the age of the smart machine – communal learning and development

Context

An embryonic African learning community

Communal learning and development is thin on northern hemispheric ground, although, and as we shall see, Shoshana Zuboff maintains that it is vital to our business and organizational functioning throughout the world, that is 'in the age of the smart machine'. In fact, as I began to digest Zuboff's seminal ideas, I realized that I had begun to implement some of them, albeit unwittingly, in Southern Africa in the late sixties.

At the time, and having recently graduated from Harvard Business School, I was returning not only to my African roots but also to the family nest. In other words, as a would-be organizational psychologist who had gained his educational and working experience in corporate planning, I was asked to take over the family business in South Africa. We ran 'Clothes-Town', in the late sixties, a chain of 21 soft-goods concessions, lodged within a group of supermarkets spread across the Transvaal province. When I became managing director a rigidly top-down organizational structure was in place. Moreover, while the white men ruled, the black and brown cultures followed!

My opportunity to change the prevailing organization, from a highly individualistic to a more communal one, came about surprisingly when we decided to computerize our sales-information system. Over a period of 18 months, in fact, involving no less than 40 weekends of 'overtime', we converted the price tickets in each of our stores to 'informated' Kimble tags. In the process, all our staff, from managing director to floor sweeper, became involved in the same kind of menial activity – that is, menial to a point.

As a result of this otherwise tedious activity a social connection was built up, across former ethnic and organizational divides, that served to create a whole new communal ethos. Working together on 'the shopfloor' was followed by sessions in one another's homes, in which we not only sampled our different ethnic foods but also got to know one another's indigenous habits and customs. By the time our database went on-line, therefore, we had established a kind of intimacy that had never existed previously. This stimulated management to let go of some of their old social prejudices, and to share information much more willingly with all levels in the organization. At the same time, the workforce became much more willing to air their own views. Unfortunately, soon after such a learning community had been informally established, our family business was taken over in 1970, and I left Africa for Europe, and business for academia.

Conducting a stage play

From the early eighties onwards I began to make regular visits to Southern Africa, thereby rediscovering my roots first in Zimbabwe and subsequently in South Africa. Having worked extensively with both businesses and business schools in those countries I had the good fortune of being called upon to undertake a consultancy assignment, in 1992, with a Southern African retailing group. Immediately it became apparent that I would be able to revisit my Clothes-Town experience. By now, moreover, a new South Africa was beginning to emerge so that our cross-cultural meetings would no longer have to be of a clandestine nature. In fact, the company whose name I have disguised under my old Clothes-Town banner was unusual, for South Africa, in that it was started by a man and a woman of two different races.

I was called in, as a consultant, to help the company evolve from its pioneering status to a rationally based organization, one which had again recently computerized its sales information. However, I immediately realized that such a conventionally, rationally and individually based institution was not generic to Africa. I knew that I would have to draw out the innately communal instincts of the majority of the employees, and subsequently draw upon them, if I wanted to make any organizational development stick. It was then that I realized that Shoshana Zuboff's work was of particular relevance. To make it palatable, though, to a communal people who loved storytelling, I decided to create a stage play, one that would chart a possible way forward based on the information I had uncovered from extensive observations, interviews and meetings.

Whereas Zuboff's concept of a learning community, therefore, comprise this chapter, the stage play is reproduced as Chapter 8. The objective of the latter was to raise the company's consciousness of the learning and development opportunities that arose out of its particular national and corporate heritage.

Introduction

The roots of communal learning

The household as a basic economic unit
The fourth and final form of learning entity is based on community. In fact for

Harvard's economic historian, Professor Badaracco, until the Industrial Revolution business was enmeshed in relationships with families, because households were basic economic units. Similarly, villages and manors were the organizing units of agriculture; guilds regulated the relations of master, journeyman and apprentice; and towns and their customs shaped and regulated the behaviour of guilds and their workers.

A communal way of life

> When I returned to Africa, after spending four years studying in Britain and America, I was able to see southern business enterprise with fresh eyes. For having previously taken prevailing forms of business forms for granted, I could now see that they were individualistic Anglo-Saxon forms implanted in communal African soils. The trouble was that such communal enterprises, lost within our northern heritage, remained equally neglected in the south.

'The core of a firm,' for Badaracco, 'is a dense web of longstanding relationships'. Ownership, hierarchical control, management power, and social bonds of membership, loyalty and shared purpose reinforce each other. Only in Britain, about two hundred years ago, did a self-regulating market of separate units appear, emerging slowly from the social and political webs that had enveloped them.

Whereas for action-centred Revans, was we saw, self-regulated learning sets could be seen to run parallel to the self-regulating markets, for feeling-centred Zuboff, as we shall see,

> the relationships that characterize a learning community can be thought of as posthierarchical in that they shift and flow and develop their character in relation to the situation, the task and the actors at hand. Managing such intricate learning calls for a new level of action centred skill, placing a high premium on the intuitive and imaginative sources of understanding that temper and hone the talents related to *acting with*.

Such talents have traditionally resided within craft-based production.

Social craft

> The impulse to computerize our sales information system at Clothes-Town was conventionally grounded in commercial logic. We wanted to improve our customer responsiveness and reduce our stock levels. Little did we realize at the time that by virtue of making sales information much more accessible to the workforce as a whole we were opening a Pandora's box. Everybody now, from the warehousemen to the sales supervisors, wanted to know why sales had gone up over here and down over there. As a result, management had to more consciously deliberate on not only who to tell what, but also how.

The industrial divide

In 1984 Piore and Sabel, two professors of economic history at MIT in Boston, wrote their seminal work *The Second Industrial Divide*. In their view, not unlike that of Badaracco, the first industrial divide came in the nineteenth century. At that time the emergence of mass production technologies, initially in Britain and then in the United States, limited the growth of less rigid manufacturing technologies, which existed primarily in various regions of Western Europe. These less rigid manufacturing technologies were craft systems. In the most advanced ones skilled workers used sophisticated general-purpose machinery to produce a wide and constantly changing assortment of goods for large but constantly shifting markets.

Craft versus mass production

Smith and Marx

Moreover, in contrast to mass production, these industries depended as much on co-operation as on competition. Unless the costs of permanent innovation were shared among firms, and between capitalists and workers, those who stood to lose by change defended their interests by blocking it. According to Piore and Sabel 'Had this line of mechanized craft production prevailed, we might today think of manufacturing firms linked to particular communities'.

Adam Smith, on the other hand, believed that the competitive market is the ideal system of exchange, and that the firm which uses special-purpose machines is the ideal unit of production. Everything that went before this optimal and social and technical organization, Smith believed, was a prelude to it, and it would subsequently disappear.

Meanwhile, Marx thought of the market and the modern factory as a prelude to socialism. Both Smith and Marx agreed that the track of human progress was narrow and unique. Throughout the nineteenth century, then, two forms of technological development were in collision. One was craft production. Its foundation was the idea that machines and processes could augment the craftsman's skill, allowing the worker to embed his or her knowledge in ever more varied products. The more flexible the machine, the more widely applicable the process, the more it expanded the craftsman's capacity for productive expression. The other form of technological development was mass production. Its guiding principle was that the cost of producing any particular good could be significantly reduced if only machinery could be substituted for the human skill needed to produce it.

The visionaries of craft production foresaw a world of small producers, each specialized in one line of work and dependent on the others. The visionaries of mass production foresaw a world of more automated factories, run by ever fewer and ever less skilled workers. Mass production offered those industries in which it was developed, and applied, enormous gains in productivity. Such gains increased in step with the growth of these industries. Progress along this technological trajectory brought higher profits, higher wages, lower consumer prices and a whole range of new products. But these gains had a price. Mass production required large investments in highly specialized equipment and narrowly trained workers. In the language of manufacturing, these resources were 'dedicated'. When the market for that particular product declined the resources had no place to go.

Best of both worlds

Yet mass production has, Piore and Sabel maintain, always necessitated its mirror image, craft production. During the high noon of mass production, craft production was used by firms operating in markets too narrow and fluctuating to repay the specialized use of resources of mass production. Craft production supplied luxury goods and experimental products.

The supermarketeer's craft

As a chain of 21 soft-goods concessions, each within a large supermarket, you would have assumed we were in mass marketing. To an extent that was true, but what I soon discovered, particularly with the help of our sophisticated sales information, was that the customer in the northern suburbs of Johannesburg was very different from her or his counterpart on the rural outskirts of Pretoria. This difference was much more marked, in clothing, than it was in foods. Because, merchandisewise, we could only be flexible to an extent, our goodwill was highly dependent on the diplomatic and social skills of our in-store sales personnel. Whereas the food counters could manage without such service personnel this was never the case on our side of the operation. Finally, we also required a lot of specialized equipment to show off the soft goods to their best advantage.

Craft producers supplied the specialized equipment used in mass production, and the standardized goods for which the demand was too unstable to make the use of dedicated equipment profitable. Craft production thus appeared either as a residual category, taking up the markets rejected by mass production, or as a limit on the pace of the introduction of mass production.

Integrated producers today have tailored their setups to exploit these possible combinations of craft and mass production. Computerized process control equipment, for example, allows firms to regulate the carbon content of steel more precisely and to add a sequence of different alloys without interrupting the flow of production. New factories are being designed to manufacture a diversity of products, using a wide range of starting materials. The institutional environment required to support them, as history shows, is very different from the one required to support mass production.

Community and enterprise

The crafts heritage

Such successful regions, historically, as the silks district of Lyons and the Prato textiles area of central Italy were defined by three mutually dependent characteristics. First, they produced a wide range of goods for highly differentiated regional markets at home and abroad, and they also constantly altered goods in order to open new markets. Second, they made flexible use of increasingly productive, widely applicable technology; and, third, they created regional institutions that balanced competition and cooperation among firms, so as to encourage permanent innovation. Technology had to permit quick, inexpensive shifts from one product to another within a family of goods. Institutions had to create an environment in which skills and capital equipment could be recombined to produce a rapidly shifting assortment of goods.

Familiasm and municipalism

Three systems, according to Piore and Sabel, can be distinguished that encouraged communal innovation through the reshuffling of resources: municipalism, welfare capitalism or paternalism; and an entrepreneurial use of kin relations that they call 'familiasm'. Any given industry might move from one system to the another as it adopted new technologies and entered new markets. Municipalism, first, involved guaranteeing the mobility of resources by protecting the firms against paralysing shocks from the market, by providing access to skills and knowledge that the firms lacked. Welfare capitalism, second, involved the industrialists in creating an extraordinary network of social institutions. There were schools for mechanized weaving and spinning, an Ecole Supérieure de Commerce in France, a savings society, and a society for maternity care. Familiasm, finally, the system *motte* (named after Alfred Motte of Roubaix, France) was to pair each family member who had come of age with an experienced technician from one of the family's firms. These two were provided with start-up capital, after which they would establish together a company that specialized in one of the phases of production that was still needed. This seemed an eminently human way to conduct business.

Family business – old and new

When I was appointed managing director, the Lessem family was very much in charge, albeit that a longstanding friend of the family was also part of senior management. I soon became aware, though, that our management accountant, a young German, was invaluable to the firm, as was our merchandising manager, a seasoned campaigner from England. Moreover, pivotal to the success of the enterprise were the sales supervisors at the branches (mostly middle-aged white women), the warehouse controllers at head office (mainly young Asian women) and the drivers (mainly indigenous young African men, who distributed the merchandise to the stores). Finally, our own concessions were an integral part of the overall supermarketing operation, as was the clothing factory in Zimbabwe that supplied most of our merchandise.

It was obviously critical, for the success of the overall enterprise, that we create an extended family network that transcended blood connections. Fortunately, while in

America, I had taken the time and trouble to study the communal orientation of the indigenous peoples of Africa, and I set out to establish a modern version of the traditional 'indaba', discussion or quality circle, that had long been in existence in our part of the world. Moreover, it had to be in a form that met with everybody's satisfaction within the constraints of a segregated South Africa. So we decided to alternate our meetings between my bachelor accommodation and the family homes of our Asian women.

The idea of humanism

The philosophy of humanism

So much, then, for the roots of communally based, craft production. Before revealing its more recent flowering in the form of so-called 'flexible specialization' and 'informated technologies' we need to probe further into its philosophical roots. In other words, if action learning is connected with pragmatism, organizational learning with rationalism, and systemic learning with wholism, whence cometh communal learning?

Badaracco provides us with a good clue. In today's world of strategic alliances, he claims, the idea of a firm as a medieval fortress that invents, owns, controls and finances all its critical assets has faded. A better image for many companies today is the Renaissance Italian city-state. Its boundaries were open and porous. Artists like Leonardo Da Vinci moved among the city-states; the Crusaders and merchants brought immigrants, goods and ideas from the Christian and Muslim worlds; Milan, Venice and Florence competed and cooperated with each other, often at the same time. The leaders of the city-states such as the Medici of Florence, in the wake of the Italian Renaissance, raised diplomacy to a high art as they forged and managed a complex, changing network of strategic alliances.

Renaissance humanism – to which Da Vinci, Michelangelo and the Medicis all contributed – was, first and foremost, a revolt against the otherworldiness of medieval Christianity, a turning away from preoccupation with personal immortality to making the best of life in this world. For the Renaissance the ideal human being was no longer the ascetic monk, but a new type – the universal man, the many-sided personality – delighting in every kind of earthly achievement. The great Italian artists typified this ideal.

According to the tenets of humanism, therefore, a society in which most individuals are devoted to a collective well-being will attain greater happiness, and make more progress, than one in which private self-interest and advancement are the prime motivation. First, a society of cooperative and socially conscious individuals will be able to achieve and maintain those higher material and cultural levels that provide the broadest foundations for happiness and progress. Second, we are gregarious creatures. Because we are social beings, we experience our deepest and most enduring joys in association with others. Third, loyalty to a worthwhile social aim can bring stability and harmony into our lives, giving us a central purpose around which we are able to integrate our personalities. While sociable humanists strive to the best of their abilities to further the good of their families, their local community – city, town or village – their state and their nation, the altruistic humanists are continually looking beyond their native lands to the world at large and thinking about the well-being of the peoples of the earth.

The family of man

> Soon after I joined Clothes-Town, valuable as I perceived the work I was doing to be, I realized that a small family clothing business based in Johannesburg would not contain my ultimate ambitions. I had a need, which first expressed itself explicitly when – as a 17-year-old at a Rhodesian high school in the fifties – I picked a book off the library bookshelf entitled *Only One Earth*. Again in the late sixties I had an urge to play my part in humanizing business across a wider, even global stage.

The philosophers of humanism

Alberti

The fifteenth-century Italian humanist, Leon Battista Alberti, believed that humanity achieves its highest expression in two arts, plastic and political. Alberti held painting to be the primary art. For it teaches us how to take the world apart, discover the relations between its parts, and then put it together again in an ideally complete form. And so too in politics. The world, for Alberti, is not primarily a place in which goods are to be consumed or a field is to be dominated. It is, rather, a field for the creation of an ideal form in human affairs. Both artist and citizen, for him, find their humanity in the encounter with the materials and in the moulding of the materials into the ideal forms which thought discovers.

Vico and Galiani

The Italian Giambattista Vico was for humanism in the eighteenth century the equivalent of Bacon for empiricism, Descartes for rationalism and Hegel for idealism. Vico argued that his contemporaries had effected great improvements in the physical sciences, but had unduly neglected those studies depicting the human will. Such studies of languages, poetry, history, law and politics involved, according to Vico, 'vicissitude and probability'.

Federico Galiani, finally, the renowned eighteenth-century Italian abbot in diplomatic employment in Paris, condemned dogmatic rationalism from the point of view of historical relativism. He called for flexible policies in line with historical and geographical conditions rather than for adherence to immutable principles of allegedly universal applicability. Similarly, Galiani's historical sense made him see value not as an inherent quality of goods but as one that will vary with our changing appreciation of them. He recognized the effect of social forces and stressed the role of fashion as a determinant of our desires and thus our values. In so doing

Galiani, and perhaps myself in my rather naive way, anticipated what Piore and Sabel term 'flexible specialization', that we are witnessing today.

Fashioning humanity

While running Clothes-Town in South Africa, I made periodic visits to our men's clothing factory in what was then still Rhodesia. One particular mission that I had overrode all others, although in the end I would have to admit defeat. For I wanted to establish a line of merchandise that was unique to our part of Africa, and yet would appeal to people around the world. It would, in other words, serve to juxta-pose indigenous Africa and modern Europe, just as Picasso had managed to do with his abstract art. So I got hold of the one local designer who was influenced by African art, though he had previously restricted his work to producing postcards, and asked him to design a line of men's shirts for me. When I returned to Rhodesia some three months later, I asked our local MD what had happened to the shirts, and he told me that the samples had been made. The trouble was, he said, nobody liked them. When I picked two of the shirts off the rail, well hidden from everybody's Western eyes, I was dumbfounded. They were extraordinary, unique, beautiful, African. I put one on myself, and rushed down to the factory floor for reactions. The workforce were in turn dumbfounded. They had never seen anything like it before. Everyone stopped to applaud.

The line of shirts, I have to say, were never manufactured. They were not the fashion, at least the one set by the fashion moguls in Europe. I just couldn't convince our merchandising manager at the time, who was too long steeped in her colonial heri-tage to see the light. Or perhaps I was much too young and naive myself to present a good commercial argument. After all, this new line of designer shirts would have required the setting up of a new production facility, and who was I – despite my family credentials – as a young upstart who knew nothing of the rag trade, to tell the experienced merchandising and factory managers what to do?

The age of the smart machine

Flexible specialization

Business and community

'Flexible specialization', for American–Italian economic historians Piore and Sabel, works by violating one of the key assumptions of classical political economy: that the economy is separate from society. Markets and hierarchies are the two categories that dominate contemporary theory and practical reflection in the organization of industry. Both presuppose the firm to be an independent entity. In market models, the firm is linked by exchange relations to other units; in hier-archy models, the firm is so autonomous as almost to constitute an industry in itself. By contrast, in flexible specialization it is hard to tell where society ends and where economic organization begins. Among the ironies of the resurgence of craft production is that its deployment of modern technology depends on its reinvigoration of affiliations that are associated with the pre-industrial past.

African management

> Instinctively I knew then, in the late sixties, as I can see more purposefully now, that the time of the South, economically speaking, will only come when it is able to forge a real connection between its longstanding communal traditions and its contemporary, individualistic influences. We are now seeing evidence of such in central Italy, and one or two such learning communities are beginning to appear in Southern Africa. Cashbuild in South Africa, for example, supplies building materials around the country and, more importantly, has a democratic constitution originally established by pragmatic humanist, Albert Koopman. The company, over the past ten years, has been dedicated not only to making significantly increased profits, but also to humanizing the practice of management throughout the communally based organization.

Specifically, within a system of flexible specialization, firms depend on one another for the sharing of skills, technical knowledge, information on opportunities and information on standards. According to Piore and Sabel, 'Structure shades into infrastructure, competition into cooperation and economy into society'. Interestingly enough, for Piore and Sabel, large firms in mature industries, like IBM, are trying to transform themselves from self-contained corporate communities into organizational centres of industrial districts. They are doing so by moving towards just-in-time production systems, which blur the distinction between inside and outside suppliers, while encouraging concentration of production.

Today, in parts of Europe as in Japan, federated enterprises hold one another's stocks and have interlocking boards of directors. Frequently, the managers of a going enterprise in the federation are despatched to serve in a new one. Sometimes the firms share financial and marketing facilities. But the group is not as integrated as the mass-production corporations, and member firms are not hierarchically arranged. Despite their large size, the modern 'solar' and workshop firms frequently treat external suppliers as collaborators. Subcontractors retain considerable autonomy; and unlike the mass producer, the solar firm depends on subcontractors for advice in solving design and production problems. These firms are large and central enough to their respective industries to supply internally many of the services that in a regional conglomeration would be supplied by the community. But firms in this category often cooperate with community institutions (for example, in research, education and welfare).

African trading

> Our family business in Rhodesia, now Zimbabwe, was termed 'African Trading', that is, before it was renamed 'Concorde Clothing'. In its original African denomination it was – upon current reflection – strangely exogenous in character. In other words,

communality was restricted to the European family that owned the business. It was never extended in any purposeful way into the surrounding community, as is the case in central Italy today. As such, it remained underdeveloped, like the country around it, in its primal state. It never became the learning community that its exclusiveness precluded. Hence I found myself, in Clothes-Town some 30 years after African Trading had appeared on its pioneering scene, trying somewhat naively to play my southern part. Interestingly enough, such communality, as we saw from Robert Reich in Chapter 1, is now becoming part of received corporate wisdom in the West.

Community and flexibility

In mass production the central problem is stabilizing and extending the market. Once this is done, the corporation as a self-contained unit has the interest and capacity to advance the division of labour through the simplification of tasks and the creation of special-purpose machines, thereby lowering production costs and setting the stage for further growth. In a system of flexible specialization, by contrast, the problem of organizing innovation just begins with the creation of a market. Because its product only appeals to a limited number of customers there is no presumption that cuts in production costs will substantially increase the market. Moreover, the very fluidity of the resources that makes the system flexible paradoxically also makes it necessary to create institutions that facilitate cooperation.

Mass production's entire division of labour routinizes and therefore, for Piore and Sabel, trivializes work to a degree that often degrades the people who perform it. By contrast, flexible specialization is predicated on cooperation, and the frequent changes in the production process put a premium on craft skills. Thus the production worker's intellectual participation in the work process is enhanced and his or her role revitalized. Moreover, craft production depends on solidarity and communitarianism.

Production workers must be so broadly skilled that they can shift rapidly from one job to another. Even more importantly, they must be able to collaborate with designers to solve the problems that inevitably arise in execution. Such craft workers are bred, according to Piore and Sabel, not born; and the formation as their identity as persons is bound up with their admittance into a group of workers, on the one hand, and their mastery of productive knowledge, on the other.

This leads us onto the work of Shoshana Zuboff, based – with her colleague Badaracco – at the Harvard Business School. Like her compatriots Piore and Sabel at MIT, Zuboff makes her communally based case, initially, by revisiting the world of craft production. Subsequently she moves us skilfully on towards her so-called 'informating' technology, drawn out of, intriguingly, sentient knowledge, in the context of a learning community.

The learning community

Sentient versus rationally based knowledge

For Zuboff the work of the skilled craftsman, prior to Piore and Sabel's first industrial divide, may not have been 'intellectual', but it was knowledgeable. These craft-based workers participated in a form of knowledge that had always defined the activity of making things. It was knowledge that accrued to what Zuboff terms 'the sentient body' in the course of its activity. Such knowledge was inscribed on the labouring body – on hands, fingertips, wrists, nose, eyes, ear, skin, muscles, shoulders, arms and legs – as surely as it was inscribed on the brain. Moreover, it was filled with intimate detail of material and ambience (for example, the colour and consistency of metal as it was thrust into the blazing fire, and the smooth finish of clay as it gave up its moisture).

These details were known, but in the practical action of production work they were rarely made explicit. Few of those who had the knowledge were able to explain, rationalize or articulate it. Such skills were taught through observation, imitation and action more than they were reflected upon or verbalized.

The agenda for scientific management, on the other hand, was to increase productivity by streamlining and rationalizing factory production from cost accounting and supervision to the dullest job on the shopfloor. Efficiency was the mania, and to achieve efficiency it would be necessary to penetrate the labour process and force it to yield up its secrets.

From African Trading to Concorde Clothing

I can well remember when, within our family clothing business in Rhodesia, we called in the time and motion experts from France to rationalize factory production. It was at the time when our men's clothing factory was renamed 'Concorde Clothing'. There were 700 workers on the factory floor. They earned a living wage. But, as a young boy, I can always remember that not one of the workers ever smiled. Africans are a communal people, and indigenous Zimbabweans radiate warmth and affability. Something had gone dreadfully awry, socially if not also economically, in this missed meeting between North and South.

In order that effort be rationalized workers' skills had to be made more explicit. In many cases skills did not yield themselves easily to codification; they were embedded in the ways of the body, in the knocks and knowhow of the craft worker. The situation is different today.

A symbolic synthesis

Intellective skills

By redefining the grounds of knowledge from which competent behaviour is derived, new information technology, for Zuboff, lifts skill from its historical dependence upon a labouring sentient body. While it is true that computer-based automation continues to displace the human body and its know-how (a process that has come to be known as deskilling), the 'informating power' of the technology simultaneously creates pressure for a profound reskilling.

In a world in which skills were honed over long years of physical experience, work was associated with practical experience and the cues they provided. A worker's sense of occupational identity was deeply marked by his or her understanding of and attachment to discrete tangible entities. It was the immediate knowledge one could gain of these tangible objects that engendered feelings of competence and control. For workers the new computer-mediated relationship was as if one's job had vanished in a two-dimensional space of abstractions, where digital signals replaced a practical reality. As the medium of knowledge was transformed by computerization, the placid unity of experience and knowledge was disturbed. Accomplishing work now depended upon the ability to manipulate symbolic, electronically presented data. Instead of using their bodies as instruments of acting-on equipment and materials, the task relationship became mediated by information.

Cedar Bluff Pulping Manager

> With the evolution of computer technology you centralize controls and move away from the actual physical process. If you don't have an understanding of what is happening and how all the pieces interact it is more difficult. You need a new learning capability because when you operate with the computer you can't see what is happening. There is a difference in the mental and conceptual capabilities that you need – you have to do things in your mind.

The thinking the operator refers to above is of a different quality from the thinking that attended the display of action-centred skills. It combines abstraction, explicit inference and procedural reasoning. Taken together, these elements make possible a new set of competencies that Zuboff calls 'intellective skills'.

> You have to be able to imagine things that you have never seen, to visualize them. For example, when you see a dash on the screen you need to be able to relate that to a 35-foot square by 25-foot high room full of pulp. I think it has a lot to do with creativity and the freedom to fantasize.
>
> (*Cedar Bluff Process Engineer*)

Once operators had established the referential function of the data, many moved to a higher feeling of complexity in dealing with the system of electronic symbols. At this level, the problem was not only to clarify the significance of individual data elements but also to construct from those elements, and particularly from their combinations, an interpretation of abstract properties of the production process. This is a process to which both Reich and Jaques have previously alluded.

Embedded knowledge

Instead of a problem of correspondence, the data now presented an opportunity for insight into functional relationships, states, conditions, trends, likely developments and underlying causes, none of which can be reduced to a practical, external referent. In other words, data needed to be translated into information, and information into insight.

Banker – global bank

> For Zuboff, the banker needs to know the structure of the data and associations, relationships and links within the data. To navigate the database you need a conceptual model of the business, the data, the logic. Users have to define their conceptual model of the bank, to make the model in their heads explicit. For the first time they will need to know the meaning of their work. The new technology makes you look at the whole.

The manager who skilfully leads a meeting uses language, gestures and deeds to shape the quality of an interpersonal event, an event that passes out of existence when the meeting comes to a close. The bleach operator who controls chemical flows on the basis of sniffing and squeezing a fistful of pulp has participated in a sentient event. The office workers who confer over the processing of an account have engaged in a conversational event. In each case knowledge is embedded in practical action that is evanescent. It leaves no trace, except for the knowhow acquired by its practitioners and the effects it has produced. As a result, it is all the more important that the manager 'acts with' his or her people, in an animated way.

Knowledge, for Zuboff, is freed from the temporal and physical constraints of action. When meaning is uncoupled from its action context and carried away in symbols a new playfulness becomes possible. Events and relationships among events can be illuminated and combined in new ways – susceptible to examination, comparison, innovation. The logician needs to be supplemented by the joker in the pack.

Informated versus automated

Public versus private knowledge

Zuboff's central idea, therefore, is that craft-based communities of old are being replaced by a new form of communal production, predicated on learning, and centred upon what she terms a duly 'informated' environment:

> In an informated environment the electronic text displays the organization's work in a new way. Much of the information and know-how that was private becomes public. Personal sources of advantage depend less upon maintaining earlier forms of private knowledge than upon developing mastery in the interpretation and utilization of the public, dynamic, electronic text. Communicative competence requires psychological individuation, which introduces a new sense of mutuality and equality into group life.

To the extent that technology is used only to intensify the automaticity of work, Zuboff maintains, it can reduce skill levels and dampen the urge towards more participatory forms of management.

Reflectivity versus activity
In contrast, an approach that emphasizes its 'informating' capacity uses the new technology to increase the intellectual content of work at virtually every organizational level, challenging the distinction between mental and manual work. Information technology thereby introduces an additional dimension of reflectivity: it makes its contribution to the product, but it also reflects back on its activities, and on the system of activities to which it is related. IT not only produces action, therefore, but also a voice that symbolically renders events, objects and processes visible, knowable and shareable in a new way.

Intelligent technology, then, textualizes the production process. When that text is made accessible to the operators, the essential logic of Taylorism is undermined. For the first time, technology returns to the workers what it took away, but with a crucial difference. The worker's knowledge had been implicit in action. The informating process makes that knowledge explicit: it holds up a mirror to the worker, reflecting what was known but now in a precise and detailed form. Such 'intellective' skill becomes the means to engage in the kind of learning process that can transform data into meaningful information and, finally, into insight.

From Concorde to Clothes-Town

> I shall never forget the day we unveiled our newly computerized system, that was after 18 months of weekend labour, and another three months of extensive debugging activity. We held a special ceremony to mourn the passing of the old manual system and celebrate the coming of the newly 'informated' one. The ceremony took place at a community centre linked to a Sikh temple, and was attended by our extended family of African, European and Asian staff members. Being in the late sixties, in Southern Africa, the age of personal computing was not yet upon us, so we all stood, worshipping at the shrine of a computer spreadsheet. We rolled it out in front of the assembled group of some 35 people. One half of it contained sales information. The other half contained a giant-sized clothes hanger, our corporate logo.
>
> What stands out in my mind, right up to the present day, was the reaction of two of our warehousemen, as they pored over the sales information. 'You mean to tell me that's the result of slaving away for 18 months, just about every weekend, sacrificing our family recreations. Lines on a piece of paper!' Obviously we had work to do. Learning, we thought to ourselves, not labour, would have to become the driving force for our future productivity.

Driving learning versus driving people
Automation preserves what is already known and assumes that it knows best. It

treats as negligible the potential value to be added from learning that occurs in the living situation. For Zuboff:

> The informating process takes learning as its pivotal experience. Its objective is to achieve the value that can be added from learning in the situation. Informating assumes that making the organization more transparent will evoke valuable communal insight. From this perspective learning is never complete, as new data, new events, or new contexts create opportunities for additional improvement, insight and innovation.

In a traditional system for Zuboff, managers are drivers of people. You focus on driving people to work as hard as possible. Within the new technology environment, she maintains, managers should be drivers of learning. Learning, moreover, requires a learning environment if it is to be nurtured as a core organizational process. Based on what we have seen of life at the data interface, a learning environment would encourage questions and dialogue. It would support shared knowledge and collegial relationships. It would support play and experimentation as it recognized the intimate linkages between the abstraction of the work and the requirements for social interchange, intellectual exploration and heightened responsibility.

Network versus hierarchy

Us versus them
The traditional system of imperative control, which was designed to maximize the relationship between command and obedience, depended on restricted hierarchical access to knowledge. It nurtured the belief that those who were excluded from the organization's explicit knowledge base were intrinsically less capable of learning what it had to offer. In contrast, an informated organization is structured to promote the possibility of useful learning among all members and thus presupposes relations of equality. However, this does not assume that all members are assumed to be identical. Rather, the organization legitimates each member's right to learn as much as his or her temperament and talent will allow. The new division of learning produced encourages a synthesis of members' interests, and the flow of value-adding knowledge helps to legitimate the organization as a learning community.

Communal versus martial
We remain, in the final years of the twentieth century, Zuboff laments, prisoners of a vocabulary in which managers require employees, superiors have subordinates, jobs are defined to be specific, detailed, narrow and task related, and organizations have levels that in turn make possible chains of command and spans of control. The guiding metaphors are military. A new division of learning requires another vocabulary, Zuboff claims, one of colleagues and co-learners, of exploration, experimentation and innovation. Jobs are comprehensive, tasks are abstractions that depend on insight and synthesis, and power is a roving force that comes to rest as dictated by function and need. The contemporary language of work is inadequate to express these new realities. The informated organization

is a learning institution, and one of its principal purposes is the expansion of knowledge, not knowledge for its own sake (as an academic pursuit) but knowledge that comes to reside at the core of productivity.

Going concentric

> At our 'informating' ceremony, held in the Sikh community centre, we had a ritualistic burning of the family tree, that is, the traditional organizational chart running from top to bottom. We replaced it with overlapping circles of colleagues and co-workers, producers and consumers, manufacturer and retailer.

The concentric organization

Learning at heart
Learning is not something, for Zuboff, that requires time out from being engaged in productive activity. Learning is the heart of productivity in the new form of labour. As the intellective skill base becomes the organization's most precious resource, Zuboff argues, as does Reich, managerial roles must function to enhance its quality. Members can be thought of as being arrayed in concentric circles around a central core, which is the electronic database.

Because intellective skill is relevant to the work of each ring of responsibility, the skills of those who manage daily operations form an appropriate basis for their progression into roles with more comprehensive responsibilities. In Figure 7.1 the activities arrayed on the responsibility rings at a greater distance from the core incorporate at least four domains of managerial activity – intellective skill development, technology development, strategy formulation and social system development.

This means that some organizational members will be involved in both higher-order analysis and conceptualization, as well as in promoting learning and skill development among those with operational responsibility. Their aim, for Zuboff, is to expand the knowledge base and to improve the effectiveness with which

Figure 7.1 Concentric organization

data are assimilated, interpreted and responded to. They have a central role in creating an organizational environment that invites learning, and in supporting those in other managerial domains to develop their talents, in the same way as Senge has indicated, as educators and learners.

Informating strategy

Learning needs to increase, as Revans initially told us, to cope with the pace of change. For an organization to pursue an informating strategy, Zuboff now argues, it must maximize its own ability to learn. In the process it needs to explore the implications of that learning for its long-range plans with respect to markets, product development, and new sources of comparative advantage. Some members will need to guide and coordinate learning efforts in order to lead an assessment of strategic alternatives and to focus organizational intelligence in areas of strategic value.

Focusing intelligence

> After our opening ceremony we ran a basic business course for all unskilled and semi-skilled members of our organizations, using pictorial examples, whenever possible, to get across the message of how the business worked. Thereafter, and among those staff members who were literate, we assigned responsibility for the monitoring of particular product lines to those people who had an innate interest in that kind of product. For example, our athletic lorry driver took a special interest in the sales of sportwear. At the same time we created 'interest groups', cutting across prior hierarchical lines, with regard to the different product lines. What struck us particularly thereafter, with one or two exceptions, was the whole new outlook on the business adopted by our manual workers. In fact, it was a group of them who initiated our first literacy classes in the warehouse.

The increased time horizons of these managers' responsibilities provides the reflective distance with which they can gauge the quality of the learner's environment, and can guide change that would improve collective learning.

Technology development

A new division of learning, for Zuboff, depends on the continuing progress of informating applications. This managerial domain of technology-related activity comprises an hierarchy of responsibilities, in addition to those tasks normally associated with systems engineering, development and maintenance. It includes maintaining the reliability of the database while improving its breadth and quality, developing approaches to system design that support an informating strategy, and scanning for technical innovations that can lead to new informating opportunities. This kind of technological development, according to Zuboff, can only occur in the closest possible alignment with organizational efforts to promote learning and social integration. Technology, then develops as a reflection of the informating strategy and provides the material infrastructure for the learning environment.

Soft technology

> Being responsible for 'soft goods' within the supermarket chain, we now also assumed responsibility for what we termed 'soft technology'. We thereby tried to interest the food side of the business in what we were doing, with only very partial success. This 'human' side of the operation was still viewed somewhat dismissively by the more traditional management, particularly in the light of the fact that our part of the organization was only just breaking even. Moreover, and in the final analysis, the culture of the foods side of the business was distinctly alien to our own. So we returned to our own operation with renewed vigour, and proceeded to expand the 'informated' applications from sales information to stock control, within the warehouse. In the process, and at the same time, we sent a group of five warehousemen, altogether, to a local management college where a course on operations management was being offered to supervisory staff. Ours were the only manual workers, albeit literate ones, on the particular programme.

Intellective skill development

The skills that are acquired at the data interface nearest to the core of daily operating responsibilities provide a coherent basis for the kind of continual learning that would prepare people for increasingly comprehensive responsibilities. The relative homogeneity of the total organizational skill base suggests a vision of organizational membership that resembles, for Zuboff, the trajectory of a professional career. This replaces the 'two-class system' marked by an insurmountable gulf between workers and managers. The interpenetration between rings provides a key source of organizational integration.

Thwarted desegregation

> Attempts to break down the divide between management and worker, via apprenticeship and educational programmes, informal discussions and social ceremonies, revamped models of concentric organization and somewhat amateurish attempts at career counselling were a modest success. We never managed to overturn fundamentally, traditionally hierarchical and racialist attitudes, but we did achieve some measure of progress. Most particularly, the skill levels of our workforce were substantially upgraded, the overall knowledge of the business as a whole went up leaps and bounds, and the general level of participation in decision making was significantly increased.

In a conventional organization a manager's action-centred skills are shaped by the demands of achieving smooth operations and personal success under conditions of hierarchical authority. In an informating strategy the relationships to be managed are both more intricate and more dynamic than earlier patterns. Entrepreneur and animator, enabler and change agent play complementary roles.

Social system development

The shape and quality of relationships will vary in relation to what people know, what they feel and what the task at hand requires. Relationships will need to be fashioned and refashioned as part of the dynamism of the social process, like

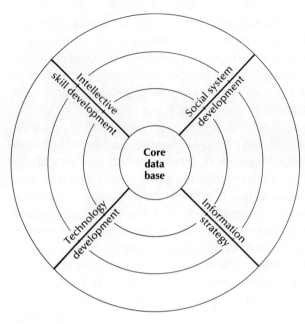

Figure 7.2

inquiry and dialogue that mediate learning. Such relationships are more intricate because their character derives from the specifics of the situation that are always both pragmatic (what it takes to get the work done best) and psychological (what people need to maintain motivation and commitment). What, therefore, is required of managers in a workplace where learning and integration constitute the two most vital organizational priorities?

Village clothes!

> The most successful social innovation, without question, was the 'clothes groups' which we established, with their particular interests in preferred product lines. In fact not only did they do an excellent job of monitoring consumption patterns, and recommending corrective actions, but we put on a panto at the end of each of two years, which went down a treat with our staff, and their families, with a storyline constructed on the basis of these patterns of product and demand. Above all, the degree of interest in our business was raised a thousandfold, and the computer printouts were brought to life in literally dramatic ways. Finally, we were able to draw upon innate social skills and animating talents of staff who otherwise would never have made the organizational headlines.

The abstract precincts of the data interface heighten the need for communication. Interpretive processes depend on creating and sharing meaning through inquiry and dialogue. New sources of personal influence are associated with the ability to learn and to engender learning in others, in contrast to an earlier emphasis upon contractual relationships, or the authority derived from function and position. The demands of managing intricate relationships reintroduce the importance of the 'sentient body'. This provides a counterpoint to the threat of hyperationalism and impersonalization that is imposed by computer mediation. The body now functions, Zuboff stresses, as the scene of human feeling rather than as the source of physical energy or as an instrument of political influence.

Human feelings operate here in two ways. First, as members engage in their work together, their feelings are an important source of data from which intricate relations are structured. Second, a manager's felt sense of the group and its learning needs is a vital source of personal knowledge. It informs the development of new action-centred skills in the service of acting with. In a traditional approach to work organization, employees could be treated as objectively measurable bodies, and, in return, they give of their labour without giving of themselves. But when work involves a collective effort to create and communicate meaning, how people feel about themselves, each other, and the organization's purposes are all critical. Moreover, each is linked to their capacity to sustain the high levels of internal commitment and motivation that are demanded by the abstraction of work and the new division of learning. Such a social system, moreover, is a vital part of the 'knowledge link', which, for Badaracco, underpins the formation of the global enterprise. This serves as the basis for our conclusion, reconnecting the regionally based family household with the globally based family of people.

Conclusion

Longstanding relationships

As we might recall, for Badaracco the core of a firm, like that of a Renaissance city-state, is a dense web of longstanding relationships. Most importantly for him,

> in an age of rapidly proliferating knowledge, the central domain is a social network that absorbs, creates, stores, sells, and communicates knowledge. Its stronghold is the knowledge embedded in a dense web of social, economic, contractual and administrative relationships. No sharp boundaries, however, separate this core from a firm's environment.

The knowledge pool

First, there is a vast pool of potentially commercializable knowledge in the world, and it is expanding rapidly. We now have more facts about the world, more scientific theories, more engineering knowhow, more branches of knowledge and more information about customers, costs, markets and sources of supply than in the past. Second, a growing number of countries, companies, universities and other organizations are contributing to the pool. Third, some of the knowledge is migratory. It can move very quickly and easily because it is encapsulated in formulas, designs, manuals and machinery. Fourth, some of the knowledge being treated in the world is embedded knowledge, which means that it moves slowly, residing in complex social relationships. A team, a department, a company 'knows' things that none of its individual members know.

Knowledge resides in team relationships

Second, just as individual craftsmen have tacit knowledge, which they cannot communicate fully to others, so do successful teams, small groups and departments in companies. Knowledge resides in team relationships in two ways. First, many tasks require too much knowledge for a single individual to grasp in its entirety – separate individuals, with partial but complementary knowledge, work together as a team, and only the team has the full body of knowledge. Second, something clicks when the right personalities, work environment, communication among team members, and leadership come together in harmony.

A firm as an embodiment of knowledge

Third, a firm is an embodiment of knowledge for Badaracco in that it can learn, remember and know things that none of the individuals or teams within it know. It is, in essence, a very large team, a confederation of teams, in which enormously complex skills and knowledge are embedded in the minds of its members and in the formal and informal relationships that orchestrate their efforts. The most valuable assets of firms, moreover, are invisible – information-based assets such as brand image, corporate culture and management skill – learned by the whole organization.

A cluster of overlapping circles

A cluster of overlapping circles, finally, may come to represent a company more accurately than a table of organization with a boss at the top. The centre of the cluster would represent a firm's core capabilities, knowledge and skills embedded in complex relationships. The surrounding circles would represent supporting skills, some owned and controlled by the firm and others managed through knowledge links (Figure 7.3). Further from the core would be the product links that supplement a company's product line, range of services or supply of components. If firms are not separate spheres but complexes linked to many other bodies in society, Badaracco argues, their political power may increase, and they may claim more persuasively to represent the broader interests of society. Hence they may authentically represent the family of people. As such, the learning community may have spread local–global.

In fact, to reinforce this final approach to business as a learning community, I want to return to my own current consulting experience within the communal terrain of the now new South Africa. As you have now seen, for 25 years I had tried, and only partially succeeded, in turning a racially segregated family business

COMMUNAL RELATIONSHIPS

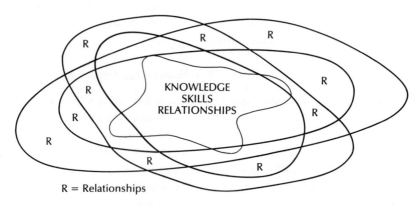

Figure 7.3 Communal relationships

into a multi-racial, cooperative enterprise. Neither the country nor I were quite ready for the task. Recently I was called in, this time as a management consultant, to help somebody else's family business to develop effectively into a learning community. To help the process along the way I created the stage play reproduced, under a fictitious Clothes-Town guise, as Chapter 8.

REFERENCES

Badaracco, J., *The Knowledge Link*, Harvard Business School (1991).
Lamont, C., *The Philosophy of Humanism*, Barrie and Rockliff (1965).
Piore, M. and C. Sabel, *The Second Industrial Divide*, Basic Books (1984).
Zuboff, S., *In the Age of the Smart Machine*, Heinemann (1988).

8

Towards the informated community

During the early part of the nineties, South Africa was engaged in an intensive (if sometimes misguided) attempt to upgrade its black cadre of management. This case study has emerged from one such attempt, which we have chosen to fictionalize because of its sensitive content. Therefore while the substance and general location of the case at hand is quite accurate, the specific context and location is not so. Let us say, then, that a management consultant was invited by the Data Processing Manager of 'Clothestown Stores' to help him to improve the quality of the service his department was offering to its internal customers.

Coincidentally, this consultant had been managing director of a similar, though smaller, operation based in Johannesburg in the early seventies. At that time he had tried, and failed, to create a genuinely non-racial corporate culture. He was too young and naive, and apartheid was still too strongly entrenched in South Africa. His family business, which was subsequently taken over, was in effect called Clothestown. The company in which the consultancy assignment was undertaken, twenty years later when a new South Africa was beginning to emerge, was based in Durban on South Africa's eastern coastline. It had a chain of clothing stores spread all round the country. Having recently become heavily computerized, it was trying to upgrade the professionalism of its operation. At the same time, and in the light of the changes going on in South Africa, it was engaged in a so-called 'black management advancement' programme.

Clothestown stores, which in the early nineties had 120 locations around the country, employing a total of 15 000 people, was unusual in that it had been started up, some thirty years ago, by an Indian and a European, together. While Meenu Sembhi was in fact half-Zulu and half-Gujarati Indian, Donald Mackay was a Scotsman who had settled in South Africa. Though prohibited from marrying one another by the country's so-called 'Immorality Act' of the time, they were like husband and wife. In fact in 1992, after the law had been changed, they finally were married, when both were well into their seventies.

The business which had been created in the early fifties had grown rapidly since then. While Donald provided the discipline and almost colonial-style organization, Meenu was full of entrepreneurial flair and southern hospitality. Once the business had grown, in the nineties, to 15 000 employees, it became necessary to professionalize the management, particularly with the onset of computerization. Ronnie Lessem was called in by the data-processing unit within the facilities department. Its personnel, of 40 people, was responsible for supplying all the Clothestown stores with up-to-date sales information. Half the department worked nightshifts.

In fact, as was discovered soon after the consultancy assignment was undertaken, there was a 'communal' African culture (predominantly nightshift) interspersed among the European professional and colonial-style autocratic ones (predominantly dayshift). While the loyalty to Clothestown as a whole was very high, the interaction with individual, internal customers at the depots and stores left something to be desired. Moreover, the overall operation was becoming progressively more automated, or informated, depending on the attitude adopted by both producers and users. As a result, there was increasing scope for a new kind of involvement, or alienation, depending upon the emergence of a learning community, or otherwise.

The consultant decided, having interviewed a major cross-section of the department's personnel, to dramatize the situation, with a view to creating a new story. In such a new story, drawing upon Shoshana Zuboff's ideas, an informated learning community would be seen to triumph over an automated production set-up. Moreover, because he had become familiar with the origins and subsequent growth of the company, and its culture, he was able to ground the story in the wider Clothestown and emerging Southern African reality. Needless to say, however, he had to exercise a fair amount of imagination, because his knowledge of the company's history was by no means complete.

Having reviewed together the script that follows, a cross-section of some 15 data-processing employees – an equal mix of Africans, Indians and Europeans – proceeded, over the course of the next six months, to build a new, service-oriented culture that was communally informated rather than divisively automated. Fortnightly input sessions, on quality and service, were heavily supplemented by project-based initiatives, aimed at renewing the computer-based community in an informated light. Considerable use was also made of imagery, drawing on formative aspects of the company culture, both past and present. The play was presented in three acts, building initially upon historical grounds. Sadly, both the company's founders had died some months before the consultancy exercise had begun.

Act I   Family matters
Scene 1   The good news

(It's a lovely day in the spring of 1971. Donald Mackay and Meenu Sembhi, happily holding one another's hands, are sitting on a park bench, looking admiringly towards the Data Processing Department.)

Bright Donald   When I look back over the years, Meenu, I can't believe all the changes we've seen. Everyone today relies on the computer.

Warm Meenu   What's so good about that, Donald? You people go overboard about technology. What really pleases me is to see the stability we have created around us. While other companies are turning over people like nobody's business our staff – black and white, brown and yellow – have been around for donkey's years.

Bright Donald   Sure that helps, but what impresses me is that we've got a really good product up front. Do you realize, Meenu, the company's got an edge over its competitors primarily because of IT?

Warm Meenu   You and your IT. What is really important is that we are still family. Can you see how these nightshifts each work together, just like a family? And their managers have been around for years and years. It really warms my heart.

Bright Donald   What's more important is that they have managed to keep up with all the changes. Credit must be due not only to them but to all those professionals we have brought in over the years to egg them along.

Warm Meenu   I knew you are enamoured by all those professional types, dear husband, most of them are white, I have to say, but where would this company be without those salt of the earth characters who man the pumps? It really does my heart good to see those school leavers, who joined us barely literate, now coping so well with those complicated machines of ours.

Bright Donald   You have a point my dear. Retail is detail, and if we lost all the knowledge contained in those years of experience we'd really be sunk.

Warm Meenu   It's our smiling customers that do my heart good, not the detail of the retail.

Bright Donald   Our customers only smile, may I remind you darling, because of the amazing systems the data-processing people have introduced over the years. Do you realize they're now giving us up-to-the-minute sales information, so we're able to respond, within weeks, to changes in customer demand?

Warm Meenu You and your sales information. You'd have me believe that they were the be-all and end-all. As far as I'm concerned, variety is the spice of life. That's what has kept our people at it over the years. In fact if I had a chance to be young again I'd want to be learning all those new things.

Bright Donald It's not a matter of learning for its own sake, of course. Those people at the sharp end of our computer operations have a vested interest in solving the problems that come up. Because if they don't, they'll be in trouble.

Warm Meenu Yes, you've always had a bit of a heavy hand, my dear husband. As far as I'm concerned it's the carrot not the stick that should be used. People must feel that they're in charge of their communal destiny, and be free to develop a sense of their own togetherness. You've always been a bit too inclined towards that outwardly imposed, autocratic outlook of yours.

Bright Donald Careful, darling. We have to be able to control change, especially in areas as complicated as information technology, or else the company would end up in a mess.

Warm Meenu I take your point, my love, as long as you don't end up controlling people in the process. All work and no play does nobody any good. Remember, people like to sing and dance in this lovely part of the world.

Bright Donald There's a time to work and a time to play. People need to know their place. Managers must manage.

Warm Meenu Hold on, Don, families need their characters. Otherwise they all become like dummies, and we've had our fair share of such characters over the years.

Bright Donald If they can help our company beat our competitors, I suppose, then I guess we need to let them get on with it.

Warm Meenu That's my Donald talking. You and I are like chalk and cheese, as different from one another as the colours of our skin. Yet we, and our business, are still here to tell the tale.

Bright Donald We've been loyal to our people, so they've been loyal to us.

Warm Meenu You're always so sensible, my darling. If it were not for me you would never have started up the business, and without you we would never have stayed solvent.

Bright Donald Hand in hand together my dear, and we've remained good friends for all those years. No wonder business is good.

Scene 2 The bad news

(It's a grey day in the autumn of the same year. Donald and Meenu are sipping cocktails at a rooftop bar, while gazing gloomily out at space, wondering when the weather is likely to turn. They have also been having a big argument. Donald, who is drinking a milk stout, when he gets angry becomes cool and detached; Meenu, who is downing a Bucks Fizz, is in a rage.)

Fizzy Meenu You just love to parcel out blame, don't you, Donald? When's the last time you paid me a compliment? It's just like I used to remember down at the shop. You'd be the first to pick holes if there were any mistakes made, but when our staff did a good job you just took it for granted.

Stout Donald You're a good one to talk. How many times did you leave me to take over from you when you were overwrought with grief, just become something fairly minor had gone wrong? I believe, in today's talk, it's called burn-out.

Fizzy Meenu You consider a major rift in our family to be a minor matter. You men are totally unable to deal with emotions. That's why we have these customer-relations problems.

Stout Donald That's rich, coming from you. You've got about as much tact and diplomacy as a bull in a china shop.

Fizzy Meenu What do you expect me to do when I break my back to get my home-baked cakes prepared on time, and you criticize me for the floor being dirty, especially when that's the cleaner's responsibility, not mine?

Stout Donald That's known as managerial delegation.

Fizzy Meenu You think you were born with a golden spoon in your mouth, don't you? I'm honest enough to call a spade a spade, and may I remind you that my own mother cleaned floors to support the family.

Stout Donald So you don't believe in being civil to people?

Fizzy Meenu You're such a gentleman, aren't you? I believe in being sincere. I have no intention of being like some Uriah Heep, as your Charles Dickens would say, or of absorbing abuse like some piece of blotting paper.

Stout Donald   Well, I have to say that, for all your merchandising skills, your upfront manner with our customers leaves something to be desired.

Fizzy Meenu   That's only when they turn nasty. Otherwise – and you know it, Don – I treat our customers just like family. And, what's more, I treat our staff like that too. In short, I care. You talk to our employees as if you were addressing a public meeting. You're just about as warm as ice in a Cape winter. And you call that service!

Stout Donald   People have to be put in their place, you know, especially when they've broken the house rules. Clothestown staff expect to be told what to do.

Fizzy Meenu   Sometimes I wonder whether you fancy yourself as a colonial policeman. We're not fighting a war, we're running a family business. Sometimes you're so remote I wonder how anybody can work for you.

Stout Donald   When you get too familiar with people, you know, they lose respect for you. That's why it's important to have rules, and systems, to set people at some distance.

Fizzy Meenu   I can tell you, Donald, that it began to worry me more and more, as our business grew, how remote we were getting from our people.

Stout Donald   That's the way it has to be. I was ambitious. I wanted the business to expand.

Fizzy Meenu   You were ambitious whatever the human consequences. I wanted our business to grow, and our love to grow, both at the same time. I never had the kind of burning ambition that you had.

Stout Donald   Thank goodness one of us had it. Where would Clothestown be today without that kind of drive?

Fizzy Meenu   It's all very well for you to say that now, while we're sitting here in retirement, but you know very well how our relationship was threatened because of your single-mindedess. You almost succeeded in breaking up the family.

Stout Donald   The trouble with you is that you never saw yourself as a manager, as a leader of men.

Fizzy Meenu   Or women, Donald. You're right. I never was an ego tripper like you. I achieved my ambitions once we had made enough for our family to live in comfort, while supporting my brothers and sisters through their schooling, not to mention our ailing parents.

Stout Donald   If I'd left it to you the business would have stagnated. It was all getting very nice and cosy, but no new blood was coming in. There was no career advancement. While I was getting on with my expansion plans, you were merely keeping things ticking over.

Fizzy Meenu   You know very well that's putting it too simply. I was bending over backwards to find a way of coping with your expansion plans, while maintaining the family atmosphere that is our lifeblood. While your answer was to bring in new blood I was trying to grow our people from within, creating an enterprising community.

Stout Donald   We'll agree to differ.

Fizzy Meenu   You and I just don't see eye to eye, do we? We're as different from one another as night from day? There's no shared vision in this place.

Scene 3   Night and day

(It's midsummer's day, 1992, twenty years later. Donald Junior and Meenu Junior, a son and daughter of the founders of the company, are sitting downstairs at the Durban headquarters. They have just heard a play about their mother and father, after having been taken on a guided tour of the new learning community, located within Clothestown's data-processing unit.

While Don Junior has a PhD in biochemistry, from St Andrews University in Scotland, Meenu Junior left school at 16 to travel around Africa, and subsequently did a University of South Africa (UNISA) Personnel Diploma, by correspondence, while working nightshifts. Don has had experience of running both stores and depots. Meenu based her project work on the unique communal setting in which she found herself. Don's ultimate aim – his hero is the Sun King – is to transform the family business into a global corporation of world class; Meenu's, whose heroine is the Queen of the Night, wants to turn such a global business into a non-racial society.)

Meenu Jr – Queen of the Night   So you think Dad and Mum were good for each other, sis?

Don Jr – The Sun King   Night needs day, and day night . . .

Meenu Jr   How are you and I going to get our act together then, Don?

Meenu Jr   By moving rapidly into the twenty-first century. Have you heard of advanced quality operations?

Meenu Jr   I have heard, while studying at UNISA, of Shoshana Zuboff and her ideas on 'informating technologies'.

Don Jr   Snap, Mee. You've read her book *In the Age of the Smart Machine*. It's absolutely up our street. Automation should be an enhancement not a replacement.

Meenu Jr   Before you rush headlong into the future though, dear brother, remember to honour your past. We can only build on strong foundations. Don't forget that half our systems were designed at the Umfolozi, our community centre down the road.

Don Jr   Don't also forget that retail is detail.

Meenu Jr   I won't. But what motivates me is people and organization not systems and technology. We have to guide and grow people into the new roles we have in mind for them. If automation is sold correctly people will understand.

Don Jr   It seems to me that you and I have to think things through together, or else we'll have double standards here.

Meenu Jr   And also feel things together, my love. You've got the professional competence; I've got the communal insight. You know how to manage; I know how to care; you are white, I am black. We have to understand one another's language.

Don Jr   The efficiency of the depot is the basis of the business though, so thank God I've managed to break through those unbelievable industrial relations problems, with a little help from your good self.

Meenu Jr   With more than a little help, Don. I know the South, and its communal culture; you know the North, and its individualistic ethos. It's like Japan and America in microcosm, or sort of. Both managers and workers can be pains in the neck, but both have legitimate needs.

Don Jr   So can we move forward into our brave new world, now we've got the basics under our belt?

Meenu Jr   Patience, love. First we have to uncover and renew the past. As you well know, originality, which both you and I value so highly, only comes out of a review of origins.

Don Jr   Lead the way, then. I must say, I've had a go at our parents' picture albums, and their press cuttings, but I'm not sure what's of real value there.

Meenu Jr Forget the materials, and listen to your own head and heart. You've heard what our founders Donald and Meenu had to say, and so have I. But nobody else has. You see, over the years, Meenu has become eclipsed by Donald, like your PhD eclipses my diploma. Her warmth, her communality, has been overshadowed by Donald's efficiency and effectiveness. That's why, while we all have a vested interest in improving our service, we, in data processing, haven't really sorted things out.

Don Jr Too much toughness and too little tenderness, as Tom Peters the American management guru would say.

Meenu Jr The balance has been wrong. And yet Meenu has lived on, not only through me but also through the shadow culture of the communal nightshift. The only problem is that she has become increasingly isolated from the mainstream. Too much love and too little challenge can lead to stagnation.

Don Jr What's caused the isolation, Meenu?

Meenu Jr Clothestown has three distinct cultures, two traditional and one modern. The modern culture is the 'professional' one that values competence and performance, and good customer relations. The traditional 'colonial' culture is the autocratic one. It's still very strong on the stores side. You do what you're told or else! Now these two toughminded cultures, of directed competence and regimented efficiency, have overshadowed the tenderhearted one, of communal togetherness and caring for one another.

Don Jr And so?

Meenu Jr If you're looking for customer care, which everybody today is calling for, you need to be able to combine together the hard and the soft, the Donald and the Meenu, you and I.

Don Jr I guess the hard side includes such things as standardization, thoroughness, meeting deadlines, not repeating mistakes, producing accurate information on time, and meeting efficiency criteria. That's the military precision.

Meenu Jr And the soft side involves caring for one another, understanding users' needs, enjoying giving people a service, promoting a culture of mutual understanding, building up a pleasant working environment, and enhancing the quality of working life – a sense of community, but an inclusive rather than an exclusive one.

Don Jr So I guess when it comes to such overall qualities as providing a composite service to the user, converting business requirements into computer solutions and enhancing the overall image of the facilities unit, soft and hard need to come together.

Meenu Jr You've hit the nail on the head, brother. And the reason that so-called black advancement goes off at half-cock here is because it is in touch with this company's toughminded origins (retail is detail) but is remote from its tenderhearted ones (we're all family). In other words, it's European rather than Indian or African. The more isolated the nightshift becomes, the more these two richly complementary sources of quality are split apart. Total quality is diminished.

Don Jr It's as if you and I can't quite make it together.

Meenu Jr We have no healthy offspring, as it were. There's us over here and them over there; guys in the know and dolls on show.

Don Jr So, come to think of it, by setting up a customer relations function run exclusively by the professionals we've perpetuated the divide.

Meenu Jr Like male versus female, individual versus group.

Don Jr We've also divided off upstairs from downstairs, the day professionals being up and the communals down – in the shadows, you might say.

Meenu Jr Let's see what our friend Nehanda [*alias Shoshana Zuboff*] has to say about all this, together with down-to-earth Choto and computer scientist Sudanshu. Nehanda, in fact, has made the amazing and indeed unique transition from African spirit medium to organizational psychologist over the course of 20 adult years.

Act II   *In the age of the smart machine*
Scene 1   Upstairs and downstairs

(*Seated on the stairs between upstairs and downstairs a small group from development and operations are huddled together, a Friday quality circle chewing the fat together.*)

Choto What have you guys got to say for yourselves today? I hear, on the grapevine, that computers are taking over from people at your place.

Nehanda It's actually more complex than that. As long as technology is treated narrowly, in its automating function, it makes it possible for work to be done more efficiently, on the one hand, while decreasing its dependence on human skills, on the other.

Choto   Sounds like what's been happening to us over the last twenty years.

Nehanda   However, when the technology also informates the process to which it . . .

Choto   Cut the jargon, Nehanda. You mean the right documentation must be supplied with it.

Nehanda   Well, more than that. You see, by informating we increase the information content of tasks, and, as a result, set into motion a series of dynamics that will ultimately change the nature of work and the social relationships that organize productive activity.

Choto   That's to say, no more bureaucracy.

Nehanda   Hold on, Choto. You're jumping the gun. You see, the work of the skilled craftsman like yourself may not have been 'intellectual' but it was knowledgeable.

Choto   You can say that again.

Sudanshu   Clothestown has, up to now, had a tendency to be anti-intellectual, you know. Retail's detail. Don't confuse us with first principles. Keep the rainmakers at bay!

Nehanda   Give a girl a chance, guys. I'm trying to make a point. You see, skilled manual work, traditionally speaking, was inscribed as closely on the hands, on the eyes and the ears, as on the brain.

Choto   What you mean to say is that we sniffed things out.

Sudanshu   In a sense. Knowledge was filled with rich detail – the colour and consistency of the babygrow material or the sound and the fury of the early Univac computer. These things were known but not made explicit. Few of those who had that knowledge were able to explain or rationalize it. Such skills were picked up through observation, imitation and action rather than being taught or put into precise words or numbers.

Choto   You mean we learnt by chatting to each other rather than being lectured by boffins like you?

Nehanda   Precisely. You see, in the old days, when we were all family, as you developed your skills so you were promoted to management ranks.

Choto   There was no them and us, bosses and workers, whites and blacks.

Sudanshu   None of that dreaded apartheid and bureaucracy.

Nehanda   Don't get too carried away, Sudanshu. You see, the trouble was that as automation gathered pace, and production jobs offered less opportunity for skill development, the boundaries between the different classes of organizational members became more rigid. That's your dreaded bureaucracy. That's colonialism!

Sudanshu   You mean skilled workers began to lose ground to bright sparks like myself.

Nehanda   The new information technology lifts skill from its traditional dependence on manual activity . . .

Sudanshu   Deskilling!

Choto   Careful, that's me you're talking about.

Nehanda   You see, in a world in which skills were honed out of long years of physical experience, a skilled worker's identity was deeply marked by his understanding of, and attachment to, particular things, such as a piece of operating equipment, or a bow and arrow. Years of service meant continued opportunities to master new objects. That immediate knowledge led to feelings of competence and control. Things worked that way in a traditional African village community, for example in the one I come from in Zimbabwe.

Choto   That's right. In days gone by, when I worked in the fields on the family farm in Zululand, I felt I was in control. Now a lot of it's out of my hands.

Nehanda   The thing is, Choto, technical advances lift skill from its traditional dependence on manual activity. The prospect is created for a profound change. The traditional separation between the subsistence and modern farmers, or the craftspeople and the pros, can be broken down, that is, if the doers are willing to see themselves in a new light.

Choto   You mean we have to go on an ego trip too, and join in with black management advancement!

Nehanda   Don't be so small-minded. If you don't exercise your own power and potential, Choto, you can be damn sure some white guy will exercise his power over you. The thing is, with the development of computer technology, there is an inevitable trend towards centralizing control. Now, if you don't have an understanding of what is happening, that is, of how all the pieces fit together, your lives will become much more difficult.

Choto   So you mean we must all go off and do UNISA degrees in computing?

Nehanda   Well, not everybody has to go to UNISA. But you've got the general message. What you do need is a new learning capacity. You need to be able to paint pictures in your mind, at work, not just on the walls of your living room at home, or in the caves, as our ancestors did.

Choto   So we all have to go off to art school!

Nehanda   That's not a bad idea, Choto. If something is going wrong with the system, nowadays, you don't go down and fix it manually, the way you used to do. You think about the sequence of activities, and how you want to effect it. Being freed from all that manual activity, you have time to think, to anticipate. So when you complete your computer run you get a sense of mental or even aesthetic achievement, rather than physical satisfaction. You then share that sense of achievement with the user.

Choto   Sounds like we're giving up our birthright, moving away from the shopfloor, or from the rural village from which we came, and hovering about in some grand ivory tower.

Nehanda   If you want to become masters of your new destiny, my brothers and sisters, you have to pick up what I call 'intellective' skills in the same way as the traditional hunter had to develop the appropriate technology to hunt animals.

Choto   You mean the sort of the sort of thing we used to do at Chidzeru by the fire at night, when we would tell each other stories of the hunt, and other people would tell us their stories, and we would pretend to go out in our mind's eye on another hunt, and so we would learn from one another?

Nehanda   I think it has a lot to do with the freedom to fantasize. You have to be able to imagine things that you have never seen. In that way bushmen trackers become cave painters, as store supervisors become scenario builders.

Choto   That should give us a great advantage over those straightlaced characters with a golden spoon in their mouths who are never prepared to fantasize, as we used to do by the fireside. Professionals, I believe they're called; storytellers, we're called!

Nehanda   Don't go overboard now. It certainly puts the old bloodhounds at a disadvantage, those characters who like to sniff problems out, the old-style colonial masters. You can't sniff out the new technology like you could the old.

Sudanshu   It seems to me that you're saying that, with this thing you call 'informating', we will have to know about subtle patterns and relationships rather than about specific causes and effects. We will need to have a picture of the way everything is connected, in our hearts and minds.

Choto   You've lost me, Sudanshu.

Nehanda   There's more to it than that, though. To navigate your way through the new systems you need to have a model of the whole business in your head, like the spirit medium and the chief had a picture of how the whole village community functioned.

Choto   So those of us who started from the bottom, and got to know the business from the grass roots, have an advantage over the youngsters of today?

Sudanshu   I'm not sure about that, Choto. The impression I get is that it's a team effort. The young professionals may have the conceptual minds and the up-to-date techniques, but you have the first-hand experience, the knowledge of the business and perhaps a feel for the rhythm of the place. You make the place hum; they make it tick. Seems to me a team effort.

Nehanda   Whatever the case, you will all need to know the meaning and the context of your work. The new technology makes you look at the whole. Gone are the days of the alienated workforce. Gone are the days of the white masters and black servants. We live in the new non-racial South Africa.

Choto   I've got the message. It seems to me that a combination of non-racial teamwork and your so-called intellective skills is what is called for. The funny thing is that us nightshift know about working together and them professionals know about that intellective stuff.

Nehanda   You're moving on too fast, Choto. The important thing to remember is that in an informated environment data and knowhow that were private become public. Whereas crudely based automation insulates and isolates people, in the informated setting the reverse is the case. Hierarchical authority is replaced by mutual exchange, and by horizontal movement. It's like the traditional village, not of the autocratic type, but the more democratic variety, where the chief was a true servant of the people.

Choto   Workers and managers, producers and users, black and white need to care for each other. No more playing the blame game.

Nehanda   What counts, in the organization I'm talking about, is not grades and suchlike status but competence and performance. Conditions must exist, in such a community, for the exercise and development of new skills. Emphasis shifts from the gaining of personal advantage to the best interpretation of shared information.

Choto   But it's always been that way in our indigenous community. What's new, pussycat?

Sudanshu   The sharing, yes. The opportunities, no.

Nehanda   Obviously, sharing can become a threat to managerial authority. That's why many attempts to automate have run into trouble. You see, automating work, for the arch-technocrat, is purely a means to cut costs, routinize work and minimize people problems. Informating involves increasing involvement at every level. Decisions, informed by understanding, therefore get spread around the organization. The old split between techie and pro, black man and white man, is broken down.

Choto   The result, I suppose you would say, is customer care.

Nehanda   Managers, Choto, need to become drivers of learning, rather than drivers of people or technology, just as it used to be in the traditional village – except we learnt different things. They should be driving everyone to use technology – as our best witchdoctors did with their herbal medicines – to get a better under-standing of ways to improve the business. The informating process, so called, holds up a mirror to the workers, enabling you or I to turn data into meaningful information or even into insight. The organization becomes more transparent, more communal. It's just like it used to be back home, except for the fact that technology has now become a friend rather than an enemy.

Choto   I am beginning to see the light. We are becoming, if we choose to see it that way, a learning community, perhaps the learning community within the company. A new kind of family feeling. To the extent that we become that, we transform our image. The frog becomes a prince. The ugly duckling turns into a swan. The bottom rung moves to the top. I like it!

Scene 2   Don and Meenu

(Don Junior and Meenu Junior, who have been listening to the quality circle, sit down together to discuss what they have heard, together with those involved.)

Don Jr   They're beginning to see the light. The colonial model of command and control was based on restricted access to information. The new learning environ-ment legitimates each member's right to learn as much as his or her temperament and talent will allow.

Meenu Jr   So if someone wants to spend all their free time playing golf or drinking beer, so be it.

Don Jr   Well, yes and no. You would need to be aware that the key to your development within the organization would be the extent to which you were able and willing to learn. You would also find, to the extent that this became a learning community, a lot of peer group pressure to develop yourself. But remember, above all else, the division between work and play will become increasingly blurred.

Sudanshu   I certainly know all about that. I presume we need a new language to represent what you are saying. Instead of bosses and workers we need to talk about colleagues and co-learners (those are fine words). Instead of work and play we can talk about exploring, experimenting, and so on, whether we are working or playing.

Don Jr   Before you get too excited, though, remember that inside this organization of ours we are not gaining, or playing about with, knowledge for its own sake. Knowledge comes to lie at the core of what it means to be productive. Learning is not just something we do in our spare time; it becomes the new form of labour.

Choto   You've lost me now. I guess I'm still so caught up with my own idea of operations, of being a black man in a white man's world, that I can't lift my vision to where you're pointing.

Don Jr   Certainly not towards black management advancement in the conventional sense. Rather, Choto, think of the members of your organization being arranged in concentric circles around a central core, as if sitting around the fireside. The fire, if you like, at least in our context, would be what we call the electronic database. Because intellective work is relevant to the work of each ring of responsibility, the skills of those who manage daily, or nightly, operations form an appropriate basis for their progression into roles with wider responsibilities. We've dispensed, in other words, with the military hierarchy. As long as it remains there, black management advancement, along with quality and service, is a non-starter.

Meenu Jr   How does that fit in with the way that we currently organize our work?

Don Jt   It fits very badly with both the military or colonial model of organization and with the more autocratic or bureaucratic form of African regime. But it blends rather well with what you might feel to be a mixture of a professionally and communally, modern and traditional, organization. You see, in a conventional factory, operations are shaped around the need to achieve smooth operations and personal success under conditions of hierarchical authority.

Choto   That sounds just like the normal business set-up around here.

Don Jr   Well, that used to be the case. In a learning community, on the other hand, relationships are more subtle and dynamic. The shape and quality of relationships will vary in relation to what people know, what they feel, and what the task at hand requires. Relationships will need to be fashioned, and refashioned, just as used to be the case in a traditional village community. They will be formed on the basis of two things – what it takes to get a particular job done and what people need to keep up their motivation and commitment.

Meenu Jr   So what kind of new skills will we need in this new environment?

Don Jr   Personal influence, for those who wish to develop, will be associated with the ability to learn and to enable others to learn. This, of course, contrasts with authority based on function and position, which underpins less well-enlightened approaches to black advancement and total quality management.

Choto   It sounds as if I will have to bring more of me into work, including those parts that I used to leave with my family at home, or with my friends in the bar.

Don Jr   You've got the message. In a colonial-style operation people give of their labour, for the money, without giving of themselves. Here it's different. How people feel about themselves, each other, and the organization as a whole is closely linked to the high levels of commitment required by the nature of the work and the learning.

Choto   It's beginning to sound, with all this emphasis on learning, that it's all head and no heart.

Don Jr   Not at all. Learning, on a shared basis, is vitally dependent on social skills, which we Northern Europeans generally have less of than you Southern Africans. In fact the physical activity of the old manually based work environment needs to be replaced by the social activity of this new learning organization. Our community centre, in Pinetown, may become the real heart of the operation.

Meenu Jr   You seem to be saying that a manager's felt sense of the group, now, as well as the group's learning needs is vital for the organization's effectiveness.

Sudanshu   Are you saying, Mee, that the body now functions as the core of human feeling rather than as a source of physical energy, or as a source of political influence?

Meenu Jr   That's certainly what I'm saying, Sudanshu. I now have to find some way of convincing Don here.

Don Jr   As long as we don't lose our heads, and keep our feet firmly on the ground, I've no objection to a display of feeling. After all, that's what's kept you and me together ever since we were kids, despite the apartheid system that tried so hard to drive us apart. Now we need to turn that same force outwards, towards the new Clothestown, in the new South Africa.

Conclusion

In the actual event, and six months after the stage play was conducted, significant moves had been made towards an improvement in quality and service and, to a lesser degree, towards the formation of a learning community. However, the company was nested within a turbulent environment, which was in need of turning itself into a learning society. The extent to which this was to be realized would be determined over the course of the next twenty to fifty years.

Putting business as a learning community to work

Introduction

In Chapter 3 we introduced you to the approach to individual and organizational learning (the inward journey) and creativity (the outward journey) that has characterized our own approach to development and transformation. In fact, from the outset of the MBA programme we became aware that many of the students' coaches, as senior managers, have had their learning appetites whetted, without having the opportunity to take direct advantage of our programme. In some instances, moreover, coaches had remained distant from our learning-oriented MBA, and we sought ways and means of getting them more involved. At the same time, we had set out from the beginning, with varying degrees of success, to position our programme among consortium members as a means of business as well as personal development and of organizational as well as individual learning.

What was therefore proposed, in the summer of 1992, was that a pilot group of selected coaches in each company, by participating purposefully in the programme, exercise a pivotal, enabling influence on their organizational learning and business development. Such a process, moreover, would be orchestrated by the so-called 'link manager' of the development programme, within each consortium company. Coaches who succeeded in this enabling respect would receive a 'fellowship', from the university, in organizational learning. To qualify as a learning fellow, the senior manager would be required, over the course of a two-year period:

- To orchestrate a major business or organizational development. In the process, he or she would be expected to foster individual learning – through his or her student(s); team learning, among the key people involved in the development; and institutional learning, affecting his or her whole division or department.
- To attend appropriate programme modules, one in the 'hard' the other in the 'soft' areas of management. The former – including operations, marketing, financial and strategic management – would be angled at business development. The latter – involving human resource management and organizational behaviour, managing across cultures and building a learning organization – would be aimed at organizational development. Whereas the written report of such a developmental activity would form part of one or more students' projects, the

171

presentation of the results would be the responsibility of the coach, together with his or her team.

- The coaches, under the guidance of the link manager, would now assume the prime responsibility for organizational learning and business development, in conjunction with the individual being assumed by both themselves and the MMBA students. The students, at the same time, would assume secondary responsibility for such institutionally based development and learning. As a result, the consortium-based company would need to take a greater interest in the success of the overall student body, as each individual part would be visibly contributing to the greater organizational whole.

Learning and creativity

To exemplify the process of organizational and corporate learning, and trans-formation, we have cited the two cases of Jean Lang and Jock Henderson, respec-tively engaged in human resource and financially based projects. In each case we invite you to project yourself into their learning-based situation.

Facilitating organizational learning

Jean Lang was one of the first newly called 'human resource managers' to be appointed in her company, in their new plant in the north of England. She had previously been personnel officer at a local distributor which had now linked up in a joint venture with Volvo. At first, the company wanted to send Jean to INSEAD, to do an MBA, but they then thought better of it – it seemed more important, at this point, that she should learn and develop from her own grass roots, while doing an 'in-company' fellowship in organizational learning.

Acquiring knowledge of human resource management

Reacting
In this new plant employing 3000 people, Jean first followed her natural instincts as an ex-distribution manager, wandering around talking, observing and generally appraising the atmosphere. In the process, duly *reacting* with her senses, Jean was able to form her initial impressions of the workforce; they seemed to be an unruly bunch, poorly motivated, and working more out of necessity than any-thing else.

Now cite your own physical reactions as you embark upon a major programme in organizational learning and development.

Responding
The next step Jean took was to visit workers at home, to be able to *respond* better to them as people. She sat around the fireside with their families, listening to stories about the old factory and the new, and about the heroes and villains. She also discovered that the test track was the only part of the works in which a real

family spirit existed – here the men actually enjoyed their work. That aside, the heart and soul of the workforce was not to be found in the 'Works' but at the local club, where a sense of tradition and community spirit thrived.

How will you go about, then, getting to know the communal environment in which the grassroots membership of your organization is based?

Adapting
Jean now wanted to find out more about the different social and working groups. First, she discovered that there was an enormous gulf between workers and management, despite the company's attempt to bridge the gap. There was an equally important disparity in expectations and behaviour between the 'shopfloor' and 'white-collar staff'. She found that she had to *adapt*, speaking almost in different languages to the two groups, which went very much against the grain, as she had always regarded herself as a woman of all the people.

Probing
Not only did Jean have to adapt to individual differences, but it became immediately apparent that she would make little progress unless she came to understand the workplace power politics. So she *probed*, both formally and informally, with a view to developing her own sphere of influence. It took her the best part of six months to make any headway – and the task ahead of her still seemed formidable – but she persevered, encouraged by the new management.

How are you probing the sources of power and influence, surrounding the development programme in which you are engaged?

Analysing
Armed, eventually with this combination of physical, social and personal knowledge, Jean began to formulate ideas for recruitment, job evaluation, training and development. But she felt very uncertain, even after almost a year, and therefore asked to be sent on a human resource management course at the business school. She was particularly keen to meet practitioners from other companies. It proved to be quite a sobering experience, as she both met a wide variety of people and applied her mind to the whole gamut of problems facing her back home.

What, then, will you be seeking to get out of a formal course on the major organizational subject of your concern that is different from what you might have learnt from experience or from your own personal reading?

Recognizing
Upon returning, Jean felt that her knowledge of the personnel role had been much improved but that she still had difficulty in placing it in perspective. After all, this was a motor company based in England, not Honda in Japan or Volkswagen in Germany. Therefore she turned to the works of Shakespeare and

Dickens. Could she *recognize* characters in the factory, or had the people been irrevocably changed over the centuries?

What kind of art or literature do you feel you need to cover to put you in touch with the particular people in the particular environment in which your development project is based?

Imagining
Jean immersed herself in English culture, from the paintings and poetry of Blake to the films of David Lean. Painstakingly, and with a little help from Reg Revans, on the one hand, and Charles Handy, on the other, and after many hours of conversations with workers and their families, she began to *imagine* the kind of organization she might wish to create.

What kind of organization do you want to create, given that it needs to be in tune with your people and their culture? Imagine its shape and form, structure and dynamics, image and identity.

We now turn from organizational learning and development to the actual transformation of, in this case, the human resource function in Jean's company.

Applying knowledge of human resource management

Transforming
Jean envisioned her auto works being *transformed* into a place where people wore smiles on their faces, achieved vast increases in productivity and attended evening classes after a hard day's work. There they would study the works of Charles Dickens, D. H. Lawrence, and Samuel Smiles, as well as Adam Smith, on the one hand; while they also investigated the ideas of Frederick Taylor and Elton Mayo, of Maslow and Herzberg, and of Henry Ford and Shoshana Zuboff. In fact, it took over a year to turn this vision into action.

How would you go about sharing your vision of transformation with your colleagues, subordinates and superiors?

Developing
In the process, and as the workers' and managers' hearts and minds were opened up, a whole series of new business opportunities were recognized, two of which were *developed* over the course of the next year. With Volvo's support, the factory diversified into machine tools and simple electronic switchgear. At the same time, a 'learning organization' was inaugurated, and the wide range of classes established to enhance individual learning was attended by no less than 85 per cent of the plant's personnel.

What kind of learning organization would you see yourself creating, as part of your overall development project?

Administering
As all these activities took off, Jean found herself having to *administer* a much-expanded human resource function, incorporating recruitment and training, job evaluation and payments administration, as well as a far-reaching programme in organization development. Jean received amazingly effective support from the company – pastmasters in personnel administration – throughout.

What administrative principles and procedures, structures and processes, would underpin your newly formed activities?

Manoeuvring
However positive all this may sound, Jean still found herself hard pressed to make her influence continually felt. The trials and tribulations of national economic and social transformation filtered down to the local level, affecting the local region and the factory alike. Jean therefore had to keep lobbying at a political level, both inside and outside the company, to *manoeuvre* herself and her department into a position of continuing influence.

What political activity do you see yourself becoming engaged in, with a view to realizing your transformational objectives?

Generating
Faced with the daunting prospect of simultaneous economic, social and technological change, Jean had to *generate* a continuing series of experiments, both socially and technically. Among innumerable training programmes, she initiated Coverdale training, management by objectives and the 'managerial grid'. She also worked closely with the company to introduce new, computerized technologies.

What kind of training programmes and information systems would form a natural part of the transformed whole?

Involving
Throughout the three years during which she retained her post, Jean continually *involved* people at all levels, both within the organization and outside it. She arranged plant visits for wives and families, as well as visits from artists, poets and writers. She even adopted the UK's Arts Council idea of an 'artist in residence'. Finally, she supplanted the conventional anniversary celebrations of Guy Fawkes with a local production festival, to celebrate not only the achievements of her most productive work group but also those of the star performers in the local economy as a whole.

What sorts of rituals, ceremonies and symbols would you be using to cement your organizational changes?

Trading
In the final analysis, and in the spirit of genuine *perestroika*, Jean was constantly

on the lookout worldwide for the best possible human resource consultants, those who were able to appreciate her company's unique situation. Over time, she became enormously astute at trading off their expertise and involvement against the enjoyment and experience she could offer them of living and working nearby during this unique period of development.

Who are the key people, from around the world, that you would want to hire in from your programme, and what might it cost you to get them involved, and how would your organization benefit?

We now turn from organizational learning, via human resource management, to the business as a learning community, with a focus on financial management.

Creativity in business

Jock Henderson was recently installed as management controller for the largest subsidiary of a diversified financial services group, based in Edinburgh. As a canny Scot, trained as a chartered accountant, Jock was eager to take up the post. At the same time, as he had been working in a medium-sized company in Singapore for the past eight years, he knew that it would take him some time to get used to this new position, back in his home country – and working for a large corporation. As a bridging process, therefore, the company's MD decided to involve Jock, from the outset, on a two-year business development programme, orchestrated by a well-known business school. His focus, therefore, was on the development of a learning company mediated, surprisingly, through financial management.

Acquiring knowledge of financial management

Reacting
When Jock took over, the Edinburgh subsidiary was in a pretty poor state. His brief was therefore to work with the new managing director to put the company back on its feet. Jock felt that it would take him a good six months to appraise the situation as it was. In fact, having spent the first week poring over balance sheets and profit-and-loss accounts, he decided to go out into the field, accompanying the insurance salesmen on their rounds. After a month of this he felt that he was almost, but not quite, able to identify the problem. His gut *reactions* were still tentatively based. While he cut 20 per cent off the expense budgets, as a gesture of stringency, he wasn't quite sure why he was doing it.

How would you react to the prospect of combining a financial reappraisal with the development of a learning company? Where would you begin?

Responding
Jock decided to get 'closer to his customers'; that is, the sales force, on the one hand, and the office administration, on the other. In effect, he took control of the

day-to-day bookkeeping, so that by duly recording all transactions himself he could get a real feel for what was coming and going. In the process, he also engaged himself in endless discussions with clerical and sales staff. The finance office couldn't understand why their boss was taking so much time and trouble to *respond* to people – this wasn't how they expected a finance officer to act!

Picture yourself taking over some of the day-to-day bookkeeping, with a view to getting to know people and things, via financial transactions, at the ground level. Describe what is going on and how it feels.

Forecasting
After three months of this mundane activity Jock felt that he had a real feeling for the whole operation, so much as that he could *forecast* anticipated revenues and expenditures for the year, on the basis of current trends; he anticipated a loss of £100 000 in the forthcoming financial year.

How might the financial forecasts which you arrived at reflect the changing flow of people and things over time?

Moulding
Jock then proceeded to *mould* together a set of financial statements based on a break-even situation. He enlisted the help of the company's IT specialist, Diane Clark, who was familiar with all the financial packages on the market. Surprisingly, in his eight-year lay-off from mainstream accounting, Jock had forgotten how to prepare these statements himself. He was amazed to find that the new packages enabled him to put a set of accounts together without more than a smattering of specialist financial knowledge.

Characterize the sorts of financial packages with which you are involved. How might you deploy them to mould your company into desired forms?

Analysing
With Diane's continuing assistance, Jock was now able to *analyse* the company's financial situation quite precisely, clearly separating out fixed from variable costs, and 'people' costs from the costs of physical things.

Picture the kinds of financial statements required to understand where the company has been, where it is now and where you would want it to go – physically, economically and socially.

Interpreting
Jock soon realized that such analyses were too sterile and difficult to *interpret* without a better understanding of trends in the industry at large. Therefore, over the next couple of months, he attended three different seminars on the financial services industry. He also made it his business to meet the most erudite academics

and consultants in the field, and to study the most up-to-date market research reports. Needless to say, he also had many long discussions with senior management in the subsidiary and with closely connected institutions in the group. Eight months after he had joined the company, Jock finally felt that he was really beginning to appreciate what was going on – the figures were merely the symptoms of a deeper underlying problem.

What kind of course would you look for, and what kinds of experts would you need to consult, in order to appreciate fully the financial and commercial position of your company?

Imagining

In his mind's eye Jock began to *imagine* a (profitably) transformed set of accounts, based on a very different operation. It was not a picture of a slimmed-down administration; on the contrary, he foresaw a group of professional salesmen carrying a much-widened portfolio of financial services. In financial terms, therefore, risks would be spread over a much wider range of activities. At the same time, Margaret Thatcher's vision of a shareholders' democracy would be reflected in the company's *avant-garde* style and ethos.

Imagine – based on a set of financial statements depicting the nature and extent of your company's past, present and future – the way the business should be going, qualitatively as well as quantitatively.

We now turn from the learning company, from a financial perspective, to its transformation, again from a commercial point of view.

Applying financial knowledge

Transforming

In effect, Jock Henderson foresaw a complete *transformation* of the business. The company he now envisaged to be in the business of 'Composite Financial Services', with one aspect complementing, or reinforcing, another. He even designed a new logo, and a colour scheme for the modernized offices – all carefully costed into his budget. At the same time, recalling some of the knowledge he had gained as a trainee accountant, Jock restructured the company's short-term investments, both to secure a better return and to improve the company's image with its bankers.

How might you reconstitute your business, in name and function, in the light of past, present and future income streams?

Developing

Jock and his managing director were now able to identify, and *develop*, a wide range of new business opportunities that had significant financial implications. In the short term, of course, the drain on cash was greater than the inflow of revenue, but this situation reversed itself within only six months.

What new and profitable areas of business – over the medium to long term – would you be liable to enter?

Controlling
Naturally, it fell to Jock to *control* the flow of finances very tightly. Unlike the development time span, which stretched between six months and two years, financial control was conducted on a monthly basis. In fact, the new computer software that they had recently installed enabled them to monitor the precise cash flows in and out of the business at weekly intervals.

How would you see the more complex business activity being financially and administratively controlled?

Manoeuvring
Control was a passive, depersonalized activity, but Jock was sometimes called upon to deliberately *manoeuvre* the flow of finances to accommodate the interests of the group as a whole, from the vantage point of quoted share price and tax liability. Like most other quoted companies of the day, the earnings per share had to be watched carefully, albeit legitimately, to minimize the risk of an attempted takeover.

What activities would your company be involved in to maintain short-term profitability at an optimal level?

Generating
Whereas such manoeuvring called upon Jock's somewhat devious 'creative accounting' abilities, his ability to tap alternative sources of funds was very much more in the intellectual mainstream! During the first two years of the appointment he lived up to his reputation by *generating* all kinds of schemes for raising finance at comparatively low cost. This very much helped the company to enter into profitable new ventures without incurring too heavy a financial drain.

How would you build into the company systems and procedures for continually reviewing the allocation of revenues and expenses?

Involving
Jock had an ability to get on with people. It was difficult at first, as established staff were suspicious of an obviously meddlesome newcomer, but he won them over (sometimes by going to such extremes as wearing his kilt – and even playing bagpipes – in the office!). Later, he took great care to *involve* the 100-strong sales force and administration staff in understanding where the cash came from and went to. Finally, after two years, he received the MD's approval to introduce a profit-sharing scheme.

How would you ensure that the workforce as a whole was continually involved in appreciating the financial base of your company?

Trading

One of the reasons Jock was able to introduce this scheme, after two years, is that the company had now grown to be very profitable. This was due partly to the new business strategy and partly to Jock's acumen in *trading* on the stock market. He had secured the MD's permission to invest 10 per cent of the subsidiary's profits, every year, and had managed to secure a fourfold return on each occasion. No-one was surprised, therefore, when it was announced that Jock was to take over as financial controller for the group as a whole, after two and a half years.

How would you build a 'tradering mentality' into your organization as a whole?

As you can see, learning and development, on the one hand, and creativity and transformation, on the other, can be extended across from both individual to institution and also across the business functions. We happen to have selected human resource and financial management, but information technology or organizational behaviour, marketing or corporate strategy lend themselves to similar learning-based treatment.

Now we turn from our particular spectral approach, modelled somewhat on Jaques's organizational stratification, to the four approaches explicitly drawn upon in this book. These four variants on business, as a learning community in turn, involve the exchange, the ordering, the development and the sharing of knowledge via – respectively – what we have termed the learning company, the learning organization, the learning system and the learning community. Here we put each to work (see Table 9.1).

Table 9.1

Management and learning

- In our rapidly changing world the most effective managers will be those who are able to *manage* and to *learn, simultaneously*.
- Management involves a path of action whereby *vision* is progressively transformed *into reality*.
- Learning involves a path of reflection whereby everyday *reality* is progressively transformed *into* personal and managerial *vision*. The old and rigid division between the job and the course is, therefore, becoming obsolete.
- Management, the outward-looking function, and learning, the inward-looking one, must be viewed as *two sides* of the same coin.
- Individual and organizational learning should be seen as *mutually reinforcing*.

Re-entering your learning organization

- The learning achieved is not so much an acquaintance with new factual knowledge as a *re-interpretation* of existing knowledge.
- This re-interpretation is a *social process* carried on by two or more learners, causing each to examine many ideas afresh.
- Within such a context, managers learn with and from each other by *mutual support, advice and criteria*.
- Through such a social process of learning, the organization makes more effective use of its *stored experience*.

Action learning – establishing a learning company

Project-based learning

Project-based learning, as we saw in Chapter 4, is a vehicle for management development and a route to organizational learning. For Revans, one cannot proceed without the other. It is critical, therefore, that the organization as a whole should subscribe to the learning objectives of the individual action learners.

If a problem is seen as requiring a project report this in no way interferes with the day-to-day operations of the company. However, if the organization is going to examine procedures, operations and methods, and subsequently, at the behest of the action learner, change them, there is a substantial threat of disruption to present operations. These, Revans maintains, must be anticipated and negotiated. Organizational commitment to learning must be developed. In any dealings between educator and institutional client, Revans has itemised 14 matters for consideration:

1. The choice of problems around which to form projects,

2. The role and responsibility of project clients,

3. The qualities and selection of project-based learners,

4. The monitoring of projects,

5. The development of set (small-group) facilitators,

6. The representation of the firm in any consortium of learning organizations,

7. The role of training,

8. The induction of students into their projects,

9. The continued academic support for participants,

10. The continued role of line management in projects,

11. The supply of appropriate technical knowledge,

12. The extension of one project into another,

13. Issues of cost and benefit,

14. The concept of the whole organization as a learning system.

An action learning consortium

While action learning has made great inroads among management in Belgium, its influence in Britain has been sporadic albeit widespread. The responsibility for spreading word and action has been largely up to individual management trainers and consultants; polytechnics, and a few companies. The trouble is, people want something tangible that they can relate to, rather than a supposed cure-all which will develop the organization as a whole. The sponsors of an Action Learning Programme Consortium, a group of companies in the English Midlands in the seventies, tried to overcome this obstacle by pointing towards some unique and yet tangible features of action learning:

1. Managers are expected not just to write reports but to initiate action towards *solution of the problems* they have been diagnosing.

2. The participating companies can maintain a *healthy balance* between problem solving and management development. The two are inextricably bound together in *action learning*.

3. The project set (group of learners) can become a *'learning community of peers'* with similarly complex problems which require action – action which must be initiated through gaining the understanding and commitment of others.

To cope with the various problems of implementation which accompany action learning, Revans has developed a formula. A decision has to be designed and then negotiated; the problem or the opportunity has first to be diagnosed and then treated. All our work suggests that the guile of realistic diagnosis – What are we after? What stops us? What can we do? – demands just less than 50 per cent of our total effect and the artfulness of effective negotiation – *Who knows? Who cares? Who can?* – most of the remainder.

Action learning in theory and practice

For Revans, as for Francis Bacon before him, the process of learning involves, at the outset, a two-way flow between *action* and *reflection*. The actor changes the system; the reflector changes the self. Neither can operate effectively in isolation of the other. You can only learn from an experience if you reflect on it. Unless you have experience, you have no foundation on which to base your learning.

The model of the learning process that Revans puts forward is a particular application of general scientific method. In encompasses a survey – reflective observation, an hypothesis – abstract conceptualization, a test – active experimentation, and an audit – concrete experience. In your own particular case, then, in relation to a subject of key concern:

• What kind of *survey* activity will need to be undertaken?
• What core *hypothesis* underlies your field of concern?
• How are you going to *test* it out?
• How will you *verify* whether you have achieved what you set out to accomplish?
• Finally, how will you *internalize* the overall learning process? (See Figure 9.1)

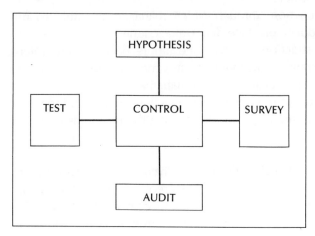

Figure 9.1 Action learning process

We now turn to our second approach to organizational learning, one which is less focused on your managerial personality and more upon your depersonalized organization.

Stratified learning – establishing a learning organization

The philosophy of organizational stratification

The functioning of social institutions depends on more than having the right individuals, according to Elliot Jaques; it depends, to begin with, on having the 'requisite' *organizational stratification*. For Jaques, depersonalized structures and functions eclipse Revans's personalized attitudes and behaviours. As far as bureaucratic systems are concerned, it is impossible to describe or define what is meant by the right person until the nature of the task has been defined and the organization designed and constructed to enable the work to be done. Finally, it is through their work at a matched level of individual and organizational cognition, Jaques argues, that individuals maintain their primary sense of reality.

Orders of information complexity are the increasingly complex groups of data which an organization must assimilate, and subsequently use, to inform its cognitive processing and thereby to solve its problems. The learning organization, therefore, is able to accommodate progressively more complex information, ranging from the specifically concrete to the universally abstract. There are, in fact according to Jaques, four orders of complexity. These are, as we established in Chapter 5:

- First-order *concrete* things, that is, specific things that can be pointed to – 'use this tool'; 'employ him, not her'.
- Second-order *verbal* abstraction, through which managers are able to run factories, design new products, produce financial accounts.
- Third-order *conceptual* abstractions involve, for example, balance sheet values that bring together a wide range of accounting categories, which can in turn be translated into specific and practical assets and liabilities.
- Fourth-order *universal* abstractions contain concepts that are grouped together into the universal ideas that are required for handling the problems of whole societies.

In our own approach to organizational stratification we have developed a spectrum of seven layers of increasing orders of complexity. Moreover, as indicated in *Total Quality Learning*, whereas upward integration from red to violet constitutes learning and development, downward integration constitutes innovation or transformation (see Figure 9.2).

Integrated learning – developing a learning system

The philosophy of systems thinking

Peter Senge, as we saw in Chapter 6, drawing upon the spirit of wholism that has predominated within a Germanic as well as oriental world view, has developed an approach to learning that befits large-scale systems. The *general systems* approach brings together disciplines for seeing wholes.

A discipline involves a system of rules which Senge has developed to cover five related disciplines. These embrace so-called 'personal mastery', the development of 'mental models', the evolving of 'shared values', the exercise of 'team learning', in conjunction with 'systems thinking' in itself.

Senge's five disciplines

- *Personal mastery* is the discipline of continually clarifying and deepening vision, of focusing energies, of developing patience, and of seeing reality objectively. As

Organisational Learning

RED	Reactor	How does your unit keep itself collectively alert?
ORANGE	Responder	How do you attract to you communities that will enhance your organisational learning?
YELLOW	Experimentor	How does your organisation maintain your exploratory stance and institutional experimentation?
GREEN	Energizer	How does your organisation continually expose itself to commercially, technologically and culturally or socially risk-laden situations?
BLUE	Deliberator	How do you continually conceptualise your unit's activities, both in part, and as a whole?
INDIGO	Harmonizer	How do you develop your powers of insight?
VIOLET	Inspirer	How do you draw out your people's and your organisation's origins, and consequent originality?

Figure 9.2

such, it is the learning system's spiritual foundation. How do you see your own work, and ultimate vocation, being transformed over the course of your working life; that is, from youth to maturity? (See Figure 9.3.)
- *Mental modelling* is the discipline of working with mental models – of people and institutions – starting with 'turning the mirror inward', that is, learning to unearth your mental pictures of the world so as to bring them to the surface and hold them rigorously to scrutiny. It also includes the ability to carry on 'learning-based' conversations that balance inquiry and advocacy. How would you mentally model your business as a learning community?

VIOLET	Create Vision	What is the far-reaching mission of your part of the organisation (your unit)?
INDIGO	Enable Development	What market or organisational potential is your unit realising?
BLUE	Structure Methodically	What definable core function is your unit carrying out?
GREEN	Compete Aggressively	What special effort and reward is particularly associated with your unit?
YELLOW	Continually Experiment	How is your unit continually learning and growing?
ORANGE	Establish Shared Values	How does your unit effect shared values, whereby people co-operate with each other?
RED	Ongoing Implementation	How are people's energy levels kept from waning?

Figure 9.2 cont.

- *Shared vision*, involves the skill of unearthing shared 'pictures of the future' that foster genuine commitment and enrolment rather than compliance. In mastering this discipline, leaders in particular organizations and in whole societies learn the counterproductiveness of trying to dictate a vision. Describe the shared pictures of your organization held by yourself and those with whom you work.
- *Team learning* as a discipline starts with 'dialogue', whereby members of a team, within and across organizations, suspend assumptions and enter into a genuine 'thinking together'. To the Greeks *dialogos* meant a free flowing of

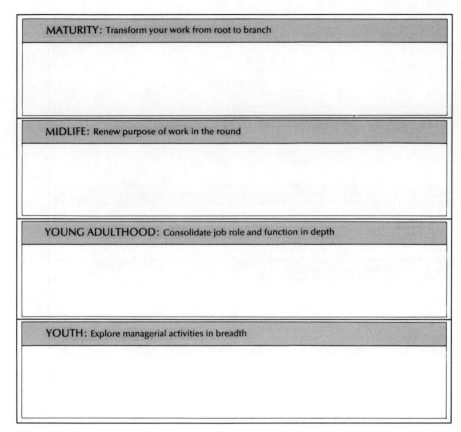

MATURITY: Transform your work from root to branch

MIDLIFE: Renew purpose of work in the round

YOUNG ADULTHOOD: Consolidate job role and function in depth

YOUTH: Explore managerial activities in breadth

Figure 9.3

meaning through a group, allowing the group to discover insights not attainable individually. Compare and contrast the discussion between, say, four people with the dialogue between them.

• *Systems thinking*, finally, is the fifth discipline. It is the discipline that integrates the four others, fusing them into a coherent body of theory and practice. For example, vision without systems thinking ends up painting lovely pictures of the future with a new, deep understanding of the forces that must be mastered to move from here to there. Systems thinking also needs the disciplines of building shared vision, mental models, team learning and personal mastery to realize its potential. Draw a picture indicating the systemic interaction between different elements of your envisaged learning system.

While Peter Senge places considerable emphasis upon individuals, if not also organizations, 'thinking together' in systemic terms, Shoshana Zuboff is somewhat more concerned with the way people 'feel together', in communal terms.

VIOLET: What is your far-reaching mission in turning your business into a learning system?

INDIGO: What business and organisational potential will you be fulfilling?

BLUE: Of what core functions will the learning system be comprised?

GREEN: What will drive you to achieve?

YELLOW: How can you ensure that the learning system will continually develop?

ORANGE: How will the systemic learning be infused with communal spirit?

RED: How will the energy level be maintained?

Figure 9.4

Informated learning – building a learning community

The concept of 'informated' work

Shoshana Zuboff, at the Harvard Business School, has made a great impact on organizational learning through her insights into so-called 'informating' – as opposed to automating – technologies. Zuboff's learning community of colleagues and co-workers, in contrast to the military terminology of line and staff, superior and subordinate, engage in four key functions:

- *Informating strategy*: For an organization or society to pursue an informating strategy it must maximize its own ability to learn. In the process, it needs to explore the implications of that learning for its long-range plans with respect to markets, product development, and new sources of comparative advantage. Some members will need to guide and coordinate learning efforts in order to lead an assessment of strategic alternatives and to focus organizational intelligence in areas of strategic value. How will you be focusing organizational intelligence?
- *Technology development*: A new division of learning, for Zuboff, depends on the continuing progress of 'informating' applications. These include maintaining the reliability of the core electronic database while improving its breadth and quality, developing approaches to system design that support an informating strategy and scanning for technical innovations that can lead to new informating opportunities. This kind of technological development can only occur in the closest possible alignment with organizational efforts to promote learning and social integration. How will you link technology development with social integration?
- *Intellective skill development*: The skills that are acquired at the data interface, nearest to the core of daily operating responsibilities, provide a coherent basis for the kind of continual learning that would prepare people for increased responsibilities. The relative homogeneity of the total organizational skill base suggests a vision of organizational membership that resembles the trajectory of a professional career, rather than the 'two-class system'. How will your professional team advance their careers, developing outwards from the data interface?
- *Social system development*: The abstract precincts of 'informated' work heighten the need for communication. New sources of personal influence are associated with the ability to learn and to engender learning in others, in contrast to an earlier emphasis upon contractual relationships or the authority derived from function and position. The demands of managing intricate relationships reintroduce the importance of the sentient body. The 'worker' now functions as a source of human feeling rather than as the source of physical energy. How will you exercise this new form of feeling-centred influence, thereby engendering learning in yourself and others?

Conclusion

The four different approaches to developing your business, as a learning community, are by no means mutually exclusive. You may well wish to mix and match along the way to your learning-based development. However, it is well to be aware that whereas Revans's action learning tends to be individually oriented, Jaques's organizational stratification is more institutionally focused. Similarly, whereas Senge has a systemic focus, Zuboff is communally oriented.

In the Anglo-Saxon world, from which most of the management literature has been derived, there is an inevitable bias towards the individual. Managers who have been educated within that tradition need to be aware of such bias and take due account of it. To that extent, the rounded approach shown in Figure 2.4 on p. 32 should be adopted. We now turn, in our final chapter, to a review of the overall implications of turning a business into a learning community.

REFERENCE

Lessem, R., *Total Quality Learning*, Blackwell (1991).

Introduction

The economics of the madhouse

As we approached this final chapter in the summer of 1992, with a view to recasting business as a learning community, I was once more struck by the headlines in Britain's leading Sunday newspapers. 'Double dip recession threat grows,' claimed the Business Editor of the *Sunday Times* on 19 July 1992. 'London's financial markets are braced for further heavy selling this week, as a clutch of gloomy economic reports suggest that the economy is threatening to plunge into a second leg of recession'.

In prompt response, the newspaper's editor, depicting 'the economics of the madhouse', claimed that 'The British economy is in a parlous situation'. Not surprisingly, therefore, he stipulated as his first requirement the lowering of interest rates, preferably within the ERM (Exchange Rate Mechanism) but, if necessary, without. Second, he advocated drastic reductions in the current sales of government bonds, which are pushing up long-term interest rates as well as a cut in the rates on National Savings. Finally, he made a plea for a genuine housing recovery package, together with public sector construction projects, locking in contractors at today's depressed costs. The only mention of 'human capital', in this *Sunday Times* editorial, is as 'locked-in contractors'! As far as the advancement of learning is concerned, that stands light years away from the editor's economic horizons. Interestingly enough, moreover, whereas more successful economies such as Japan and Germany have a far better trained workforce than their Anglo-Saxon counterparts, their 'economic' debate continues to be couched in such conventional terms.

As a result, the economic debate among the G7 countries is again focused upon interest rates, with the German Bundesbank being the current villain. The advancement of the learning society, which is at least implicitly a much stronger part of Japan's agenda than Britain's, does not feature explicitly on the global economic agenda. In other words, and in Peter's Senge's terms, we are missing the key point of leverage within our present-day economic system.

The next economic frontier

The limits of monetarism

For Robert Reich, as we may recall from Chapter 1, the old entrepreneurial era has had its day. A similar point was recently made by a professor of economics at Columbia University, in his book on *Business Organization and the Myth of the Market Economy*. For William Lazonick, Reich's entrepreneurial era coincided with what Lazonick terms 'proprietary capitalism':

> Relying more on markets than managers to coordinate industrial activity, and hence more on external than internal economies to cut costs over time, British industry gained international competitive advantage. It was the institutions of market-coordinated proprietary capitalism, including heavy reliance on a self-reproducing supply of skilled labour to coordinate as well as execute work, that permitted British manufacturing to dominate world markets in the late nineteenth century. Britain's rise to industrial dominance arose without investments in managerial structures that could develop firm-specific organizational capabilities.

Whereas it will always be necessary and desirable for entrepreneurs to play their part in the economic whole, their heyday – at the turn of the nineteenth century – has gone. Monetary incentives, therefore, which formed so strong a part of Reaganomics, of Thatcherism and of the entrepreneur's motivation, have only a minor role to play in processes of long-term economic renewal.

In other words, such incentives are necessary to give an economy the proverbial 'kick start', but such brute force will never provide ongoing momentum. Enduring force is derived from the inner-directed human needs for long-term meaning and purpose, rather than from the outer-directed ones for short-term financial gain. Finally, what applies to the individual is equally applicable to whole societies. Britain was at its political and economic height when it genuinely perceived its sense of purpose in the world. That was before the management era came upon us.

Fiscal limits

Entrepreneurship for the first three-quarters of the twentieth century, at least in America, was replaced at the leading economic edge by management. Interestingly enough, America and Germany grasped that managerial nettle much better than did Britain, by establishing large-scale, depersonalized enterprises, buttressed by schools of engineering, and – in America – by schools of business administration.

According to Lazonick, again, during the first decades of the twentieth century, proprietary capitalism gave way to managerial capitalism as the dominant engine of industrial development. Using managerial structures to plan and coordinate mechanized production processes and to apply scientific knowledge to industry, US corporations had, by the twenties generated a second Industrial Revolution. Proprietary capitalism proved inadequate to deal with the technological complexities and the attendant high fixed costs of the new industrial era. Through managerial coordination, industrial corporations were able to develop the combined productive capabilities of human and physical resources in ways that market coordination, with its unplanned interaction of specialized producers, was unable to do. The more technologically complex the process or product and the less it relied on external resources, the greater the need for the organizational capability to plan and to coordinate.

Coincident with this second era were the forms of economic management, or fiscal policies, that were conceived by the great British economist, John Maynard Keynes, and popularized by America's President Roosevelt in his famous 'New Deal' in the thirties. Keynes's approach to demand management, whereby in times of recession governments intervened by upgrading purchasing power, is revisited in the above-mentioned *Sunday Times* editorial in terms of the housing and construction projects advocated.

While Thatcherism operated at the level of individual inventives, assuming that personal capitalism lives on, Keynesianism operates at the level of mass demand and production, assuming that managerial capitalism prevails. Moreover, while the former is geared towards the individual entrepreneur, the latter addresses the mass of consumers. Neither monetary nor fiscal policies address the capacity or motivation to produce of the workforce as a whole. This may be due, as Lazonick again intimates, to the conceptual limitations of Anglo-Saxon economics:

> In defining the economic problem as the allocation of scarce resources, neoclassical economics ignores the analysis of how individuals, firms and economies create more value with the same amount of human and physical resources, and thereby overcome scarcity. In short, neoclassical economics has a theory of value allocation, but it lacks a theory of value creation. A theory that simply assumes that the greatest economic prosperity is achieved when organizations are subservient to market forces, as neoclassicists argue, cannot explain the ways in which invested resources have been transformed into higher quality products.

Not surprisingly, therefore, for Reich as for Lazonick, the managerial heyday came to an end twenty years ago, when the era of mass production began to be eclipsed by so-called 'lean' manufacturing and flexible specialization.

Human capital

Japan's skilled workers
Interestingly enough, and in an evolutionary sense, we can see that both pragmatism, personified in entrepreneurship, and rationalism, embodied in management, have had their pre-eminent day. Seemingly, and drawing upon our portfolio of philosophically based factors of production, wholism and humanism are poised to enter centre-stage. In the process, we advance from labour as a commodity and people as a resource – eras past – to human capital and, ultimately,

human being – eras present and future. For Lazonick, the era of human capital is embodied not in proprietal or managerial but in 'collective' capitalism, most vigorously embraced by Germany and Japan. As he points out, over the past two decades, Japanese manufacturing has outperformed America in the mass production of most lines of consumer durables:

> Over the long run Japanese organizations will, in my view, continue to outperform their US counterparts because of organizational integration that extends beyond the limits of the planned coordination of the specialised division of labour, as practised under managerial capitalism. First, organizational integration in Japan extends across vertically related companies to a much greater extent than in the US. Second, within the dominant Japanese enterprise, organizational integration extends further down the corporate hierarchy to include male, blue-collar workers. Both extensions of organizational integration significantly enhance the organizational capability available to Japanese enterprises. Japanese practice, then, is in marked contrast to the US managerial concern with using technology to take skills and the exercise of initiative off the shop floor. This practice goes back to the late nineteenth century when the success of US production was dependent on breaking the power of the craft workers and transferring to management the sole right to plan and coordinate the flow of work.

Despite the existence of militant unionism in Japan at various points in the first half of the twentieth century, there was never any attempt by Japanese workers or their organization to establish craft control on the shopfloor. As a result, Japanese employers never had to confront established craft positions of workers, as was the case with US manufacturers at the turn of the century. Nor did they have to resign themselves simply to leaving skills on the shopfloor in the hands of autonomous craftworkers, as was the case in Britain.

Historically, the problem facing Japanese capitalists was not to rid themselves of skilled workers who might use their scarce skills to establish craft autonomy on the shopfloor. Rather, their problem, coming into the twentieth century, was an absence of a self-generating supply of workers with industrial skills. To overcome this constraint, industrial capitalist employers had to make the investments that would transform unskilled into skilled workers and then retain them by integrating them into the organization. Out of the exigencies of developing and utilizing workers with industrial skills were laid the social foundations for the current permanent employment system. For Lazonick:

> If there was one lesson to be learnt from the comparative history of three industrial revolutions, it is that, now more than ever, industrial innovation requires the long-term commitment of resources to organizations that can plan and coordinate the development and utilization of productive capabilities. If, in a particular social environment, private enterprise cannot itself create the organizational conditions for the appropriate education, mobilization, and coordination to occur, then public intervention is required.

Germany's organizational ecology
Walter Streek, a German economist, takes on where Reich and Lazonick leave off. On the face of it, Streek maintains, Germany appears to be an advanced case of what used to be called 'Euro-sclerosis'. Collective bargaining has remained centralized at the industrial level; the legal complexities of running enterprises under co-determination continue to puzzle managers and labour lawyers; involuntary dismissals of workers in large firms are still very difficult by comparison with other countries; the vocational training system with about four hundred nationally standardized occupational profiles is a bureaucratic nightmare by liberal standards. But in spite of these institutional rigidities, Germany is, in terms of international competitiveness, one of the world's two or three most successful economies.

The explanation appears to be that, whereas German institutional rigidities have largely foreclosed adjustment to price-competitive markets, they have at the same time, and instead, forced, induced and enabled managements to embark on more demanding, high value-added, diversified quality production strategies. The resulting 'organizational ecology', in Streek's terms, produces:

- A system of rigid wage determination, operated by strong and well-established trade unions and employers associations, that keeps wages higher, and variations between wages lower, than in a free labour market. Unless employers are willing to move production elsewhere, this forces them to adapt their product range to non-price competitive markets capable of sustaining a high wage level. A high and even wage level makes employers more willing to invest in training and retraining.
- A policy of employment protection that compels employers to keep more employees on their payroll for a longer time than many might, on their own, be inclined to do. High employment is imposed on firms through collective agreements, co-determination and legislation. To compensate for such external rigidities, firms have to increase their internal flexibility. By foreclosing ready access to the external labour market institutional rigidities thus force as well as enable firms to invest in long-term human development.
- Having an assured 'voice' in the management of the enterprise makes it possible for the workforces to forego short-term advantages for larger, long-term benefits, without having to fear that they may not be around to collect those when they materialize. This, in turn, enables managements to invest in longer-term projects.
- A training regime that is capable of obliging employers to train more workers and afford them broader skills than required by immediate product or labour market pressures. The result is an excess pool of 'flexible', polyvalent workers and skills that constitutes an important advantage in periods of fast technological change. Firms' training activities are closely supervised by quasi-public chambers with compulsory membership and far-reaching powers. By being forced to

invest in expensive skills, firms find themselves further induced to move into non-price competitive markets for high value-added products. As a result, they use new technology in a way that makes the most of a firm's potential for flexible retooling, adopting an organization of work that allows workers to use discretion, and complying with a regime of employment protection that also protects their human resource investment.

- In combination with high and even wages, high employment security, co-determination and training, the imposition by unions on employers of non-Taylorist work rules impedes the use of new technology for purposes of rationalization. It also encourages a modernization strategy of industrial adjustment that is highly conducive to diversified quality production.

Streek's central claim, then, is that a regime of free markets is not enough to generate and support a pattern of diversified quality production. Such a pattern is conditional, rather, upon an industrial order or organizational ecology that transcends contractually based arrangements. Where such a regime is fully developed it is the outcome of a collective, cultural choice crystallized in a set of social institutions. This is because diversified quality producers thrive in an organizational ecology, or community, where other firms engage in the same kind of production. According to Streeks:

> Unlike the Fordist 'cathedrals in the desert', firms engaged in diversified quality production are neither self sufficient, not can they in their own interest hope to become so. In fact they perform best, if, rather than relying on their own endoskeleton they build on, submit to, and invest in a common public institutional exoskeleton to guide their decisions and facilitate their activities.

Where a firm's best interest, then, is no longer in the competitive elimination or hierarchical incorporation of other firms, but rather in being part of a rich, diversified, polycentric economy, forms of governance are necessary that allow for cooperative upgrading of technological capabilities. Such forms serve to protect the mutual confidence in one other's goodwill that is central for holding down transaction costs, and for enabling firms to shift flexibly from competition to cooperation and back.

Similarly, if small and medium-sized firms are to become full participants in diversified quality production, enabling institutional mechanisms are needed that provide for an efficient inter-firm transfer of technology and know-how. This is all a long way from the present economic policies of America or Britain. Moreover, a Ministry of Organizational Ecology, or of Human Capital, does not even exist in Germany and Japan, never mind in Britain or America. Seemingly, we are in a 'catch 22' situation. We continue to depend on the Anglo-Saxons for our leading-edge economic theories, and yet they are falling well behind the Germans and Japanese, who are now at the cutting edge of business practice. Let us turn, now, to business, in theory and practice.

Continuity and change

The path of business evolution

In the same way as British Chancellors of the Exchequer, and American Secretaries of State for Commerce and Industry, continue to thrive – in stature if not in achievement – despite the passing of the entrepreneurial era, so the business enterprise continues to maintain its essential, 300-year-old identity. Although trading companies of old have been transformed into modern-day multinationals, we have not advanced, constitutionally, beyond the original joint stock company. At the same time, we continue to refer to such factors of production as raw materials and land, labour and enterprise, as if they had remained unchanged. Moreover, as Lazonick has indicated, it is no wonder that we Anglo-Saxons face difficulties in adding value to our enterprises when we have no economic theory to support us. That having been said, the 'real world' has been rapidly changing. We are evolving, as Reich has indicated, from successively entrepreneurial and managerial eras towards an era of human capital.

Lazonick, similarly, has intimated that a move from a proprietary to a collective form of capitalism is a prerequisite for success in today's world. The only trouble is that micro-economic, or even management, theory, has not caught up with practice. So the *Sunday Times* can get away with its archaic statements because the business world, at large, has not found a way of reconceiving itself. We have attempted to make a start in this book by revisiting our business spheres – west and east, north and south – and reconnecting each with our four seminal philosophical systems – pragmatism and wholism, rationalism and humanism. Each of these reconstituted factors of philosophical production, moreover, can be seen in an evolving light, giving birth to new forms of enterprise:

- First, in the Borough of Ealing, individually grounded in the western sphere of pragmatically based *experimentation*, the concept of *action learning*, oriented towards the *learning company*, prospectively replaces professional services and marketing management,
- Second, in Lecroy Electronics, institutionally grounded in the northern sphere of rationally based *abstraction*, the concept of *organizational stratification*, oriented towards the *learning organization*, prospectively replaces management control,
- Third, and prospectively in the Norwich Union, grounded conceptually if not actually in the eastern sphere of wholistically based *systems thinking*, the concept of *general systems*, oriented towards a learning system, may replace operations management,
- Fourth, in Clothestown (South Africa), societally grounded in the southern sphere of humanistically based *collaboration*, the concept of *informated work*, geared towards a *learning community*, replaces human resource management.

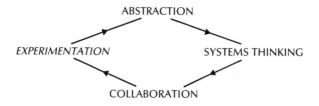

Figure 10.1

We shall now review each of these in turn, in the hope of synthesizing the overall argument contained in this book.

From free enterprise to learning company

In Britain local government is caught upon the horns of a dilemma. On the one hand, in being invited to throw off its bureaucratic shackles so as to become an enterprising community, it is being offered something it cannot culturally refuse. The 'experimenting' West in general, and England in particular, has always found depersonalized bureaucracies to be unsuitable for their individualistic orientation. In fact, bureaucratic town halls have grown up almost by default, as a necessary evil – if you like – rather than as a welcome development. Mary Coles herself personifies this highly individualistic and, in her case, deeply reflective side of Englishness. Whereas her father had been something of a self-made man, an experimenter in the outer world, Mary – as a self-made woman – is more inclined to explore her inner world, alongside that of others.

Whereas the English have always felt at home with small-scale enterprise, in both the private and the voluntary sectors, large-scale organization runs against the Anglo-Saxon cultural grain. Improvization rather than collectivization have inevitably been favoured, and rules that can be liberally bent rather than religiously obeyed have always been preferred. As a result, bureaucracy, in its Western essence, is, at best, a 'way-station' between free enterprise and the advancement of learning, the former being critical to Britain's Industrial Revolution and the latter central to its post-industrial society.

To the extent that the Borough of Ealing – like all other local authorities – is being induced to become an 'enabling' rather than a bureaucratic authority, all should be well. Such an enabling authority would set out to create an enterprising community by facilitating both commercial and voluntary activity. Moreover, enabling activity, seemingly dear to Western hearts, would be not only economic and technological in nature but also social and psychological in orientation. Yet therein lies the rub. For, and on the other hand, a Tory government in Britain, somewhat blinded by its pragmatically based materialism, believes that a bureaucratic organization can be turned into an enabling one simply by contracting out services to the most economical source of supply.

The government, in fact, has lost sight of the whole, that is, the enabling organization, by concentrating on the part, which is the contracted-out unit. In other words, the government has focused, essentially, on the allocation of value rather than upon its creation. For added value is primarily created by the new organization, as a whole, and only secondarily by its constituent services, each in part. As Lazonick has indicated earlier, the proprietal focus is inevitably on fostering markets rather than on facilitating organization.

Mary Coles, however, has focused on a new form of local organization, one that would function as a learning company. Out of a strong admixture of nurturing, inherent within the profession of social work, and of scientific inquiry, intrinsic to action learning, an enabling organization would emerge. This, in its turn, would add enduring value to the social services, and to the professional workers. Moreover, inner-directed learning, particularly of the inductive variety, accommodates the pragmatic cultural grain as much as does outer-directed enterprise. In addition, it adds value to enterprise in that, within the context of the learning spectrum, it lends insight and imagination, as well as organization and animation, to activity, flexibility and initiative. The learning company, moreover, is able to bring all those elements to bear upon communal activity by enabling every individual to realize his or her unique potential. It is that inner-directed, psychologically based motivation that conventional political wisdom completely bypasses.

In fact Revans, in championing the development of the individual, made a special plea that 'comrades in adversity' learn from one another. It is, in essence, this evolutionary movement, from the exchange of visible goods and services to the exchange of invisible knowledge, that is a mark of real progress. Toynbee, as we recall from Chapter 4, termed it a process of 'etherialization', whereby materially based achievement is replaced by spiritual advance. This process he identified historically to be the mark of an ascending civilization. More tangibly, Revans has commented upon the coincidence of scientific method (i.e. science), and intelligent counselling (i.e. nurture) with successful achievement, all under the aegis of ongoing action learning.

Such is our equivalent in Britain, if only we realized it, of quality circles in Japan and of Total Quality Management in the United States. For in the truly enabling organization not only is every employee a learner – experimenting and abstracting, thinking systemically and collaborating socially – but so is every citizen. Now there's a citizen's charter of real British worth, albeit that old-fashioned bureaucracy still stands in the way of its ultimate realization!

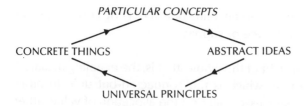

PARTICULAR CONCEPTS

CONCRETE THINGS

ABSTRACT IDEAS

UNIVERSAL PRINCIPLES

Figure 10.2

From bureaucracy to 'requisite organization' (Figure 10.2)

The place to enhance the functioning of bureaucracy is more likely to be France or Switzerland than Britain or America. Appropriately, therefore, Lecroy Electronics' European base is in Geneva. Scientists and engineers, moreover, engaged in high-technology businesses are well used to dealing with complexity. That having been said, their professional training, often as electronic engineers or as biotechnologists, is more likely to sensitize them to complexity in relation to practical things, or to particular physically based concepts, than with respect to abstract ideas or universal principles covering people or organizations.

Interestingly enough, the moment Conrad Fernandez joined our programme he took to the idea of a learning organization like a duck to water. It was as if his affinity with universal ideas, coming perhaps from the Indian part of his heritage, was being given permission to express itself. At the same time, the American company Tektronics, in which he was originally based, encouraged the entrepreneurial side of him. When he changed jobs, moving from London to Geneva, the organizational climate altered significantly. Although Lecroy Electronics was also American owned, the European operation was strongly influenced by Gallic rationality. Whereas America and Britain are blood brothers, when it comes to business philosophies, this is not the case for America *vis-à-vis* continental Europe.

In fact Conrad soon found himself challenged, by European rationality, to frame his entrepreneurism managerially. Having initially resisted these 'bureaucratic' incursions upon his entrepreneurial flair, he was subsequently drawn to Elliot Jaques's work on organizational stratification. For he could see, thanks to the concept of 'requisite organization', that he had to adapt his approach not only to the different tasks at hand but also to the varying layers of complexity. He also discovered, along the way, that Lecroy had not yet made explicit the uppermost layers of complexity required of its business, were it to come to grips with the authentically long-term future.

To the extent that Lecroy was to become a learning organization, Conrad then realized that it would need first, and at the most basic learning level, to know how to survive in the short term. This involved being able to 'run' the specifics of the business, including particular men and materials, money and machines, well enough to survive against the competition. A second level of learning, though, involved knowing how to manage such abstractions as the planning and control, direction and coordination of its entire factory, efficiently and effectively.

To the extent that its learning was even further intensified, moreover, the business would become able both to compete and also to cooperate with other firms, while its employees gained both economic and psychological fulfilment from their work. Finally, as a highly evolved form of learning organization, Lecroy would ultimately be contributing to some wider economic and social, psychological and ecological purpose than that of its own survival, thereby serving some universal cause.

The trouble was, of course, that Lecroy was not yet large enough, as, for example, IBM would be, to reach these upper echelons of learning. Moreover, because the many different European nationalities employed in Geneva were treated somewhat more like a homogeneous melting pot than as a heterogeneous group, the diversity of philosophies remained implicit rather than explicit. Conrad decided in his next Management MBA project, therefore, to tackle the heterogeneity head-on with a view to recognizing the authentic unity-in-diversity in his company. This, in its turn, would set his organization on a newly enriched path of learning.

Conrad felt, moreover, that such an acknowledgement of diversity and complexity was the key to turning what was otherwise perceived as something of a Swiss–American bureaucracy into a 'requisite' European organization. His MBA colleagues from the Norwich Union were faced with different – more overtly systemic – kinds of problems and opportunities. Brian Johns, an actuary by profession and a manager by craft, was one of Conrad's colleagues.

From closed to open system

In the individualistic west, and according to Revans, in order to change a system, at least in a fundamental way, you have to change yourself. Such change comes about, moreover, through an internalization of scientific method. Robert Reich's processes of experimentation, abstraction, systems thinking and collaboration are thereby applied to individual learning. The subsequent 'learning organization' is a sum of the individually learning-based parts, albeit mediated by the learning group of 'comrades in adversity'. Mary Coles saw it as her pragmatic task, therefore, to set such individual learning in motion, anticipating that the resulting sum of personal changes would inevitably lead to organizational learning.

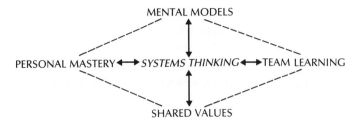

Figure 10.3

In the home of reason in the institutionalized north, embodied in the work of Elliot Jaques, individual learning and development is preconditioned by organizational circumstances. Bureaucracy, therefore, is not a constraint to learning. Rather, through the organizational stratification that it facilitates, people become able to manage complexity. Organizational learning, therefore, is a reflection of progressively higher levels of cognitive capacity built into the institution. To the extent that the institution, through its organizational stratification, matches the cognitive capacity of its personnel, so it will be 'requisite' in its functioning.

Whereas pragmatism is individually oriented and rationalism is institutionally focused, wholism is transpersonal, transnational and – if there is such a word – 'transorganizational' in orientation. The learning entity, in this 'eastern' case, is the interdependent system. Whereas before the Second World War both Germany and Japan were inhibited, in their inter-organizational learning, by the predominance of closed cartels, the post-war injection of Western-style freedom into these 'Eastern' societies produced a more learning-based amalgam! What, you may well ask, has all this to do with Brian Johns and with the Norwich Union?

In fact, the forerunners of actuarial science in the early part of the nineteenth century were well aware of the *gestalt* in which insurance was contained. Thomas Bignold, the founder a century and a half ago of what was to become the Norwich Union, was not only motivated by the need to protect himself from highwaymen on his East Anglian journey, as the company's history tells us. In fact he was also impelled to create an insurance business because of his innate appreciation of the principles of mutuality that underpinned his new product. For the realization that no man is an island, so that the insurance of one is dependent on the contribution of many, came naturally to those in nineteenth-century Britain who were drawn to the mutual provident societies.

These societies, at least within the Anglo-Saxon world, were the forerunners of the extensive co-partnerships that are developing across the global stage in business today. They were born out of a combination of systemic thinking and shared values, now championed by Peter Senge, and developed further as in the case of the Norwich Union by team learning and mental models, albeit of a somewhat rudimentary kind. Undoubtedly, though, such Quakers as George Cadbury and Seebohm Rowntree in England in that particular era had developed inordinate degrees of personal mastery. Moreover, the call for intensive dialogue, alongside extensive discussion, was readily received by those very Quakers who duly 'quaked' when something of real substance was being spoken.

Brian Johns, in our present day, particularly within an Anglo-Saxon world where independence supersedes interdependence, has to struggle to find authentic evidence of Senge's 'fifth discipline'. For contemporary actuarial science is largely cut off from its mutualistic origins, and the notion of 'union' tends to be pragmatically viewed 'really' rather than wholly grasped 'ideally'. Nevertheless, the potential remains for a genuine union to be created between life, as a whole, and insurance, as a part, or indeed vice versa.

Insurance products, established almost two centuries ago, when life could be short and highwaymen stalked the roads, were properly based on the need to protect life and property. While today we still live in an insecure world, our everyday tensions – at least within the industrialized countries – are as much social and psychological as physical and economic. In that respect, insurance companies have failed to move with the times, hence becoming interactive, learning systems. I am unaware of any products currently on the market to insure the development of my social or psychological being, as opposed to the maintenance of my physical or economic well-being. Similarly, our ecological uncertainties remain, as yet, uninsurable, reflecting the unsystemic nature of many insurers' world views. At the time of writing, in fact, the Lloyd's insurance market is in a parlous state, reflecting symbolically, through the losses of its famous 'names', the perils of personal independence in isolation of organizational interdependence. For each insurance broker for some three hundred years, like each individual 'name', has been left to paddle his or her individual canoe. Managerial or collective capitalism has not yet caught up with the birthplace of insurance. Hopefully, its state of crisis will precipitate a transformation and a due process of systemic learning.

As such, and to the extent that the mutual insurers are touched by this, they will evolve from something of a closed system to much more of an open one. Such openness, ideally, will result in a new sense of union, leading to the reaping of psychological and ecological as well as technological and economic synergies. For one thing, Norwich Union may now seize the opportunity to return to Southern Africa, where not only do opportunities for new insurance products abound, given the societal insecurity there, but the communal environment of the indigenous people could serve to enhance the sense of union.

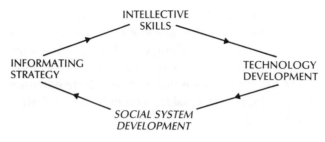

Figure 10.4

From patriarchy to informated community

Southern Africa, of course, is my own home ground. Twenty-five years ago, having recently graduated from the Harvard Business School, I was asked to take over the managing directorship of 21 clothing concessions, located within a small supermarket chain in South Africa. As this was an offshoot of our Southern African, Lessem patriarchy, I consented, despite my tender years – I was 26 at the time – and my unfamiliarity with the rag trade.

During the two-year period I spent in the family business, before that particular part of it was taken over, we not only installed a computerized information system but I also made an ill-conceived attempt to create a multi-racial, cooperatively run enterprise. I say 'ill conceived' because neither did I yet have the resilience, nor apartheid South Africa the magnanimity, to allow me to succeed. Little was I aware at the time, though, that I would be able to make a second attempt, this time as a management consultant, in the newly emerging South Africa, 25 years later.

The family business I was called on to assist, in the early nineties, was founded upon genuinely multi-racial lines, one of the very few enterprises in South Africa to bypass the colour bar. Moreover, whereas the original founders were innately non-racial in outlook, their children had become purposefully communal in their approach. Furthermore, because the business now employed some 15 000 people it had become a complex organization. It was ripe for evolution from a family business into an 'informated' community, particularly because newly networked systems were being installed 'in the age of the smart machine'. For an organization like Clothestown to pursue an informating strategy, Zuboff tells us, it had to focus organizational intelligence on areas of strategic value. The more this intelligence, including an appreciation of what adds up to 'strategic value', is spread around the organization, the better for its collective learning. The way I chose to make strategy accessible was through storytelling, a medium that was indigenous to Africans and also inherently communal.

A new division of learning, for Zuboff, depends on the continuing progress of informating applications. It includes, as we may recall from Chapter 6, maintaining the reliability of the database while improving its breadth and quality, developing approaches to system design that support an informating strategy, and scanning for technical innovations that can lead to new informating opportunities. This kind of technological development can only occur in the closest possible alignment with organizational efforts to promote learning and social integration. It is for this reason that I likened the database that had been established to the collective storytelling that went on by the fireside in a traditional African village. Fortunately, moreover, we were blessed with a systems analyst within the company who was also a traditional healer, so she could make the creative leap between tradition and modernity.

The intellective skills that are acquired at the data interface nearest to the core of daily operating responsibilities provide a coherent basis for the kind of continual learning that would prepare people for increasingly comprehensive responsibilities. The relative homogeneity of the total organizational skill base suggests a vision of organizational membership that resembles, for Zuboff, the trajectory of a professional career that replaces the 'apartheid system', separating conventionally black workers and white managers. The interpenetration between rings provides a key source of organizational integration. The African image of *ubuntu*, that is, a harmonious circle, replaces the European notion of authority, allied to hierarchy. Finally, and most importantly for Zuboff, relationships will need to be fashioned and refashioned as part of the dynamism of the social process. The abstract precincts of the data interface heighten the need for communication. New sources of personal influence are associated with the ability to learn and to engender learning in others, in contrast to the Anglo-Saxon emphasis upon contractual relationships or the authority derived from function and position.

With the body now functioning, Zuboff stresses, as the scene of human feeling rather than as the source of physical energy, or as an instrument of political influence, I was able to change the perception of technology among the workers, again through the medium of storytelling. The introduction of extended data-processing facilities was reconceived as a collective effort to create and communicate meaning. Don and Meenu, in the storyline, were symbols not only of genesis but also of man and woman, individual and community.

What, then, does this all imply for business as a learning community?

Business as a learning community

Differentiated learning

We now need, having journeyed west, north and south – if not also east – to return to the overall theme of this book, whereby we have reconceived business as a learning community. In the process, and as was indicated in Chapter 2, business as well as business executives, together with their supporters and detractors, consciously evolve in four directions.

From self-help to self-development

- A market-based enterprise, marked by a horizontal exchange of goods and services, is transformed into a *learning company*, dominated by a negotiated exchange of knowledge.

The path of evolution, in the Anglo-Saxon world, would seem to be from Victorian-style, market-oriented self-help to modern-day, knowledge-oriented self-development. In other words, Adam Smith's wealth of nations would slip into the background, while Francis Bacon's advancement of learning was allowed to advance into the foreground. Now there's a turnabout for the political agends, one which would do a local authority like the Borough of Ealing no end of good, if only it saw the light. In effect, self-knowledge would replace self-aggrandisement or self-effacement as an order of the new day. Moreover, such knowledge of ourselves and of others could only be acquired through ongoing, experientially based exchange of information and ideas, challenge and support. As such, it would not preclude the creation of wealth, through avowedly esoteric pursuits, but, true to Anglo-Saxon pragmatic form, would enhance both wealth and well-being. In other words, as Bacon originally said, knowledge would produce works, and that includes self-knowledge as well as knowledge of other people and things.

From functional administration to structural management

- A bureaucratic hierarchy, marked by a vertically stratified organization of people, is transformed into a *learning organization*, characterized by a cumulative ordering of knowledge.

Bureaucracies, like the Borough of Ealing, inhibit their professionals' self-development because their functionally administered organization is structurally underdeveloped. In fact pragmatically based cultures generally have an empathy for the 'deep structures' of individuals and only for the 'surface structures' of institutions. Rationally oriented cultures, on the other hand, tend to be the reverse. Moreover, whereas function is visible – on the surface, structure is hidden – in the depths.

In a heartfelt letter to me, written in response to our Chapter 6 covering his 'structural' ideas, Elliot Jaques said:

> I have been seen as concerned more with organization than with people, and with an undue emphasis on organization structure. My actual aim is to understand organizations of all kinds in relation to people, and individual behaviour as influenced

by the organizations we inhabit . . . I believe that organizational work suffers from the failure to keep structure and process together. In particular, however, structure is not included because there is an almost total ignorance of structure. Our field, with its total inability to differentiate between the managerial hierarchy and, for example, a partnership, or a university tenure staff organization, or a church or clergy hierarchy, is like a biology that does not know the difference between elephants, frogs, butterflies and coral colonies, or between different plant species – or like physiology without any knowledge of the anatomy of various processes [that produced barber surgeons].

Conrad Fernandez, therefore, has used Jaques's concept of organizational stratification to identify the deep structures of Lecroy Electronics, in sympathy with his Genevois colleagues. In that respect he has transcended the surface appreciation of functional management, contained within American-style 'business administration'. In recognizing, and reforming, the layered structure of his organization, Conrad is acting as a business manager rather than a functional administrator. In re-ordering complexity, within his business institution, he is giving expression to its progressive learning, from surface concreteness to universal depths. A similar process of ordering is intrinsic to our own spectral theory, spanning both individual and organizational learning. All too often, Gallic rationality, duly depersonalized, is disconnected from Anglo-Saxon pragmatism, innately personalized. The gap between these two inevitably inhibits managerial learning, which arises out of an interaction between the person and the institution. Genuinely systemic learning is, again, something else.

From organizational differentiation to systemic integration

- An industrial system, with interdependent business functions and economic enterprises, is transformed into a *learning system* characterized by combined knowledge disciplines.

The pragmatist focuses on the individual, so that a learning company becomes the non-synergistic sum of parts. The rationalist focuses on the institution, so that the learning organization becomes divorced from both the individual and the environment. The wholist, with whom we are now concerned, is oriented towards the integrated industrial, social and ecological environment, of which the individual and the organization are differentiated parts. Not surprisingly today, it is in Germany that we find a 'whole' new approach being adopted, in this case to recycling. According to Parkes:

Germany's messianic environment minister, Mr Klaus Topfer, has a way with words. In his book, rubbish is not garbage. It is, for him, a secondary raw material. In his mind's eye he sees product cycles not as lines fettered with ups and downs, but as near-perfect circles . . . The aim of his 'circulation economic law' is to force manufacturers and distributors to take their end products back at the ends of their useful lives.

Wholism, in Germany or in Japan, is oriented towards the integrated process that underlies their differentiated economic, technological, social and ecological functions. In structural terms these are considered to be interdependent, one of the other, in circular terms. In process terms, learning takes place through a series of dialectically interacting crises and resolutions. In fact, because of his somewhat Anglo-Saxon, American orientation, Peter Senge has been able to grasp the systemic circularity of his 'fifth discipline' but not the evolutionary dynamic. This is more clearly represented in the Germanic *weltanschaung* of Marx and Hegel, Lievegoed and Schumpeter (see Chapter 6).

The development of knowledge, therefore – through Senge's systemic combination of personal mastery, mental modelling, team learning and shared vision – needs to be extended from firm to industry and technology to ecology and society. The individually differentiated learning company, and the institutionally differentiated learning organization, need to be integrated within a more widely interconnected learning system. For the Norwich Union this would need to encompass a much more extensive and intensive 'union' than it currently envisages. Norwich Cathedral, on the Norwich Union's present logo, would need to embrace the churches and cathedrals, mosques and synagogues of a more inclusive world. Its insurance base would need to be extended, through a cross-fertilization of actuarial, socio-psychological and anthropological disciplines. Linkages between the United Nations, the European Community, the British trades unions and the Norwich Union would need to become systemically apparent.

Finally, unlike the challenge and support undergone by individually interacting action learners and the progressive ordering of complexity involved in organizational learning, systemic learning involves an acceptance of differentiating crisis as a means toward integrating resolution – given a systemic awareness and a visionary orientation. Now, and finally, it is time to turn south.

From family business to socio-economic network

• A family business network, with reciprocal personal and commercial relationships, is transformed into a *learning community*, characterized by the sharing of social, technical and economic knowledge.

Whereas wholism submerges self within society generally, humanism subordinates self to a particular community. However, communal learning across the world has hitherto been largely inhibited by isolation or domination. On the one hand, communities which have isolated themselves from 'Western' technology, have, notwithstanding their intrinsic humanism, remained 'primitive'. As a result, their learning has been localized, intense but parochial. On the other hand, communities, other than the Japanese and perhaps the South Koreans, which have accommodated 'Western' progress, have lost their primal identity. Such a primary sense of identity, moreover, is a prerequisite for durable learning and authentic development.

Shoshana Zuboff has charted a path through what she terms 'sentient' knowledge towards an ongoing learning community. The process of 'informating', contained within, transforms a process of domination and exclusion into one of accommodation and inclusion. Through acting with people, the emergent animator, via the sentient realm of the traditional craft worker, transforms the ability to act on things, which is no longer required, into a new and appropriate skill. Within that communally learning-based context I was able to work with a group of indigenous and exogenous Southern Africans to turn a database into a perceived extension of a village community. The key to such communal learning lies in the retention of that fragile connection between people and technology, now and then. The modern technologists and the traditional spirit healer need to be able to converse with one another.

Inevitably, however, the leap from family business, or subsistence economy, to socio-economic network, underpinned by modern technology, is huge. Elements of individual, organizational and systemic learning need to be accommodated if the learning community that ensues is to transcend its parochial limits. This, in effect, is exactly what has happened in the case of Benetton. Central Italy, as a whole, is uniquely poised between the rationality of the north and the communality of the south, albeit lacking in some of the individuality of the west and the integration of the east.

Ironically, and when it is able to restabilize itself, South Africa has the potential to release all four factors of philosophical production – British pragmatism, French Huguenot rationalism, Dutch wholism and African humanism – from within itself. Therein lie the seeds for integrated learning.

Integrated learning

Conceptualize the whole of learning as a cycle
In the final analysis we shall have grossly misled readers if we had implied that the four separate learning entities contained within this book could be practically set apart. Whereas in theory this can indeed be the case, in practice, as you build up your business as a learning community you will want to combine conceptual forces. After all, this is exactly what we have done within our own development programme. As is therefore indicated in Figure 2.4 the best way of reconceptualizing learning as a whole is in terms of a cycle.

Beginning by establishing action learning sets
A natural place to begin, as a pragmatist, is with action learning sets, preferably and gradually spread throughout the organization. As each individual engages in

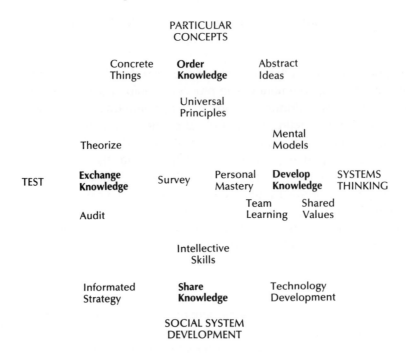

PARTICULAR
CONCEPTS

Concrete **Order** Abstract
Things **Knowledge** Ideas

Universal
Principles

Mental
Theorize Models

TEST **Exchange** Survey Personal **Develop** SYSTEMS
Knowledge Mastery **Knowledge** THINKING

Team Shared
Audit Learning Values

Intellective
Skills

Informated **Share** Technology
Strategy **Knowledge** Development

SOCIAL SYSTEM
DEVELOPMENT

Figure 10.5 The knowledge based organization

exchanging with others, that is, through surveying the field, auditing their own experience, testing it out in new situations, and conjecturing or theorizing upon the results, so a learning company will be set in behavioural train. Such a company is a necessary but not a sufficient condition for business as a learning community.

Reconstitute your organization in layers of increasing complexity

For the institution to be learning it will need to be fully reconstituted, along with the individuals. This is an overtly rational as opposed to pragmatic process. The establishment of a learning organization requires the ordered stratification of knowledge, along cognitive lines. For both Jaques and ourselves, seven such strata of progressively evolving complexity seemed to be in order. The resulting combination of behavioural and cognitive change produces both functional and structural learning. Yet we still have a long way to go.

Orchestrate interdependence across your organizational ecology

The most demonstrably effective businesses, as learning communities, are the successful Japanese ones. The reason, in part, is because of the way that personal mastery, as in the case of Honda or Sony, have been combined with team learning.

Where, for a start, would Honda have been without Fujisawa, or Morita without Ibuka? Moreover, the Japanese have been uniquely adept in recent years in combining team learning, on a micro-scale with shared vision on a macro-scale throughout the organization. Ultimately, however, systemic learning is dependent upon the degree of integration within the *kereitsu*, or enterprise group, inclusive of bank and manufacturer, trading company and subcontractor, and, of course, MITI itself. The German economy, in fact, is similarly integrated, as a so-called organizational ecology'. So, as we can see, in developing business as a learning community we need to orchestrate interdependence.

Share communal knowledge from a sentient base
In our beginning is our end, at least according to T. S. Eliot. The birthplace of the human race was in Africa, and communality is still strongest in the southern part of the world. Similarly, within Europe it is in Italy and Spain, Greece and Portugal that family businesses are most strongly rooted. The progression from family business to socio-economic network, moreover, represents a series of profound learning steps, around the cycle, from west and north, to east and finally south. This movement around the entire business sphere has been strongly inhibited until now. For communal learning, of such a wholesome character, requires a unique bonding of enterprise and community, of tribal group and nationally based institution, of personalism and collectivism. The sharing of knowledge, from a sentient base, underpins such a development.

As, at the time of writing, the guns keep on firing in Sarajevo and township violence flares up again in South Africa, the urgency of our task intensifies. In facilitating the cycle of learning we are not only revitalizing business and renewing the much-jaded Anglo-Saxon economies. We are, in effect, truly harnessing the physical and intellectual, emotional and spiritual resources of the business sphere.

As I complete this particular book I look forward, with eager anticipation, to my visit home, to Southern Africa. I remain optimistic that the time of the south will come, and my home territory, the birthplace of the human race, is likely to play its leading part in our world renewal. At the same time, and bearing in mind the result of the 1992/3 US election, we can only hope that Bill Clinton, alongside John Major, will see the learning-based light. As a resident of Britain, a country I dearly love, we can only hope that as Anglo-Saxons we can enhance Toynbee's process of etherealization, whereby our civilization advances from self-help to self-development.

Finally, as the great American management thinker Mary Parker Follett once said, 'if you don't make your unique contribution to the world, you cripple the world'. The same goes for the individual as for your organization, for industries as for societies, at least for those that dedicate themselves to the advancement of learning that bears fruit in work!

REFERENCES

Jaques, E., Personal communication, 15 June 1992.

Lazonick, W., *Business Organization and the Myth of the Market Economy*, Cambridge University Press (1991).

Parkes, C., 'Bonn crusader shares vision of circular rubbish', *Financial Times*, 20 July 1992.

Streek, W., 'On the institutional conditions of diversified quality production', page 32, Matzner and Streek (1991).

Index